TO
LHASA IN DISGUISE

TO
LHASA IN DISGUISE

A SECRET EXPEDITION THROUGH MYSTERIOUS TIBET

BY

WILLIAM MONTGOMERY McGOVERN

D. PHIL (OXON.)
Lecturer in Chinese and Japanese at the School of Oriental Studies,
University of London

ILLUSTRATED WITH PHOTOGRAPHS

GYAN

Published by

GYAN

Gyan Publishing House
5, Ansari Road
Daryaganj, New Delhi-110002
Phone: 011-47034999, 9811692060
E-mail: books@gyanbooks.com

Distribution Network
gyanbooks.com
India, USA, Canada, UK, Australia, France

ISBN : 978-81-212-4121-2 (PB)
First Published, 1924

2nd Impression 2020

Printed at: Gyan Press, Delhi.

TO LHASA IN DISGUISE

A SECRET EXPEDITION THROUGH MYSTERIOUS TIBET

BY

WILLIAM MONTGOMERY McGOVERN

D. Phil. (Oxon.)

Lecturer in Chinese and Japanese at the School of Oriental Studies, University of London

ILLUSTRATED WITH PHOTOGRAPHS

GROSSET & DUNLAP — *Publishers*

by arrangement with The Century Company

Dr. William Montgomery McGovern

TO WILLIAM DEDERICH, ESQ.

DEAR MR. DEDERICH:

It would seem to me quite wrong that this book should go out without being dedicated to you, for not only were you the kindly patron through whose unfailing support and coöperation the whole journey through Tibet was made possible, but it is entirely owing to your insistence that the present book has been written.

I had intended to write a somewhat technical volume dealing with the scientific results of my journey through Tibet with special reference to anthropology, both physical and social, omitting all matters of merely personal reference, but you have persuaded me that you and perhaps some others would be interested in reading a plain account of some of the personal experiences which my secret expedition to Tibet entailed.

It certainly was interesting to be forced to see Tibet and the Tibetans from the Tibetan point of view, to live as a Tibetan for months when a false word or act would have given me away, to be forced to study their quaint customs, not merely from a dry, dull, scientific standpoint, but also that I might journey among them without being detected; and so I have given way to your arguments and, departing from my custom with previous books, have tried to describe some of the varied experiences which I encountered during my secret expedition to the sacred city.

I have therefore put off to a subsequent volume discussion of the more technical side of my exploration work, detailed notes on the physical geography of the country, and the comparative anatomical measurements which I made, with the view of ascertaining the exact racial position of the people. In the same way I have postponed detailed treatment of the minute points of Tibetan Buddhist philosophy, a subject which greatly interested me, and have tried to make the present volume one which can be read with interest and enjoyment and not merely used as a book of reference.

At the same time I have tried to include in this work, something which would make it of more lasting worth, numerous notes of personal observation of various aspects of the country and the people. I have tried to weave through the record a general but accurate description of manners and customs and beliefs, including some of the extraordinary institutions which exist in the government of Lhasa. Finally, I have tried to give an adequate description of the great transformation which has taken place in Tibet the last few years, so that I hope it can be claimed that my book gives to the general public its first exact information concerning the present diplomatic, political, military, and industrial situation in a country which occupies such an important strategic center that it is of interest to all students of Asiastic and world affairs.

This work is sent out in all true humility. I make no pretense to style or to fine writing, but if you and others can get any pleasure from reading of adventures which took place and observations which were made on the Roof of the World, I shall feel more than repaid for all the trouble which the writing of this book has entailed.

You and I both know how much I am indebted to Mr. J. E. Pryde Hughes for his constant and efficient help in the labor of composition.

WILLIAM MONTGOMERY MCGOVERN.

CONTENTS

CHAPTER		PAGE
I	Tibet and the Tibetans	3
II	The First Attempt: The Journey to Gyangtse	10
III	Preparations for the New Attempt: The Journey Through Sikkim	62
IV	Trapped in the Passes	92
V	First Days in Tibet	116
VI	We Join a Tibetan Caravan	181
VII	Shigatse and Beyond	227
VIII	Through the Rong Gorge	265
IX	On the Last Lap—But Suspected	289
X	The Last Fifty Miles	314
XI	The Goal Achieved—We Arrive in Lhasa	334
XII	Life in the Forbidden City	370
XIII	A Prisoner of State	409
XIV	Last Days in Lhasa and the Return to India	451

LIST OF ILLUSTRATIONS

Dr. William Montgomery McGovern . . . . . . *Frontispiece*

FACING PAGE

The Dalai-lama, at window: unique photograph taken when the Dalai-lama was in flight from the Chinese invaders . . 4

Tibetan troops being drilled by Indian N. C. O. 5

Tibetan troops of the old army 5

Tibetan beggar woman 12

Tibetan princess in gala dress 12

The Kung Kusho and his A. D. C. The Kung Kusho, a near relative of the late Dalai-lama, ranks as prince and general in the new Tibetan army 13

Reconnaissance of Mount Chumolhari (left), twenty-four thousand feet above sea-level 13

Phari reservoir with island shrine 32

Phari Ozong 32

Bhutanese princess and husband 33

Dongtse monastery 33

Natives of Gyangtse posing to cinematography 48

A prayer-wall along which one must walk to acquire merit . 48

The portable gramophone carried by the first expedition proved of great interest to the Tibetans 49

A Tibetan city store 49

FACING PAGE

Tibetan woman weaving thread 64

Dr. McGovern in disguise as Tibetan coolie 64

Map: dotted lines, first expedition; black line, Dr. McGovern's route to Lhasa in disguise 65

The first halt 65

Group at Yatung, Tibet: the British trade-agent and family, Bhutanese visitors and members of first Expedition: Dr. McGovern in lama dress standing third from right . . 80

Inspection of coolies selected for the first expedition . . . 80

Dr. W. Montgomery McGovern on his return 81

Dr. McGovern on a voyage to India 81

A typical Sikkimese village 96

The takin: the rarest animal in the world, found only in the mountains of Tibet; it is a mixture of many species, goat, cow and boar, etc., breeding now as a distinct species; less than a hundred exist 96

Dr. McGovern in mountain kit 97

The Depön Kusho: Tibetan trade-agent, who is also a general in the Tibetan army 97

Tibetan official and wife watching a lama dance 112

The road to Gyangtse 112

Glacier from Mount Chumolhari 113

Gyangtse, the third city of Tibet, and capital of the province. Castle on hill; Golden Chorten (shrine) on right. Here the first expedition awaited permission (which was refused) to proceed to Lhasa 128

Gyangtse plain with castle on hill 128

Abbots' gallery at Gyangtse cathedral; these effigies of departed abbots of the cathedral exhibit exceptional workmanship 129

FACING PAGE

Two of the gods, guardians of the four quarters of the world at the doors of Tibetan cathedral; there are four gods to defend the cathedral against evil spirits 129

William Dederich, F.R.C.S. (organizer) 144

Tibetan lama devil-dancers in masks 145

Devil-dancing at a small monastery 145

Wall-engravings in Tibetan cathedral 192

Engraving of devil in Tibetan cathedral 192

Phari rest-house early morning 193

Yaks transporting wool to Lhasa from Tibetan provinces . 193

Sacred chortens, or shrines, on the road to Shigatse . . . 240

Tibetans with the native four-horned ram 240

Procession with palanquin of Trashi-lama, Shigatse . . . 241

A typical Tibetan village 241

Superstition: prayer-flags and the horns of the Ovis Ammor (blue sheep of Tibet), a species of wild sheep deemed sacred, are placed on the roof of the house to protect it against evil spirits 292

Tent dwelling of the wild Tibetan yak-herders 292

Skull (front); Skull (top); Skull (side) 293

The oracle of Tibet. He prophesied the month and the year the Great War would end two years before the armistice. The Tibetan Government will not act without his soothsaying 300

The Tibetan oracle as he is normally, with attendants . . . 300

Gera monastery near Lhasa; the second largest in Tibet . . 301

Shigatse; the monastery, home of the Trashi-lama, the supreme abbot of Tibet 301

Medical college, Lhasa, on hill 336

FACING PAGE

Frozen ground and lack of wood or vegetation for fire drive the Tibetans to cut up their dead in the hills and leave the remains to the vultures 336

His Holiness the Dalai-lama 337

Over the roofs of Lhasa, with Potala in background . . . 352

One of the main streets of Lhasa: Potala in background, right; cathedral, center; medical school on hill, left . . 352

Lhasa: the Potala 358

The Potala, official court and palace of the Dalai-lama at Lhasa 358

The monastery of Dreföng, near Lhasa, the largest in Tibet, housing about eight thousand of the turbulent, red (or fighting) monks 400

Dongtse monastery 401

Sons of *lönchen* (or prime minister of Tibet) the younger on left, is an official; the elder on right, a monk 416

Tibetan women with traditional head-dress 416

Exterior of Gyangtse cathedral; monks at morning prayer . 417

The cathedral of Lhasa 417

LIST OF MAPS

Map of Asia showing Tibet 9

Map: dotted lines, first expedition; black line, Dr. McGovern's route to Lhasa in disguise 65

Dr. McGovern's route through Sikkim 91

To Lhasa in Disguise

To Lhasa in Disguise

CHAPTER I

TIBET AND THE TIBETANS

FOR many years Tibet has been the mysterious unknown country, and Lhasa, its capital, has been the Forbidden City of the Buddhas, into which entrance by many adventurous explorers has been sought in vain.

Both nature and the inhabitants have coöperated to make entry into the country well nigh impossible. A huge table-land, whose average altitude is fifteen thousand feet above sea-level, it is surrounded and intersected by even greater mountains, many of them over twenty thousand feet high, shrouded in perpetual ice and snow.

Tibet has an area of over one million square miles; but though it lies between the two fertile countries of India and China, so bleak and so cold is it that nearly the whole land is a desert devoid of trees and plants, producing only patches of sparse grass which serve to support the deer, the wild ass, the yak, and herds of cattle and sheep. Barley, a hardy plant, is the one cereal grown, and even this flourishes only in the milder parts, but hidden within Tibet's ample bosom are vast and almost untouched stores of natural mineral wealth.

Scattered over this huge territory are groups of natives fiercely jealous of every intruder. Many of them are nomads moving here and there with their flocks. Others form communities dwelling in settled villages. Nearer the larger towns, perched on high hills or precipitous cliffs, are to be found gigantic stone castles of quaint old-world design which frown upon the country-side.

Even more numerous than the castles are the monasteries, for Tibet is the country of monks. One man out of every four is a priest, and such persons dwell together in vast buildings placed far away from other habitation. But such institutions instead of being havens of peace are the centers of turmoil. Many of their inhabitants become what are known as fighting monks and spend their time in brawling.

Wild, reckless men they are. Sometimes one monastery will wage war against another, and sometimes these ecclesiastical swash-bucklers will pour into the towns and seize and hack to pieces some unpopular governor. The monasteries, having hundreds and in some cases thousands of inhabitants, overawe the districts in which they are placed.

It is the monks who are fiercest in hatred of outsiders; it is they who present the greatest danger to the would-be explorer of the inhabited portion of Tibet, for in their foreigner-hating zeal they are apt to ignore

The Dalai-lama, at window: unique photograph taken when the Dalai-lama was in flight from the Chinese invaders

Tibetan troops being drilled by Indian N. C. O.

Tibetan troops of the old army

any safe-conduct which might be granted by the civil authorities to a stranger.

In the very heart of this gloomy land is the sacred city of Lhasa. Here lives the Dalai-lama, who is both the emperor and the high priest of his people, who regard him as an incarnate god. In his magnificent palace, the Potala, he dwells on public occasions, surrounded with all the pomp that befits a living deity, and receives in audience the pilgrims who come from every part of Tibet to bring rich offerings and to adore.

He who would seek to penetrate into Lhasa must first overcome the tremendous physical difficulties which bar the way to the threshold of Tibet; and even if he rise victorious over ice and snow, gnarled crag and precipitous cliff, he finds upon arrival on the plateau an angry populace which bars the way and insists on an immediate return.

In the old days various well-known explorers tried by means of devious routes and various disguises to escape being turned back at the frontier and succeeded indeed in passing far into the interior, only to find that sooner or later they were detected before reaching Lhasa, the abode of the gods. Among the most noteworthy of these explorers was the Swede, Sven Hedin, and the illustrious American scholar, W. W. Rockhill.

In the last few years a few have been more fortunate. Sir Francis Younghusband, Sir Charles Bell, and General Pereira, for example, have been able to throw a great deal of light upon many hitherto unknown aspects of Central Tibetan life. The Younghusband military expedition of 1904 to Tibet particularly was destined to alter the whole internal history of the country. But in each case the torch-light which has illuminated for a moment the Tibetan darkness has been extinguished; and once again, and in fact more than ever, is Tibet the mysterious unknown country and Lhasa the Forbidden City of the Buddhas.

In recent years both country and capital have become more particularly worthy of study, owing to the curious developments which have taken place there. While retaining the glamour of mystery which belongs to a country ruled by monks, many of whom are worshipped as gods, and which excludes all intruders from without, Tibet is now worthy of the interest of the student of diplomacy, politics, and economics.

We are all aware of the extraordinary transformation which Japan underwent during the course of the latter part of the last century, when from a quaint kingdom of fable, closed to the outside world, it became a first-class modern power, with all the equipment and organization of the West.

A similar transforming movement is now taking place in Tibet, a movement which may have an important influence upon the political future of Eastern Asia. Until 1912 Tibet was a vassal of China, without a standing army or adequate munitions of war. To-day the Chinese have been expelled, and Tibet stands alone and independent. She has a new army, an army ever growing in numbers, well drilled, well disciplined, and armed with rifles, either imported from Europe or made in the Lhasa arsenal. Regular postal communications have been opened between the principal towns, and

Lhasa itself is possessed of telephone and telegraph—quaint and crude, to be sure, but workable—and that last instance of modern European culture, paper money, is now being printed.

The Government has also undergone considerable transformation. The Dalai-lama, the supreme pontiff of Tibetan Buddhism, is now in fact, as his predecessors were in name, the absolute ruler of the country. Tibet has long been possessed of two curious bodies, a council of shapé or secretaries of state, constituting a cabinet, and a Tsongdu or National Assembly, the Tibetan Parliament or Congress; but in the last decade both these bodies have undergone an interesting evolution, making them correspond more closely to their European counterparts, and even in distant Tibet constitutional crises are by no means unknown. What is most curious is that these modern movements seem to have had little effect in rendering Tibet less exclusive; in fact, in some ways the ring grows tighter. In former years the Chinese at least were admitted to Lhasa, and now even these are excluded. Even the new institutions, such as the post and the telegraph, are employed as the most efficient means of keeping the unofficial European intruder out as in this way constant communication between the frontier and the capital is insured.

To the adventurer and the explorer, therefore, Tibet at the present moment presents a fascinating field of research. In my own case I was equally interested by Tibet as the luring past and as the womb of the unborn to-morrow. As an anthropologist I became fascinated by the Tibetan people with their customs, their language, their religion, and their literature, all of which are in some way unique. As one who had studied the modern developments in diplomacy and statecraft in the other countries of the East, I was anxious to study the changing institutions of this hidden theocratic empire and to see what effect these might have upon the relations of the surrounding peoples.

In bygone years I had devoted much time to a theoretical study of the Tibetan language and customs, in the hope that this would the better enable me to carry on exploration at first-hand. But it was my privilege to utilize this stored-up knowledge and to continue my studies under very peculiar conditions. Circumstances forced me to cross an eighteen-thousand-foot pass into Tibet in midwinter, a time when it was blocked with snow and supposedly closed to all travelers, even natives. Arrived in Tibet, I was required to disguise myself as a Tibetan coolie and to travel as such through the heart of the country. During the latter part of this secret journey the Tibetan Government learned of my escapade and ordered a sharp watch to be kept for me at all the villages. The caravan with which I was traveling in the humble capacity of servant was several times stopped and examined without my being discovered.

At last I arrived in Lhasa. Here I was foolish enough to reveal myself voluntarily to the authorities, with the result that the Lhasa monks led a popular riot against me, and the civil government, in an attempt to protect my person, was forced to declare me a prisoner of state until the popular clamor had subsided.

After a six weeks' stay in Lhasa, I was permitted to return to India, an escort being given me in order to insure my safety. In this way my adventure came to an end, but in the meantime I had been able to secure numerous priceless manuscripts, had met or seen all the principal persons in the sacred city, and had had unequaled opportunities for studying the inner life of the Tibetan people and the working of their institutions.

CHAPTER II

THE FIRST ATTEMPT: THE JOURNEY TO GYANGTSE

THE adventure which was destined to have this adventurous end started in a much more conventional fashion. It was in fact but the sequel to an earlier open expedition consisting of five Europeans engaged on scientific research, which penetrated one hundred and fifty miles inside the Tibetan frontier and managed to acquire a great deal of scientific material before it was stopped and turned back by the order of the Tibetan authorities. It was only through this expedition, of which I was a member, that I gained the necessary experience and information to enable me to carry out my journey in disguise, so that it is necessary in the first place to give a short account of this first attempt to reach the Forbidden City.

In 1921 Mr. George Knight, F.R.G.S., conceived the idea of organizing a research mission to Tibet to carry out a thorough survey of the country and the people.

It was first of all necessary to get in touch with some one who was in a position to organize and finance such an expedition. After several disheartening failures to secure such support, Mr. Knight obtained the hearty coöperation of Mr. William Dederich, F.R.G.S., who was a friend of the late Sir Ernest Shackleton and had rendered that great explorer practical help in the organization of Shackleton's 1914 Antarctic expedition. Mr. Dederich is not only a generous patron of scientific exploration but a man whose administrative ability renders him of great assistance to an expedition faced with the complicated problems of equipment and organization. By his aid the idea was soon placed on a stable basis, and active steps could be taken toward sending out the exploring party.

At first the personnel of the new expedition consisted of four persons; viz., Mr. Knight himself, the leader, who was also to look after botanical and zoölogical research; Captain J. E. Ellam, the co-leader, who was to devote himself to the study of the political and religious institutions of the country; Mr. Frederick Fletcher, who was to act as geologist and also transport officer to the party; and finally Mr. William Harcourt, who was appointed cinematographer, for it was realized that in modern times a living pictorial record of the land and the people should form an integral part of every scientific expedition.

At a somewhat later period, in fact only a short time before the date fixed for departure, I was asked to join the mission as general adviser, as it was thought that my previous residence in the Orient and my knowledge of Tibetan language and customs might prove useful. Through the kindness of Sir E. Denison Ross I was able to secure leave of absence from my university and was thus enabled to accept the invitation.

We had then to decide upon the direction from which Tibet was to be entered. Three places at once suggested themselves. One was to enter Tibet from the east through China. Another was to go from the west through Kashmir and Northern India. The third was to start from Darjeeling in the south and to pass through the small semi-independent state of Sikkim, which lies between the larger countries of Nepal and Bhutan.

This last was the route eventually selected because it would bring the expedition into immediate contact with the central portion of Tibet with its two great cities, Shigatse and Lhasa. This route was the preferable one because as a result of the Younghusband expedition the Indian Government had secured the right to send certain specially selected persons to two places inside of Tibet itself. The first of these was the town of Yatung in the Chumbi Valley, just inside the Tibetan frontier. The other was the city of Gyangtse, a hundred and fifty miles in the interior. Persons permitted to travel to either place were required to go in a direct line without deviating in any way from the main trade-route.

The India Office and the Government of India were approached on the subject, and after some negotiation they gave us the necessary permission to travel to Gyangtse to apply to the Tibetan Government for further permission to proceed to Lhasa and other portions of the interior but refused to give us any further support or recognition.

In July, 1922, the party set sail for India. It was

Tibetan beggar woman

Tibetan princess in gala dress

The Kung Kusho and his A. D. C. The Kung Kusho, a near relative of the late Dalai-lama, ranks as prince and general in the new Tibetan army.

Reconnaissance of Mount Chumolhari (left), twenty-four thousand feet above sea-level

found impossible for all the members to go out together, and so it was agreed to make Darjeeling our rendezvous. Fletcher and Harcourt, however, accompanied me on the S.S. *Nellore,* and after touching at Malta, Port Saïd, Colombo, and Madras, we arrived at Calcutta in the middle of August. It was then, of course, the height of the Indian summer, and on many occasions the thermometer registered 110 degrees in the shade.

I have always had a fondness for tropical heat, but my companions suffered so much from it that after collecting the boxes which had been sent out from England and making a number of further purchases necessary for camp life in Tibet we went on by rail to Darjeeling, where before long the whole of our party assembled.

Darjeeling lies on an outer spur of the great Himalayan range. It is more than seven thousand feet above sea-level and even in summer is delightfully cool. For this reason it was made the summer capital of the province of Bengal, Calcutta, of course, being the winter capital. The chief objection to Darjeeling is its great rainfall, most of which occurs during the summer months, these forming the rainy season all over India.

Sixty years ago Darjeeling (properly Dorjeling, the temple of the thunderbolt) consisted of an insignificant village, forming part of the territory seized by the British Indian Government from the little independent hill-state of Sikkim by way of reparations. Reparations in those days seem to have been a matter more easily and quickly settled than they are now.

Darjeeling has had a very rapid development and is now a flourishing city. A large portion of the land seized along with Darjeeling, and which is known as British Sikkim, is laid out in tea-plantations, supervised by Europeans who use Darjeeling as their supply-base and frequently ride in for dances and other festivities. Their club, the Planters' Club, is a very important institution.

Apart from these, the resident European population is very small. The more important officials of the Bengal Government have summer villas scattered along the hillsides, but these are occupied chiefly in summer, at which time the hotels and boarding-houses are also packed with visitors. The native population is much larger and is more permanent.

The great Darjeeling market-place is the famous meeting-place for people of every race and caste. There is a substratum of the old Sikkimese population. Sikkimese are really Tibetans, who, in comparatively modern times, have migrated and settled south of the Himalayas. They have kept the appearance, the language, and the religion of their Tibetan ancestors, and for their benefit there are three lama (Tibetan Buddhist) monasteries in the neighborhood of the city. In recent years numerous settlers have arrived from the Indian plains. These, of course, are either Hindus or Mohammedans, and for their benefit there has been erected a temple and a mosque in the heart of the city.

An even larger number of people come from without the bounds of British India. These include immigrants from the still independent parts of Sikkim and from Bhutan, Nepal, and Tibet. Tibetans are to be seen all over the town and attract a good deal of the tourists' attention. Many of them have brought down curios from their native lands which are sold at enormous profit to European visitors.

Our party stayed for some three weeks at the Labyrinth, a small residential hotel, and it required all of this time to complete our preparations. Knight and the other members of the expedition frequently visited the market-place in order to secure those supplies which had not been procured in either England or Calcutta. I for the most part was engaged in "going native," spending long hours with the Sikkimese and Tibetans who are resident in Darjeeling. A number of the Tibetans were lamas or priests who had come down to India to go on pilgrimages to the holy places of Buddhism. Buddhism has long died out in India, but it is frequently visited by Buddhists of other lands, who love to walk in the footsteps of their Master, dead these two thousand five hundred years.

These long conversations served both to practise my Tibetan colloquial and also to add to our scanty stock of information about the conditions existing in the Forbidden Land. The good manageress of our hotel, a dear stout old Scotch lady, of strict Presbyterian doctrine with singular views on "the heathen," often lifted up her hands in horror when she saw my private sitting-room crowded with weird pilgrims who had come from north of the passes with the odor of the mountains still strong upon them.

The umdze or dean of one of the local Sikkimese temples was one of the most frequent of my visitors, and as he had already been to Shigatse and to Lhasa, the goals of our journey, and therefore knew the way, I at length engaged him as my secretary, and procured for him leave of absence from his temple so that he might come with us. It is considered very impolite in Tibet to call a man by his name when he possesses a title of any sort, and so he should have been called umdze-lā (literally *lags*), lā being a term of respect which may mean either Mr., Mrs., Miss, or Master. But this was too much of a mouthful for our party. So they christened him Toby, and Toby to the end of the journey he remained.

One of the most useful of our informants in Darjeeling was Laden La (literally *legs ldan lags*), a very well known character in this part of the world. The son of an insignificant Sikkimese landowner, he entered the police force while a boy, became a police sergeant, and eventually was given a commission as captain and became deputy and acting superintendent of police. Shortly after our arrival in India he was made an honorary A.D.C. to Lord Lytton, the governor of Bengal, a unique honor for a native. His unofficial position, however, is even greater, and we found him the uncrowned king of the whole Darjeeling district. All natives in the place are absolutely under his thumb, taking, changing, and losing their posts at his command. It is almost entirely at his order that Darjeeling remained nearly free from the Gandhi movement that swept over the whole of India. In accordance with Oriental custom and tradition, his position has rendered it advisable for the natives to offer him "slight tokens of their esteem" from time to time, so that he is now in the possession of a considerable fortune.

Chance has brought him into very close touch with the highest Tibetan officials. The two great potentates of Tibet, the Trashi-lama of Shigatse and the Dalai-lama of Lhasa, have both made visits to India, and in both cases Laden La was lent to them by the Indian Government to act as a guide and guard. As a result of this, Laden was made an honorary chamberlain of the Dalai-lama's court and was given the rank of depön or general in the new Tibetan army, and a few months after my return from Tibet he was actually called to Lhasa to organize for the Dalai-lama a police force of his capital.

We found him an exceedingly acute and able man, and as he was good enough to grant us his favor we found things mysteriously expedited; for not only did he give us letters of introduction to various people in Tibet, but he arranged that we secure able and faithful servants.

We had next to arrange for our transport. Wheeled traffic of any sort was of course impossible over the passes and is unknown anywhere in Tibet. For ourselves and our bearers we secured ponies, and for the major portion of our transport, mules. We intended to keep to the great highroads even after entering Tibet. Along these highroads it is always possible to hire animals, and as this was cheaper and less troublesome, we decided against purchasing any, particularly as any animals we might purchase in Darjeeling would be unfit for use on the high plateau of Tibet. For the first part of our journey riding-ponies were to cost us five rupees and transport mules three rupees a day.

We were now in a position to start on our journey. In any case we should have to pass through the little independent state of Sikkim on our way to Tibet, but it was decided that our main party should take the short cut which lay through the southeast of this little country, while I was to start a few days earlier and make a detour in order to visit the maharaja or king of Sikkim at his capital of Gantok, rejoining the main party at Yatung just inside of Tibet.

I was anxious to start on September 5, but this was an unlucky day, according to Tibetan calculations, and Toby insisted that I wait until the next, which was more auspicious. The Tibetans are grossly superstitious and arrange all their affairs with reference to lucky and unlucky days. These are calculated both with reference to the days of the month and also the days of the week. Thus for example Tuesdays, Thursdays, and Saturdays are bad days on which to start some new undertaking, while Mondays, Wednesdays, and Sundays are considered auspicious. The ninth, thirteenth, nineteenth, and twenty-ninth days of the month are considered of particularly good omen, and Toby pleaded that we postpone our departure until Sunday the nineteenth, a doubly favorable day. He seemed very much surprised that I refused to sacrifice two weeks in order to start things properly. At last he consented to come on the sixth, a Wednesday, provided that we started at nine o'clock, which the calendar declared to be an auspicious hour.

In case urgent business makes it necessary for a Tibetan to start a journey on an unlucky day he will have a hat or some other article of clothing sent on a mile or two ahead on the road on a lucky day preceding, because it is thought that in this way the gods can be beguiled into believing that the man himself started on the correct occasion.

I was told a good tale of a Tibetan who took a long journey with his wife. He so arranged the matter that he reached and left each town en route on a lucky day. While still on the journey the poor wife died (was this part of the good luck?), and the delay caused by this event upset the whole schedule, so that the man was hung up for several weeks at a little village en route waiting for an auspicious series of dates to come round again.

On the sixth a special service was held in Toby's monastery at daybreak, and at his earnest invitation I attended this ceremony in order to receive the special blessing of the abbot. Armed with this blessing I returned and made the final preparations for the departure at the fateful hour of nine. This took place without mishap. Toby, Lhaten, my "bearer" or personal servant, and I trotted away on our ponies, and we were followed by two coolies on foot to carry the baggage, for I was traveling light and required no mules.

At first the way lay through the damp, hot, luxuriant forest, which characterizes the southern slopes of the Himalayas, in such marked contrast to the bare, treeless, plantless, lifeless plateau of Tibet, which lies just north of that magnificent range of mountains.

From the Tibetan point of view our start may have been very auspicious, but personally I considered it very unfavorable, for after we had gone a mile or two it began to rain and in fact continued to pour the rest of the day. This very much hindered our progress, and we had to stop at the little village of Peshok. The next day we continued on our way. An important milestone was reached when we came to the Tista river. It was spanned by an imposing-looking bridge, but one which is really ramshackle and unsafe. There is a cart-road which goes as far as Kalimpong and Gantok, but when the carts reach this bridge they have to be taken apart and hauled over. Here I was instructed by Toby on two important points of Tibetan etiquette. He would not allow me to ride over the bridge but insisted that I get off my pony and walk across as a sign of reverence to the gods of Tibet.

In the middle of the bridge we found a number of paper prayers fluttering in the breeze. Toby brought out three such printed prayers which he had carried with him and tied them on to the others, and at the same time threw a couple of copper coins into the river as an offering to the deities which dwell therein. This last is an important custom which the Tibetans share with the ancient Romans.

We next ascended a long slope and found ourselves in the afternoon in the town of Kalimpong. This is the last outpost of the British Indian Government and an important city of trade. It has been called the

Harbor of Tibet, for while neither European nor Indian traders are allowed inside of the heart of the forbidden land, the Tibetans are free to come down to India and sell their goods, chiefly wool, and take back with them cheap knickknacks for sale in the markets of Shigatse and Lhasa. Kalimpong serves as the meeting-ground of Indian and Tibetan traders, just arriving or returning to Lhasa, the Secret City; so that to see the caravan merchants coming in from the North was like having communication with another unseen, half-fanciful world.

In order to promote such trade, the local authorities organize various fairs in Kalimpong which are attended by hordes of people of all races, chiefly Bhutanese, Sikkimese, and Tibetans, and the anthropologist has only to go to Kalimpong to find abundant material for the study of types.

Kalimpong differs from Darjeeling in many ways. In the first place, Kalimpong is part of the territory seized not from Sikkim but from Bhutan and is, therefore, the center of the district known as British Bhutan. It is some two thousand feet lower than Darjeeling (being five thousand feet above sea-level) but has the advantage of being much less damp than Darjeeling.

The social distinction between the two towns is even greater. Darjeeling is essentially an official post, and there the missionaries play a very minor and subdued part even in the social life of the place. In Kalimpong, on the other hand, things are very different. Here the missionaries reign supreme. All the important buildings belong to the Scotch Presbyterian mission, which also owns large tracts of land in the district. The senior missionaries, therefore, form the local aristocracy, overawing even the British-Indian officials; and Dr. Graham, the head of the mission, is the uncrowned king of Kalimpong, the arbiter and dispenser of justice even to those not inside the Christian fold. Dr. Graham has won this unique position largely as a result of his forceful and tactful personality, for from the purely missionary point of view the Tibetan peoples form a singularly unpromising field, and very few converts have been won.

Considering this and other facts it is curious that the Tibetans prefer Kalimpong to Darjeeling as the base of their communications with India, but certainly the fact is undisputed, and there is, therefore, good reason to suppose that Kalimpong will gradually rise and Darjeeling sink in importance.

From Kalimpong the caravan road leads on direct to the Jelap Pass and the Chumbi Valley in Tibet. This was the road destined to be followed by my main party, but in order to visit Gantok I had the next day to descend once more to the Tista Valley and follow for many miles the Tista River. In the afternoon we reached the frontier of Sikkim. Here we were stopped by some Sikkimese frontier police and had to show our passes permitting us to enter Sikkimese territory.

For many years the British Government has had diplomatic relations with Nepal and Bhutan, but both these countries have maintained their independence. Sikkim, on the other hand, though also nominally independent, has come much more closely under British influence and control. The maharaja of Sikkim recognizes the nominal suzerainty of the emperor of India. An English political officer is resident in Gantok, the capital, and wields a great deal of influence, but Sikkim, in common with other so-called native states, is still entirely autonomous on nearly all local and internal matters, possessing her own laws and courts of justice, her own ministers of council of state, her own system of taxation, and her own defense force, and no European can pass within her borders unless armed with a special official pass.

I noticed, however, that the gendarmes or soldier police who demanded our passes were Nepalese, who, though in the pay of the Sikkimese Government, could not even speak the Sikkimese language.

Soon after we crossed the frontier it began to rain very heavily, and so we halted for the night at the village of Rangpo, situated in the heart of the warm, moist Tista Valley. This part of Sikkim is very famous for malaria and other tropical fevers, and so we took great care to boil our water and to wrap ourselves up with mosquito-nets, for the air was black with these germ-carrying insects.

The next day we continued on the Gantok road and halted at another little Sikkimese village that evening. On the way we stopped to rest for a few minutes, and on these occasions we began to be troubled with leeches. These horrible blood-sucking little creatures were hidden in the undergrowth, but they must have smelled our presence, for as soon as we stopped they began coming toward us with great rapidity in their curious form of locomotion. Although they look like black earthworms, instead of gliding along the ground in snakelike fashion, they rise on their tails until they are absolutely perpendicular, then, arching their heads down to the ground, bring their tails up to their heads. They thus measure their distance along the ground. It is really comical to see these tiny creatures without legs walking along a path, the head and tail taking the place of legs.

In spite of my vigilance, two or three attached themselves to my body and began thirstily sucking blood. I wanted to tear them off, but my bearer Lhaten would not allow me to do this, as the flesh comes off with them and leaves a nasty wound which refuses to heal for many days thereafter. In accordance with his instructions, therefore, I had to allow the creatures to continue their ghastly work until he prepared a little bag filled with salt and, dipping this in water, let the brine trickle down on them. This had a magical effect. The leeches shriveled away into seeming nothingness, leaving only a little clot of blood, which we easily wiped away.

We found the road surprisingly good; our day's destination proved to be an insignificant little village, but we stayed in comfort at the little government rest-house, fitted out in an entirely European style. The official rest-houses are scattered all over the inhabited part of Sikkim.

When the Indian Government carried through one of its punitive expeditions against Sikkim, it forced the maharaja's Government to undertake to construct and to keep under repair, a number of high-roads throughout the country, in place of the casual tracks which were hitherto to be found, and also to erect a number of these official rest-houses. All the people of Sikkim benefit from the roads, but for the most part they gain nothing from the rest-houses. For although the maharaja himself and one or two of the higher members of his court are permitted to use them, they have been erected chiefly for the benefit of the British political officer and his staff, and also for other European travelers who are given permits from the Government. This system of rest-houses (or dak-bungalows, as they are called) forms part of the general policy of the Indian Government, which has forced a number of rulers of other native states to erect similar institutions.

These dak-bungalows are really dainty little villas, with a sitting-room, two or three bedrooms, and out-houses for the use of the travelers, servants, and animals. They are nicely furnished, though, in accordance with Anglo-Indian custom, every traveler brings his own bedclothes, and also a retinue of servants, who cook for and serve him, as each rest-house has only a chowkidar or caretaker in attendance. Supplies must be procured by one's own servants in one of the local bazaars.

Early the next morning we continued our journey. We had for some time a level road, and I tried to get my pony to canter and so found that these hill ponies have only one pace, viz., an amble, something between a fast walk and a trot, and nothing will induce them to break into either a real trot or a gallop. They are able to keep up their amble all day, however, and are able in the long run to outdistance any pony with more orthodox styles of locomotion.

The summer rains had washed portions of the road away, and I noticed a number of laborers repairing it. These, also, I noticed, were Nepalese and not Sikkimese. In fact during the last few years the number of immigrants from Nepal has been so great that the Nepalese inhabitants of Sikkim far outnumber the Sikkimese.

In the early afternoon we began another long ascent and a few hours later found ourselves at last in Gantok, the capital of Sikkim. I duly installed myself in the dak-bungalow, and a few moments later the private secretary of the maharaja called to welcome me in the name of his master and to state that his Highness would receive me in audience the next morning at eleven. Later in the evening five servants arrived from the palace bringing presents of food, so that I was made to feel something of a guest of state.

The next morning at the appointed time I walked along the ridge over to the maharaja's palace. This consists of two buildings, one built in Tibetan style and the other in European style, but it is significant that the European house is the only one now in use.

I found the maharaja a very affable young man of about twenty-five, pale, thin, and rather nervous and anemic-looking, and obviously not particularly interested in the affairs of state, which, however, he felt bound to take as seriously as possible. His hobby is photography, and he spends a good deal of time in playing with his pet animals. Much more impressive and imposing was his wife the maharanee, a Lhasa woman, who obviously had a good deal to say in the government of the household.

The maharaja was educated at St. Paul's School, Darjeeling, and speaks excellent English, but in deference to his lady we spoke a good deal of Tibetan. The maharaja spoke Tibetan with a marked Sikkimese accent, using a number of local words, but was quite intelligible. What he thought of my accent Heaven only knows.

The present ruler of Sikkim came to the throne quite unexpectedly. His predecessor was his brother, a young man of great talent and charm, who was educated at Oxford and who had traveled very widely. He was very much struck by Japan and was very anxious to marry a Japanese woman. The India Office for obvious diplomatic reasons refused to permit such a match. It is interesting to note that the India Office had the power to do this. The young maharaja then tried in vain to marry a Burmese princess, but in the end he was forced to take a Lhasa lady.

In spite of his modernist tendencies, his secular position, and his state of marital bliss, he enjoyed the distinction of being regarded as an incarnation of divinity by both Sikkimese and Tibetans. This was the result, not of his kingly position, but of a rather interesting chain of circumstances, which deserves narration.

It is well known that the abbots of the leading

temples in Tibet are regarded as incarnations of various deities, or more technically of various buddhas and bodhisattvas. When such a person dies he is supposed to be reborn again almost immediately as an infant. A search is made for the sacred child, who, when found, is at once recognized as the new abbot, a regent being appointed to administer his duties during his minority.

In some cases the selection of the child is done purely by lot. In other cases the old abbot shortly before his death will give some indication of the place or family in which he intends to be reborn.

On one occasion many years ago one such living deity grew very fond of a little Sikkimese girl and declared shortly before his death that he would be reborn as the first male child to whom she would give birth. After the death of the old man, the then maharaja of Sikkim, learning of the prophecy, married the girl, who in due course gave him a son and heir, who was thus regarded as a deity while his father was still on the throne.

It is surprising that the young ruler whose character was thus swathed in the atmosphere of this quaint old-world divinity should have developed into a man so modern and European in his ideas. In fact he proved too progressive for his country and his people, and not long after he returned to his native land he died suddenly and mysteriously. Rumor had it that some of his old-fashioned ministers, disturbed by fear of too radical changes, gave him enough poison to insure that the divinity move on to still another incarnation, in order that his younger brother in this life, who was likely to prove more pliable, might come to the throne.

My morning audience with the present maharaja was not the last meeting I had with him, for, learning that I was eager to push on the next day, he invited me to tea that afternoon in order that I might meet the Englishman who acts as his personal assistant.

This tea-party proved very entertaining, for it was quaint to have such an orthodox English meal in the midst of such other-world surroundings. The personal assistant proved to be a bluff, jolly man of great simplicity whom I liked immensely. He had, I think, been for many years a non-commissioned officer, doing clerical work, and had only recently, upon semi-retirement, taken over his new post.

His position threw an interesting light on the relations between Sikkim and the Indian Government. The senior British official in Sikkim is the so-called political officer, appointed directly by the viceroy of India, and he exercises an enormous amount of power. In theory, however, his post is entirely diplomatic, his office corresponding to that of a minister or ambassador, so that it is impossible for him to interfere too much in the details of every-day internal administration. As a further check on native malpractices, therefore, the maharaja is given an English "personal assistant." He is nominally a servant of the native ruler and in theory can be engaged and dismissed by him, but in practice he holds his post at the pleasure of the political officer. It is the duty of the personal assistant to act as secretary and adviser to the maharaja on all matters of state (though in theory his advice may be disregarded) and also to superintend the wheels of the administration and to see that no serious corruption or malpractice takes place.

In theory the entire control of matters of state lies in the hands of the maharaja, aided by his council of state, which consists of various ministers in charge of separate departments and of nominees chosen from the Sikkimese landed aristocracy. All the members of his body are of course natives, and it is the wise policy of the British Government to allow the native officials to carry out their duties according to their own desires, so long as there is no flagrant injustice and so long as they do not touch on diplomatic affairs.

Very occasionally an important point of policy will be forced on the country by the political officer. One such point was an importation of Nepalese settlers into the country.

A few decades ago the population of Sikkim consisted of three or four thousand Lepchas and a slightly larger number of Sikkimese. The Lepchas are supposedly the primitive inhabitants of the country. A timid, spiritless, nature-loving, childlike folk, they still try to dwell in the hidden forests, far away in the hills. They are probably distantly, but very distantly, related to the Tibetans, but they possess a language and a primitive culture entirely their own.

The so-called Sikkimese are Tibetans, who in the last three hundred years have swept down into the country from the north, conquering and displacing the Lepchas.

Great strapping creatures most of them are, but

incurably shiftless and lazy. Sikkim is rich in resources, but neither Sikkimese nor Lepcha could be made to develop these. Consequently the political officer of the time, Mr. J. C. White, forced the Sikkimese Government to import Nepalese laborers and other settlers, and now there are nearly ten Nepalese for every one Sikkimese, even in Sikkim. This has proved enormously beneficial to the wealth of the country, but needless to say it proved unpopular among the Sikkimese, who were forced to work in competition with a keen and industrious people. So far, however, the Sikkimese have kept official posts entirely in their own hands.

The maharaja urged me to stay in Gantok for several days longer, but I told him that it was imperative for me to go on with my journey the next day. He was then kind enough to suggest that I dismiss the ponies and the coolies I had brought with me from Darjeeling, as he would supply me free of cost mule transport for my party to Yatung in the Chumbi Valley, the great Tibetan outpost.

I was very glad to avail myself of his offer, and the next morning set out for the three days' journey to the passes. This consisted of a long continuous ascent along a narrow trail which had been cut into the side of the cliffs. In some places the road was only two feet wide, and we had a sheer drop of two thousand feet below us. It was a very exciting journey, as the mules would insist on walking along the extreme edge of the road on the very brink of nothingness. In summer the road is frequently washed away and in winter the path is completely blocked by snow, so that spring and autumn are the only times one can count on getting through. Even in September I found the road in a very bad state and saw numerous Nepalese coolies busy repairing it.

Gantok lies six thousand feet above sea-level. The next day brought us to Karponang, nine thousand five hundred feet; the day after to Changu, with its beautiful lake, twelve thousand six hundred feet above sea-level; and early the next morning we came to the Natu Pass, which at this point divides Sikkimese from Tibetan territory, and which lies about fourteen thousand feet above the sea.

The last day the climb was so steep that it was impossible to ride, and the sharp ascent had to be made on foot. At such an altitude this climb was terribly fatiguing, and to make matters worse we began to suffer from mountain-sickness, a gruesome exaggeration of the symptoms felt in seasickness. I was reminded here of the story of the poor British soldier who took part in the 1904 military expedition against Tibet and who remarked on the way up that he had always heard that Tibet was a table-land, and that if so the road up to it must constitute one of its legs.

Very bleak and forlorn is the Natu Pass. In the winter it is covered with thirty feet of snow, and it seems to be the center of great wind- and thunderstorms. Nevertheless the view gained from the top was worth all the trouble, the pain, and the fatigue of the ascent. In the distance we could see the snowy cone of the sacred mountain of Chumolhari, at the

Phari reservoir with island shrine

Phari Ozong

Bhutanese princess and husband

Dongtse monastery

base of which we knew the real Tibetan plateau started. Immediately below us was the Chumbi Valley, the curious outpost of the Tibetan Empire which only at this point stretches south of the Himalayan ranges.

We had first of all to make our way down into the thickly populated valley in order that later we might work our way up its sides until we came to the barren table-land of Tibet proper.

The descent proved nearly as difficult as the ascent. To make things easier the steeper portions of the road, if it could be dignified by this name, wound round and round in a singularly sinuous fashion, for even a mule cannot maintain his hold when his tail is vertically over his head. Even so, there are a great many casualties every year among the mule caravans that make their way over the passes.

This was September, and no snow had fallen since the preceding winter, but here and there we came across great patches of snow which even the fierce summer sun had not been able to melt away.

At last, however, we came to the bottom of the valley, and I was able to see something of its picturesque villages and their inhabitants. In many respects the Chumbi Valley is quite unique and is unlike any other part of Tibet. A valley on the south side of the Himalayas, it is a narrow wedge of Tibetan territory lying between the states of Sikkim and Bhutan. Like these latter countries, and unlike the barren plains of Tibet proper, the sides of its hills are covered with trees, and it receives a very heavy annual rainfall, something which is entirely unknown on the Tibetan plateau.

Owing to the severity of its climate, the only crop which true Tibet can grow is barley. In Sikkim, on the other hand, the staple crop is rice; hence its Tibetan name of Drenjong, or the rice country. In the Chumbi Valley the main crop is wheat; hence its Tibetan name of Tromo, or wheat country.

Ethnologically, as well as geographically, Chumbi is quite distinct from Tibet; for though the Chumbi people in common with the Bhutanese and Sikkimese are of Tibetan origin, they have a dialect and many customs entirely their own.

They have the deserved reputation of being the most beautiful of all the peoples of Tibetan stock, and many of the young men and women I passed were really remarkably handsome. Unlike the true Tibetans, with whom filthiness is a virtue esteemed by the gods, the Chumbi people are occasionally known to wash themselves.

I was particularly interested in the Chumbi Valley, because it is only by an accident that to-day it does not form part of the British dominions.

After the success of the Younghusband expedition in 1904, it was arranged that Tibet should pay reparations to the extent of seven million five hundred thousand rupees (or five hundred thousand pounds) to the British Government. And, pending the full payment of the amount, the Chumbi Valley was to remain in the hands of the British Government. It was originally arranged that this sum was to be paid in seventy-five annual instalments, which meant that England would have a seventy-five-year lease on the Chumbi

Valley; this was practically equivalent to annexation, but things were destined to turn out otherwise.

In the first place, the Liberals came into power in England and in a burst of anti-imperialism voluntarily reduced the reparations claim to one third of the original amount. Secondly, China, anxious to get rid of British occupation anywhere in Tibet, came forward and arranged to pay the whole sum immediately on behalf of Tibet. This was agreed to in the end, and so the British occupation of Chumbi came to an end, though the Indian Government reserved the right to keep a trade agent there and to station a small body of Indian soldiers to act as his body-guard; but the administration of the district was handed back to the Tibetan officials.

The British agency is placed in the village of Yatung (properly New Yatung), called by the Tibetans Sashima, which I reached that same afternoon.

Immediately on arrival at the village I saw a house with a union jack flying over it; and, knowing this to be the British agency, I at once set off there to make an official visit. I must confess that I went there with a certain feeling of undeserved shame.

In order to protect myself from the bitter morning cold of the passes, I had put on an airman's helmet, which completely covered all of my face except my nose. In this very highly rarefied atmosphere any portion of the body exposed to the sun becomes terribly sunburned in spite of the intense cold, and so when I pulled off my mask before making my visit I found that my face as a whole had retained its pallor, while my nose was a most fiery red. I looked, indeed, like a confirmed toper and determined to make a firm display of teetotal principles immediately on meeting the British agent.

My meeting with the trade agent turned out to be unexpectedly pleasant and informal. The term "trade agent" is somewhat misleading. His duties are exactly those of a consul, but he is given his title because he is appointed by the India Office and not by the Foreign Office.

The present occupant of the post is a most charming Eurasian by the name of MacDonald. His father was a Scotch tea-planter near Darjeeling. His mother was a Sikkimese. His wife is a Nepalese, while one of his daughters has married an Englishman, so that his family can be called truly cosmopolitan. His mother's language being but a variation of Tibetan, he speaks that language with great fluency, which makes him an ideal figure for his post, that of intermediary between the Tibetans and the Indian Government; though it is interesting to note that because of his Scotch blood, and in spite of his personal friendship with the Dalai-lama, the supreme ruler of Tibet, he also is not allowed to go outside of the so-called trade-route, the narrow strip of land that connects Yatung with the city of Gyangtse, still further in the interior. Even to him, apart from the two towns of Gyangtse and Yatung and the direct road which runs between them, Tibet is the Forbidden Land.

There was a rest-house at my disposal at Yatung, but Mr. MacDonald very hospitably insisted upon my staying with him until my main party should arrive from Darjeeling, and in the course of many long conversations with him I secured much useful information.

The next day brought a little excitement in the arrival of Major F. M. Bailey, the political officer in Gantok, who has also complete charge of diplomatic negotiations with the states of Bhutan and Tibet.

The British trade agent may be called the consul, or even the consul-general, while the political officer is the ambassador, save that he is not allowed to visit Lhasa, the capital of the country to which he is Great Britain's diplomatic representative.

In the old days there was an equal ban upon his visiting the little kingdom of Bhutan, but this is gradually being lifted by reason of some very astute diplomatic moves. The Bhutanese were to the surrounding peoples what the Scots robber barons were to the English at one time. No near-by district was free from a raid, and they spread terror and desolation wherever they went. During the last century they gravely mistreated a British envoy, and the invasion of British India by some of their marching bands forced the Indian Government to take action and seize a good portion of Bhutanese territory, which is now known as British Bhutan, paying as a sort of rent, however, a yearly sum of money to the Bhutanese Government on condition that it kept its subjects in order.

Trouble continued for some time, however, because of the weakness of the central Bhutanese Government. There were two "kings" of Bhutan; one was the dharmaraja or spiritual overlord, and the other was the secular head, but neither possessed any efficient control over the *pönlops,* or district governors, who were hereditary semi-independent barons.

It was obvious, therefore, that a change in policy was necessary. In 1904 one of these magnates, the Tongsa *pönlop,* had become the most influential person in Bhutan. He rendered very valuable diplomatic assistance to the Younghusband expedition while in Tibet; and largely on the advice of Mr. White, the previously mentioned political officer in Sikkim at that time, not only was the Tongsa *pönlop* made a K.C.I.E., but the Indian Government decided to give moral backing enough to allow him to declare himself the first hereditary maharaja or king of Bhutan. This change was duly made, and under the new ruler's strong hands Bhutan has been welded into a coördinated and centralized state.

The new ruler did not forget his gratitude, and though Bhutan has remained closed to the ordinary Englishman, the political officer in Sikkim has on several occasions made a state visit to the capital of Bhutan. Major Bailey was just returning from one such visit. On this occasion he had been accompanied not only by his wife but by his mother-in-law, Lady Couzens Hardy, and rumor has it that the journey was not without amusing incidents from internal as well as external causes.

The next day I paid an official visit to the Baileys, and they were kind enough to invite me to lunch. Later events were to bring me into very violent political conflict with Major Bailey; but personally our relationships were always of a very friendly character, and certainly he is a most interesting and capable man, a great sportsman and traveler. He has in the past also taken several secret journeys through Tibet, though he only got to Lhasa in company with the Younghusband expedition.

He had only recently secured the post of political officer, and I was much interested to learn from him something of his policy toward Tibet; as in his hands lie, to a large extent, the future relations between India and Tibet. From a personal point of view this presents a very great contrast to that of his predecessor, Sir Charles Bell, and well illustrates two different ways of handling Orientals. Sir Charles Bell aimed, not at overawing the Tibetans, but at securing their close sympathy and friendship. In order to do this he thought it necessary to conform to certain aspects of prejudice and superstition. Thus, for example, he neither fished nor shot. He abstained from tobacco as the Tibetans regard the use of tobacco with horror. When in contact with Tibetans he abstained from eating fish and chicken, as the Tibetans regard these foods as unclean. This extraordinary regard for native susceptibilities is not always successful, but in the case of Sir Charles it seems to have worked wonders, and I was later to find that many Tibetan officials have an unusual affection for him.

Major Bailey has followed the more ordinary lines of British administrators, who believe it inconsistent with the maintenance of dignity to pander too much to native ideas, but certainly his policy has not decreased

British prestige in this part of the world. But I believe that there is no great love lost between the past and present political officers, and as Mr. MacDonald, the trade agent and nominally Major Bailey's subordinate, is a protégé of Sir Charles Bell, the relation between the political officer and the trade agent has sometimes an interesting side.

A day or two later my main party arrived in Yatung, and shortly afterward Major Bailey and his party returned to Gantok, but not until he had given us final and rather unexpected orders. As previously stated, he has authority to grant special passes permitting Europeans to go on to Gyangtse, several miles further in the interior, and these he handed to us, but only after extracting from each of us a solemn promise that we should not depart from the main direct route to Gyangtse, and further that in the event of the Tibetans' refusing us permission to go further we should return immediately to India. This was a serious blow to the scheme which I had already in mind of going on in disguise from Gyangtse in case we were refused permission to go on to Lhasa. Equally vexatious was the promise we were forced to make that even if we could extract permission from the Tibetan officials to go on to the Forbidden City we should leave our cinematograph camera behind at Gyangtse. For scientific purposes we had very strongly wanted to get a living record of Lhasa life, but we were completely in the political officer's power and had to sign the necessary guarantee.

We were now in a position to move on, but before

doing so our reunited party decided to pay an official visit of courtesy to the Tibetan *depön* or general, who was the chief official of the Chumbi Valley, and who was placed there to carry on any necessary negotiations with the British trade agent.

We rode down the valley for a bit and soon found ourselves in front of his house. It was a substantial mansion of typically Tibetan formation, being built around a courtyard. Its walls were of stone and were four or five feet thick. The door only was of wood, and was painted in gaudy Chinese design.

Entering the courtyard we ascended to the second story, which was the residential part, and met the *depön,* who proved to be a most beguiling old man, trained in the school of Chinese diplomacy. He assured us that since we had come to Tibet its desert wastes would bloom with lotus-flowers. Secretly he wrote a letter to the Lhasa Government advising them to have nothing to do with us. Nevertheless, we got an excellent and free lunch out of him.

Returning that evening to Yatung, we found that a Bhutanese chieftainess had arrived with three of her husbands; all people of Tibetan stock practise polyandry, of which more hereafter. They were on a visit to Mr. MacDonald. They had been invited to attend the wedding of his daughter and had arrived exactly a month too late—a typically Oriental way of keeping an appointment.

I noticed the husbands were very meek and tame-looking, and I heard that the husky damsel had the reputation of being something of a bully.

Both men and women in Bhutan wear very short dresses, so that the chieftainess exposed to sight a vast quantity of leg but seemed not in the least discomposed about it.

In contrast to the elaborate head-dresses of the women in Tibet proper, the Bhutanese women wear their hair bobbed, and it was really comical to see so modern an English custom on so primitive a woman. It was obvious that she was not only wealthy but strong, for she wore around her neck a great necklace of coral, which weighed more than fifteen pounds. Her conversational abilities were limited, and her favorite amusement was chewing betel, which she spat out with great gusto upon some of Mr. MacDonald's fine carpets. Her aim was remarkable and reminded me of the performance of certain Kentucky colonels with chewing-tobacco.

She was very courageous generally but very much afraid of dogs. On one occasion we were out in the garden, and a puppy ran up and barked. The Bhutanese chieftainess gave one shriek and ran for protection, not to one of her husbands, but to Mr. Harcourt, the cinematographer, the youngest and handsomest member of our party. She clung so desperately that all the breath was squeezed out of him before I had time to pick the puppy up and put him in his kennel.

After this episode we began to fear that Mr. Harcourt would be kidnapped and added to the lady's harem, and so we decided to leave the next day on the road for Gyangtse.

Shortly after leaving Yatung, and while still following the narrow ravine which leads from the Chumbi Valley to the Tibetan plateau, we came to the great Chumbi Monastery, well known on account of its learned abbot, and also because of the famous oracle, or prophet, who is housed therein.

I was shown all over the monastery, and then with two of our party had lunch with the abbot; and we had a high time talking over fine points of Buddhist theology. The old man, though educated at the great Trashilhumpo monastery at Shigatse, was born in Mongolia, and so I was able to win his affection by talking to him in his native tongue, which he had not heard for many years.

Our whole party then assembled to see the oracle. Like the late O. Henry, I am not superstitious in that I refuse to believe in black cats, palmistry, or the weather forecasts in the newspapers, but certainly our prophet friend turned out to be very interesting.

Although at present the most famous of them, he is not the only oracle Tibet possesses. Formerly there was in Lhasa itself an oracle renowned for his prophecies, but in the course of a long life he made one mistake. At the beginning of the Younghusband expedition—the Tibetans dignify it with the title of the war between India and Tibet—he foretold that Tibet would be successful and drive the barbarians away. After the final defeat of the Tibetans and the flight of the Dalai-lama, he went the way of all false prophets and had his head removed from his shoulders, whereupon he ceased to prophesy.

I observed the Chumbi oracle very closely and

found that his methods correspond in general to those used by mediums in the West. He goes into an ecstatic trance, frequently accompanied by epileptic symptoms, and while thus obsessed delivers semi-coherent words which foretell what is to happen. Generally, like the Delphic oracle of old, his prophecies are delightfully vague and can be made to fit the event however it may turn out; but it is remarkable that halfway through the great World War he foretold the exact year and month in which hostilities would cease.

Not long after leaving the monastery we came to the village of Gautsa, the last village of the Chumbi Valley. Here we bade good-by to trees. Hereafter we were to live on the desolate Roof of the World. The next day we emerged from the ravine-valley formation and found ourselves on the great Tibetan table-land—broad, treeless, plantless plains, bordered by rippling, even hills; hills, however, which were eighteen to twenty thousand feet above sea-level.

Continuing along the plateau for some hours, we at last came in sight of Pari Castle, situated in the center of the great Pari plain, with Chumolhari, the sacred mountain, looming in the background.

On reaching the town of Pari, the first thing that came to our attention was a tiny sacred island in the middle of a frozen lake. Here were erected prayer-flags which, as they fluttered in the breeze, wiped out the sins of man, according to Tibetan belief; and here morning and evening was burnt incense, the sweet odor of which was supposed to appease the dark demons of the night.

Behind the island of prayer and protected by it was the great castle of Pari, the giant outpost fortress guarding this part of the Tibetan frontier. Armed as we were with special passes permitting us to go as far as Gyangtse, the local officials were unable to turn us back and so made the most of a bad job by inviting us to a state luncheon, which lasted for four hours. Most of the food was in Chinese and not in Tibetan style (Chinese cooking is in Tibet what French cooking is in England and America), but we were forced to consume enormous quantities of Tibetan tea.

I was very much amused by one incident. The use of tobacco is very strictly prohibited in Tibet. The smoking of tobacco is regarded there in very much the same way as the smoking of opium is in Europe (it is curious that the Chinese never taught the Tibetans to smoke opium), but one of the two governors of the castle had contracted a great liking for cheap English cigarettes, two or three of which he smoked while we were there. During the lunch he sidled up to me and in a whisper implored me to say nothing about his smoking in Lhasa, because if it were known he would inevitably be dismissed and disgraced.

After lunch was over we ascended to the roof of the castle and gained a panoramic view of the town of Pari, which has the well-earned reputation of being the filthiest town in the world. Because of the fact that refuse has continually been thrown into the streets, these streets are now nearly on a level with the roofs of the houses, which look as if they were built underground. Pari is, in fact, buried in its own filth.

Picturesque it certainly is, however, for on every roof there was a prayer-flag or two, and on many of them a heap of barley-straw and yak-dung.

On the outskirts could be seen fields sown with barley, but being nearly fifteen thousand feet above sea-level and exposed to the full Himalayan cold, this barley very seldom ripens, and its stalks can only be used as animal fodder. No other cultivation is possible, so that the local inhabitants must get their living from their flocks and as carriers on the great caravan route between Lhasa and Kalimpong. Most of the precious wool which Tibet sends down to India comes through Pari.

While continuing our march the next day, we were very much struck by the great beauty of the near-by mountain, Chumolhari. This peak is twenty-four thousand feet high, and its steep sides and proudly precipitous glaciers render it one of the most difficult mountains in the world to ascend. The natural grandeur of Chumolhari has impressed itself even upon the stolid Tibetan, and he worships the mountain as a goddess, as the fair lady of the everlasting snows; on its sides, he believes, dwell the gnomes, the demons, and the goblins, who play such an important part in Tibetan folk-lore.

For the most part our way lay along the great, bare, desolate plains, occasionally intersected by mountains. Sometimes the plain narrowed down to a valley between such mountain ranges. Properly speaking, there are no roads in Tibet. The officials need all the tax money for their own private requirements and have none to spend on public works; but though Tibet excludes outsiders, the Tibetans are great travelers inside of their own country, and the great caravans going to and fro in Tibet have worn out for themselves a settled route. In some places the ground is too sandy for the yaks or mules to leave any tracks, but in other places, where the ground consists of mud or clay, one sees huge ruts or tracks through which the animals pick their way. Wheeled traffic is completely unknown. The only cart which the country possesses is used to transport an idol inside the city of Lhasa, and this has to be pulled by men.

We were traveling slowly, as we wished to see something of the country, and so en route we were overtaken and passed by Mr. MacDonald, who was also going to Gyangtse to look after us while we were there. Formerly there was also a British trade agent at Gyangtse, but for some time past Mr. MacDonald has been in charge of both posts, so that frequently he has to go from one place to the other.

A day or two later Toby, my lama secretary, became very ill. We thought he had pneumonia, which in Tibet, because of the rarefied atmosphere, is nearly always fatal, and so we thought we were in for a bad time. The next day he grew worse, and as the main party could not delay they went on, leaving me and Lhaten behind to nurse Toby, and if necessary to bury him.

There was nothing we could do except to feed him with cod-liver oil and malt, and wait for the crisis. One afternoon a couple of days later, while Toby was asleep, I got out some of my Tibetan books—all books in Tibet are of a religious character—and began chanting from them, as I thought it was the best way to kill time, and also to go on with my Tibetan studies. This continued about two hours, and by a curious coincidence, when he awoke, we found the crisis had passed and that he was much better. By the natives the benefit of the cod-liver oil was forgotten and the "cure" was put down to my religious incantations, and I was put down as a "holy man," a reputation that was later to stand me in good stead.

A day or two later we were able to go on again, and by traveling double stages we soon caught up with our main party. Our long journey to Gyangtse was broken each evening by our stay in one of the official rest-houses, erected at the order of the Indian Government, in order to establish a line of communication between their two outposts in Yatung and Gyangtse, and to serve strategic purposes in case of a renewed outbreak of hostilities. At each camp we spent some time in trying to gain the friendship and confidence of the natives. In this part of Tibet, in this narrow six-mile strip reaching to Gyangtse, they had become inured to foreign barbarians but were apt to be sullen; but we found that music has indeed charms to win the savage breast. We had with us a small portable gramophone, and the villagers crowded around to hear the weird noises that came out of the box. In fact, after the ice had been broken, they even entered into a competition to see who was the first to learn the tango, the fox-trot, and the shimmy.

Natives of Gyangtse posing to cinematography

A prayer-wall along which one must walk to acquire merit

The portable gramophone carried by the first expedition proved of great interest to the Tibetans

A Tibetan city store

At this time it was autumn, and as we passed through occasional straggling villages we could see the peasants hard at work harvesting their crops. Tibet is far too bleak and cold to be an agricultural country, and the one thing that can be grown in any quantity is barley, an unusually hardy plant. The threshing was carried on by the process which has come down from time immemorial and consisted of the whole family walking on the barley-stalks and stamping out the grain. Round and round they went, wife, husbands, and children, aided by the slow-moving Tibetan cattle, a cross between Indian cattle and the indigenous yak of Tibet.

On many occasions as we went along the road we passed by some shrine or sacred image. One of these, the famous Red Idol, as it is called, is quite imposing, and I noticed with particular interest the heap of tiny stones in front of it. As Tibet has no flowers to present to the idols, the Tibetan peasants will carry little pebbles and heap them up before the image—certainly a very curious way of showing their respect. Beyond is the Red Idol Gorge, named for the image; here I caused my servants a great deal of uneasiness by galloping on ahead of our party and alone. This gorge is noted for its bandits and highwaymen, and Tibetans will only go through it in large parties. As I passed through I noticed one group of horsemen who did indeed look somewhat suspicious, but instead of trying to avoid them I made straight for them, and to my surprise they immediately turned tail and scampered away.

Two days later we came to a little village where the narrow valley widened out into a plain once more, and we could see ahead of us in the distance the town of Gyangtse, our immediate goal.

Gyangtse is about 147 miles inside the frontier. It is the third largest city in Tibet, and is the seat of an important administrative district. In common with other such places, the town itself was dominated and rendered almost insignificant by the great stone castle, which is on the top of the hill in the very center of the plain. The castle is one of the most imposing anywhere in Tibet, and certainly deserves to rank with any of the medieval European castles, although it has only recently been rebuilt.

A mile and a half away from the castle the Indian Government has erected a strongly fortified fort where are housed the British trade agent and his escort of soldiers. It is necessary to keep this armed escort here in order to see that no attempt be made on the life of the British agent by any of the fanatical peasantry.

We found Mr. MacDonald, the agent, waiting for us, and he gave us lunch and a warm welcome. The fort is connected by telegraph wires with Yatung and Kalimpong, so that it is possible for the agent to communicate at once with the Indian Government any event of especial importance which may take place in Tibet, though communications are much handicapped by the fact that no British representative is allowed to reside in Shigatse or Lhasa, or anywhere within the interior, and the agent has to rely very largely upon the vague rumors which find their way down to Gyangtse.

The establishment of the British agency and fort here is the direct result of the Younghusband expedition, which was of such far-reaching importance that just a word must be said concerning it.

Because of the close proximity of Tibet and India, the British Indian Government tried for many years to enter into diplomatic negotiations with the Tibetan hierarchy. As far back as 1774 Warren Hastings, the first and greatest of the governor-generals of India, sent a diplomatic mission to the Trashi-lama in Shigatse, under George Bogle, and followed this up by another mission in 1783 under Turner. Neither of these had any permanent effect, and neither of them got to Lhasa. Gradually Tibet became more rigid in her isolation, and the relations between India and Tibet grew worse and worse. This was accentuated by various boundary disputes, and by the effort of each country to exercise paramount influence in Sikkim.

A final peaceful settlement was rendered difficult because the Tibet officials refused even to negotiate; special letters which were sent by the viceroy of India to the Dalai-lama and couched in the most complimentary terms were returned unopened. In 1903 the British sent a special commission under Younghusband to Kampa Dzong, just inside the Tibetan frontier, and asked the Tibetan Government to send down representatives with whom they could negotiate. This request was ignored; and as at the same time the Dalai-lama was coquetting with Russia, it was decided to send an armed expedition into Tibet in support of Colonel Younghusband's mission, to see that no harm befell the members of this mission as they continued on to the interior, in order to negotiate a treaty of peace with the Tibetan Government.

Instead of marching forward from Kampa Dzong, it was decided that the expedition should move forward into Tibet along the very same line which we had followed. Skirmishes took place between the Tibetans and the British forces at Guru and at one or two other places between Pari and Gyangtse, but the most serious engagement took place in Gyangtse itself, where the Tibetans delivered a serious attack and heavy fighting took place, in which, in the end, the Tibetans were worsted.

For some extraordinary reason the Tibetans still refused to enter into serious negotiations, and it was necessary for the mission to continue its march from Gyangtse to Lhasa, at which it arrived in August, 1904, only to find that diplomatic negotiations were still difficult, as the Dalai-lama, the supreme pontiff, and many of his important officers had fled.

It was obviously impossible to pursue the Dalai-lama and bring him back, and the rapid approach of winter made it necessary for the British troops to return to India as soon as possible. After several weeks of delay, Colonel (now Sir Francis) Younghusband eventually got the leading people in Lhasa together and forced them to sign a treaty of peace.

The terms of the treaty were very simple. It provided principally for the opening up of the trade-centers of Yatung and Gyangtse, and also in Gantok in the extreme west of Tibet, to which British officials were to be appointed, and to which British subjects approved by the Indian Government could go.

Fearing Russian and other encroachment, it was stipulated that Tibet should not sell or lease any of her territory or resources to any foreign power. The Indian Government was anxious to secure the right to keep a diplomatic representative in Lhasa, but the Tibetans raised such a storm of protest against this suggestion that it was waived, but only on the condition that no other representatives or agents of any foreign power should be admitted to Tibet.

Immediately after the signing of the treaty, the Younghusband expedition returned, and the close isolation of Tibet continued apart from three places specifically mentioned in the treaty.

As we were anxious to go further into the interior, and even to be accorded permission to go on to the capital itself, it was necessary for us to apply for special grace on the part of the Tibetan officials. Sooner or later the matter would be referred to Lhasa for final decision, but it was necessary to carry on negotiations with the officials resident in Gyangtse, and in order to secure their recommendation we were advised to accompany our request with a little personal "keepsake" in token of our regard.

Mr. MacDonald was kind enough to advise us which persons were the proper ones to approach. In the first place we climbed up to the castle and paid a ceremonial visit to the governors there, but even more importance was attached to a state call upon the *kenchung,* who is generally called the Tibetan trade agent, as it is his duty to negotiate with the British trade agent in Gyangtse. The old *depön* in the Chumbi Valley is more of a consul, and the *kenchung* may be termed the Tibetan ambassador to Great Britain, although his ambassadorship keeps him inside of his own country.

He is only three fourths Tibetan, having Chinese blood in his veins, and several years' residence in China has taught him how to conduct negotiations in the wiliest of ways. I was surprised to find that though he speaks Chinese fluently he was unable to read or write a word of it. I was later to find out that this is true of most of the Tibetans who claim to have a knowledge of Chinese. There are quite a number of such people, owing to the long period of Chinese domination in Tibet, but they are nearly all confined to the official classes.

One of the few serious mistakes which Kipling made in his "Kim," that most fascinating of all books, is to suppose that the Tibetan lamas or priests are conversant with Chinese or quote from it for ecclesiastical purposes. In Tibet I never met a single priest who had any knowledge of literary Chinese, not even of the Chinese Buddhistic literature.

In the old days the *kenchung* must have spoken Chinese very fluently, but I found that he was getting rusty, as he had not used it for ten years. As is generally known, until 1912 Tibet had to acknowledge the suzerainty of China. Two Chinese *ambans* or official residents were kept in Lhasa, and numerous petty officials and soldiers were scattered throughout the country. There had long been a strong nationalist movement in Tibet; and eventually, taking advantage of the Chinese revolution of 1911, the Tibetans were able to overcome their Chinese masters. Many of them they killed, and the remainder were sent back to their native country, and Tibet declared herself absolutely independent and refused even to have Chinese diplomatic representatives in Lhasa. This has greatly simplified British negotiations with Tibet, as in the old days one never knew whether to communicate direct with the Lhasa officials or with the Chinese overlords, and the dual sway was made the excuse for much treaty evasion.

The *kenchung* received us with a great deal of state and, after hearing our desires and requests, informed us that he was powerless to give or refuse permission to go on, but that he would send by courier a communication to Lhasa, stating our whole case. Pending the ultimate decision we were not to advance a step further into Tibetan territory, but we had his permission to wander about the city as much as we pleased.

We were very glad to avail ourselves of his invitation. The period of waiting continued much longer than we had anticipated and in fact extended over a period of nearly two months, but so busy were we adding to our experiences that the time passed very quickly. Official visits to various local notabilities in an attempt to ingratiate ourselves with the natives took up a good deal of this time, but in addition many hours were spent in casual wanderings through the busy market-place and through the teeming irregular streets of the city.

The market-place and a large portion of the residential section of the city belongs to the monastery which is built on the slope of the hill that arises just behind the town. This monastery, needless to say, was visited by us on several occasions.

As monasteries go in Tibet, the Gyangtse monastery is not particularly large, as it has only a thousand monks within its walls, but historically it is both famous and important. These monks have at their disposal some twenty or more buildings. Of these the most important is the Du-Kang, or great assembly-hall, in which are placed the principal images. It is here that every day all the monks gather together to read their liturgy and perform their religious ceremonies.

At each side of the great doorway are two large images representing in all the four great guardian deities of the four quarters of the world. The Tibetans believe that by placing these fearsome images at the entrance-hall of the temple they prevent evil spirits from entering the temple itself and disturbing the pious monks at their prayers within.

The images inside the temple were equally interesting, some of them being remarkably well made. The principal image was that of the historical Buddha, the Indian sage who walked the earth preaching the doctrine of emancipation from the wheel of life more than two thousand years ago. Strangely enough, such images are rare in Tibet, as the Tibetan prefers to worship at the shrine of some purely mythological deity, one of the so-called non-human or Dhyani buddhas.

Another image showing fine craftsmanship was that of the bodhisattva Maitreya. A bodhisattva is a being who in some near future birth will gain the crown of buddhahood or supreme enlightenment. Maitreya, the compassionate, is the next Buddha destined to be born in the world and is adored by nearly every sort of Buddhist. He is frequently portrayed almost as a European. I have sometimes seen representations of him with white skin and blue eyes, and in nearly all cases his image is sitting on a chair in European style as opposed to the Oriental cross-legged attitude assumed by the other Tibetan deities.

What, however, proved the most entertaining was a small chapel on the third story, the hall of the abbots with numerous images representing the past bishops or archbishops of the Gyangtse temple. The curious miters which some of them wore were particularly striking, as were also the high and even aquiline noses of some of these departed worthies in such great contrast to the broad flat noses of the modern Tibetan peasant.

Immediately to the left of the Du-Kang, or the assembly-hall, was a great gilded shrine called by the Tibetans a chorten, and popularly called the Golden Pagoda. This is the object of pilgrimage on the part of the peasantry for hundreds of miles around.

Let into the walls of the lower part of the pagoda

were a number of revolving barrels. These were the famous Tibetan prayer-wheels. It is the duty of every man as he passes along to stop and twist these wheels, causing them to revolve. This, it is believed, causes a man to acquire an enormous amount of merit and rids him of all his sins. Certainly in Tibet salvation from sin seems extraordinarily easy, and it is, I think, a facility which is greatly needed by its inhabitants.

From the bottom of the great shrine we could look up the hill and see numerous other monastic buildings. At the top of the slope was the great storehouse where there is kept a huge supply of dried yak's meat and barley-flour for the use of the monks during winter. A little below it was the residence of the Lama-trodampa, or the abbot of the whole monastery.

I put on the full ecclesiastical outfit given me by the great Buddhist cathedral of Kioto, as a token of my honorary Buddhist ordination, and paid the old lama a visit. He received me with great courtesy. We had a long conversation, in the course of which he remarked that in order to understand Tibetan Buddhism one required a knowledge of Sanskrit, the classical language of India. By chance the little gift which I had brought with me to present to him was a Buddhist book in Sanskrit; so after his statement I thought it a good chance to give it to him, but I found that the old gentleman had been bluffing, because he understood not a word of it in spite of his exalted position.

In spite of this little misunderstanding we got along together very well, and he was kind enough to let me have the use of the temple library with its thousands of valuable and long-forgotten manuscripts. These were brought to our rest-house from time to time, and I was able to make a number of interesting finds. This made me feel all the keener to get on to Lhasa, where of course the literary material was much greater, and all of us waited from day to day in anxious expectation of favorable news from the capital.

Alas! all of our hopes were suddenly blighted. One morning we received a visit from the *kenchung*, who informed us that a definite answer had now been received from Lhasa, and that under no circumstances would our party be permitted to journey there. This was indeed a very sad blow to all our fond expectations and meant decisive and absolute failure. Anxious to grasp at any straw that presented itself, we decided to make one more desperate attempt to carry out part of our ideas. We thought that possibly the Lhasa Government had been affected in its decision by the comparatively large number of Europeans in our party. Consequently Knight, Fletcher, and Harcourt immediately returned to India by the same way by which we had come, though they stopped en route to make a closer survey of the environs of Mount Chumolhari and managed by their surveys to add many interesting details to our geographical knowledge of the country.

Ellam and I remained in Gyangtse a short time longer in order to send in a further petition to the Lhasa authorities, asking that they reconsider their decision and allow us to come to the Forbidden City, or, failing this, that we be permitted to visit Shigatse, the second largest city in Tibet, the seat of the famous Trashi-lama, and the center of an important ecclesiastical organization. We further requested that, should both these favors be denied, at least we be given permission to remain for a few months in Gyangtse in order to continue our researches there. Another two weeks brought us an answer to this petition in no uncertain terms.

All three requests were given a decisive refusal, and we were peremptorily ordered to leave the country immediately. I was very much put out by this curt refusal and the way it was handed to us, and was eager immediately to start my attempt to reach the Forbidden City in secret and in disguise. I had here numerous native friends and sympathizers who would have aided me in my attempt. But I remembered my promise given to Bailey that I should return to India in case of refusal, and rather than break my word I decided to return to Darjeeling with Ellam, and so we turned back on our weary way, rendered all the more weary by the sense of failure and disappointment.

We crossed over the Jelap Pass into India at the end of November just in time, for we met with a snowstorm which continued for many days and which eventually stopped all traffic for many weeks thereafter.

Once back in Darjeeling (we arrived December 9), I was entirely free from my spoken bond and began making active steps for a new undertaking, for I was determined that come what might I should make one more attempt to reach the sacred city of the Buddhas, if necessary even by stealth and by disguise, and to trust to luck to help me through the dangers of detection and possibly of violent treatment at the hands of the religious fanatics in the land of seclusion.

CHAPTER III

PREPARATIONS FOR THE NEW ATTEMPT: THE JOURNEY THROUGH SIKKIM

I was determined to keep my promise, however great the cost, and so had come back to India before starting on my new undertaking, but even during our long stay in Gyangtse I had not been entirely idle. Every day while there I had been making special studies which would enable me to undertake, with some chance of success, the new journey in disguise. By this time I was so well known personally on the Yatung-Gyangtse road that I definitely decided not to use this route again; so it was necessary to learn something of the other roads and passes leading from India into the interior of Tibet, and this knowledge had to be secured very delicately, as the Tibetan authorities were already suspicious of my movements. Consequently long hours were wasted in casual conversation in order that I might slip in seemingly purposeless questions about other parts of the country.

Gradually my cipher note-book was filled with a huge mass of miscellaneous information concerning towns, roads, snowfall in passes, and the severity and laxity of various officials in different parts of Tibet, but much was still lacking that in order to carry out my designs it was desirable to know.

As the journey would have to be done in disguise with grave danger of detection, it was necessary to train myself to act as a Tibetan. The renewal of intensive study of colloquial Tibetan since August had, of course, greatly added my fluency in speaking. I could now converse for several hours on end with no great difficulty, but this was far from the ability to speak as a native. More particularly, apart from orders to servants, all my practice of the language had been with my native secretary, local officials, and other persons who spoke what is known as the "elegant language."

I decided to travel as a servant in order to attract less attention, and so it became necessary to make myself proficient in "Coolie talk." Consequently, rather to the scandal of the other members of the party, who as yet were completely ignorant of my design, I made frequent excuses to go to the kitchen and listen to the servants talking among themselves, making careful note of their tones, their slang, the manner in which they spoke of their own and other masters, and, last but not least, the exact way in which they squatted, spat, quarreled, and carried on flirtations with local dames and damsels.

This was as far as I could go while I remained in Gyangtse, but once I was back in Darjeeling, in India, I could go on with active preparations.

Up to that time I had kept the idea of a secret journey entirely to myself, but immediately after arriving in Darjeeling I revealed my plans to my four English friends. This led to tremendous discussion, but in the end the proposition won the favor of all, and thereafter my friends gave me enthusiastic support throughout all of my difficulties. At first it was proposed that I be accompanied by one of the other members of the late mission, but eventually it was unanimously agreed that I should attempt the task of getting to Lhasa alone, inasmuch as I was the only one who could speak Tibetan at all fluently. This meant that I was forced to spend some time in learning from Harcourt the art of cinematography, as I was very anxious to secure a film of the Sacred City.

It took exactly a month to get everything in order. This included the purchase of transport animals and the hire of servants. A secret visit to the city of Kalimpong enabled me to secure three mules and three ponies. In Darjeeling itself I engaged four servants who I thought would be suitable for my present purpose. These were, first, a native secretary who was later to play the part of my master on my arrival in Tibet. By reason of certain delinquencies in character he received from me the sobriquet of Satan. The second was my bearer, or personal servant, who had already accompanied me to Gyangtse and had proved his efficiency and loyalty. The third was a syce or groom who was to have charge of the animals. The fourth was a poor, stunted, half-witted boy whom I called Diogenes and who was to act as "odd man."

All these were Sikkimese. Ethnologically speaking Sikkim is a province of Tibet, for the true Sikkimese

Tibetan woman weaving thread

Dr. McGovern in disguise as Tibetan coolie

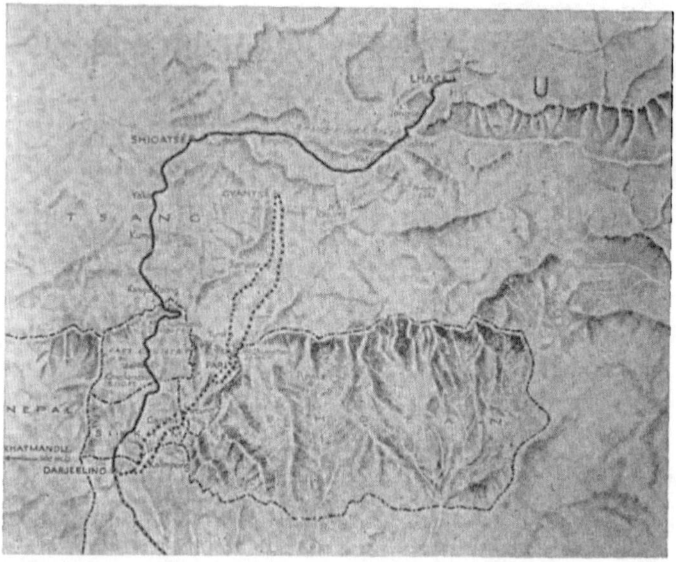

Map: dotted lines, first expedition; black line, Dr. McGovern's route to Lhasa in disguise. **See p. 67**

The first halt

are Tibetans who have migrated in modern times to the south side of the Himalayas. Their kinship is acknowledged by the Lhasa authorities, so that they are allowed to go to the Sacred City at will. Inasmuch as my servants were Sikkimese, and as the Sikkimese dialect differs somewhat from that spoken round Lhasa and Shigatse, I considered it safer to go myself as a Sikkimese rather than an inhabitant of one of the central provinces. Slight deficiencies in Tibetan etiquette and difference in pronunciation would thus be explained away by a story of Sikkimese origin.

One of my great difficulties in engaging servants was the necessity of employing them under false pretenses. It was absolutely necessary to have all of my plans kept secret, as otherwise the Tibetans would certainly have heard of the project, and everything would have been frustrated. At the same time I knew it was impossible to make a secret departure from Darjeeling. A mysterious and sudden disappearance would have excited suspicion immediately and a search have been made for me. It is always useful to make one's secret preparations under the limelight. Consequently I gave it out that I was going on a two months' tour through Sikkim, exploring the unknown regions and climbing some of the out-of-way mountains in order to carry on geological work. This would allow me to disappear for several weeks on end without exciting comment. At the same time it permitted me to test the caliber of my new servants. If they were frightened at the idea of climbing twenty-thousand-foot glaciers in midwinter, it was obvious they would not serve my purpose.

Finally the question of equipment had to be considered. All the camp-kit of the ordinary explorer had necessarily to be done away with, but food, clothes, and materials for disguise had to be purchased. Food-supplies were cut down to an absolute minimum, since I intended to eat nothing but native food once I was in Tibet, and even in Sikkim, through which once more we would have to journey, to rely entirely upon local provender. As a sort of last resort I packed away three tins of Quaker Oats and five pounds of sugar. The sugar was a luxury, my sole compromise with hedonism, to be used along with native food, as the Tibetans never employ it or any substitute, being one of the few people who manage to exist without any form of sweets. The rolled oats were a necessary stand-by. In the past I have been able to exist for a considerable period on porridge alone when no other food was available, and I knew we would be in some danger of starvation should we be caught in the passes by a snowstorm and be unable to go forward or to return.

The selection of clothes required a great deal of care. I had already purchased or been presented with several lama costumes and also costumes such as were worn by native officials, but none of these would do in the present instance, as I had to be clad in the poorest garb. In the end I secured three coolie dresses, one new and specially made to order, and two old ones which had already seen long service, as the possession of a whole wardrobe of new clothes would have been certain to excite suspicion.

Materials for disguise including hair-dye, a mixture

of iodine and walnut-juice to stain the skin, dark goggles, two lemons, and a small bottle of glue to be used to camouflage the color of my eyes. The use of these last two articles will be explained hereafter.

No one outside the five Europeans of our Gyangtse party had any inkling of what was being done. To make surety doubly sure, Knight agreed to go out into Sikkim on an independent tour in order to distract attention from me. Ostensibly both of us were to make by different roads for Pemayangtse, the largest monastery in Sikkim.

In a quiet, unostentatious manner our small party took its departure from Darjeeling on January 10. No one, not even my erstwhile companions, knew exactly the route I should take, though I had already worked out the journey in great detail. I was able to follow this plan almost without alteration, except for several unforeseen stops en route and for slight deviations when the road became vague or when detours were necessary for some reason or other.

The rough outline here will show with greater clearness than words the line of march.

I was anxious to see both Shigatse and Lhasa, the two great cities of Tibet, but it obviously would be better to visit Shigatse first, as I intended to reveal my identity on arriving in Lhasa, after which I knew that further rambling about the country would not be permitted.

The journey along the Pari-Gyangtse road being out of the question, I decided to take the more direct though more hazardous route straight through the heart of Sikkim, marching due northward over the passes, entering Tibet proper near Kampa Dzong; the path would continue north through the Tsang province until Shigatse is reached and, just beyond it, the Brahmaputra River. After this I had in mind to follow the Brahmaputra River on its downward course to the east until we reached a point where we could again branch off to the north and proceed straight to Lhasa. It was on this stretch that I found eventually the marches could not proceed to plan, as will be explained later on.

This is a little-known route, occasionally used by petty Tibetan traders in preference to the main Pari-Gyangtse-Lhasa road, but it is supposed to be closed in winter, as the pass, eighteen thousand feet high, or four thousand feet higher than the Jelap Pass, is as a rule completely blocked by snow except during the short midsummer period. Provided, however, that we could force our way through this pass in the depth of winter, the official closing of the road would prove of great advantage, because naturally during this time the passes would not be so strictly watched.

For the first day or two my path would coincide with a road leading to Pemayangtse (Pemionchi), my ostensible goal, as I had allowed it to be generally understood, which enabled me to make a semi-public departure from Darjeeling. On the actual day of my departure the usual irritating last-minute details cropped up, so that we could not get away until nearly eleven o'clock. Therefore, I decided to go only as far as Manjitar, just over the Sikkim frontier, and there rest for the remainder of the day.

All sorts of people were hanging around, and I arranged with Knight to have one of his servants sent after me with some trifling object which I had left behind, so that, as I was leaving, I might shout out to him to keep the article until we met in Pemayangtse some two weeks or so later. I heard afterward that this little bit of play-acting was the subject of gossip in the bazaar and succeeded in side-tracking all suspicions as to my real intentions.

The whole of the first day our road lay straight downhill, and it was so steep that it was quite impossible to ride. In fact, the fresh-fallen rain made it more of a slide than a walk. Lhaten carried the cinematograph camera, always an awkward load, and once fell very heavily. I was afraid that the apparatus was damaged, but after the tightening of a screw or two all seemed to be well. In the late afternoon we got to the bottom of the mountain and arrived at a bridge crossing the Rangit River, which marks the boundary between Sikkim and British India. On the other side of the bridge was the town and frontier station of Manjitar. Halfway across the bridge we were stopped and had to go through the troublesome business of presenting passes. One of the police officials was particularly anxious to know whether I had sent in my guarantee not to attempt to get from Sikkim into Nepal, Bhutan, or Tibet, but at this point I took refuge in pretended stolid ignorance of Sikkimese and all other native tongues and refused to understand a word. In the East, especially, ignorance is frequently more valuable than wisdom, so "'t is folly to be wise." In the end the official gave up the matter in despair. In this way I escaped having to commit myself to anything. I noticed, however, that the police were much more vigilant than previously. Had I given a guarantee not to pass over the Sikkim frontier into any other state, or had I been forced to admit that I had not entered into a guarantee, I should have landed myself in a pretty kettle of fish. It would have meant that I should be making my effort for nothing, for I should have had to renounce my desire to get to Lhasa or even Shigatse.

Glad I was to get away from this ominous frontier station, and instead of resting in the village I hastened my small caravan through the place and beyond, camping that night in the open, half a mile from any habitation, at a suitable spot where we were able to secure all necessary supplies. Besides water, the daily requisites were wood for fuel, bamboo leaves for animal fodder, milk for myself, and marwa beer for the servants. The other food, such as meat, rice, eggs, and tea, we carried in stock and only replenished from time to time. Generally speaking, in the inhabited parts of Sikkim all these things are easily procurable, but on the present journey Manjitar proved to be the only place where milk could be purchased, as nearly all the Sikkimese cows were affected by foot-and-mouth disease and were either dead or incapable of giving milk.

During these early days in Sikkim our camp routine was nearly always the same. First of all, the tent was erected and I ensconced therein. A place was also found inside for Satan, Lhaten and the other three servants sleeping outside in the open; while the syce prepared the animals for the night, Lhaten and the others prepared the evening meal. Our cooking utensils consisted of two tin boilers, a frying-pan, and a tea-pot. The tea-pot and one of the boilers were communal property, for I ate the same rice and drank the same tea as the servants, save that, in accord with Oriental etiquette, I had always to finish my share before the servants began theirs. The frying-pan was used exclusively for the scrambling of my eggs; my diet at this stage consisted at all meals of only scrambled eggs and rice. The remaining boiler was used to prepare the servants' stew, meat and greens finely chopped and then boiled together.

For some unknown reason I have never been able to eat either boiled or chopped meat with any pleasure, and so I contented myself with eggs, but I had so accustomed myself to eating with my fingers that even my eggs and rice I ate in Sikkimese or Indian fashion and had brought neither fork nor spoon along with me in my meager outfit.

Food having been finished, the marwa beer was prepared and slowly drunk to the accompaniment of the eternal chitter-chatter of Eastern servants. I occasionally sucked at a marwa pipe myself, though I preferred my milk, but always joined in the conversation in order to improve my dialect, as only Sikkimese was spoken. And then, after about two hours of this sort of thing, to sleep.

To return to the day-by-day narrative, on the morning of January 11 we started on another short journey, the seven-mile ascent from Manjitar to Namtse (Namchi on the maps). Because of the precipitous nature of the road and our consequent snail's pace interspersed with halts, this took us five hours. As usual there was a marked change in the temperature between early morning and midday. We started muffled up in overcoats and ended on the doubtful side of modesty. Halfway up the climb we stopped at the village of Kyitam for tea and sugarcane, while Satan called on a friend to renew a row over the payment of an old horse deal. As usual the "silent, unemotional" Orientals managed to raise a terrific shindy, and the heat of their arguments brought together the whole of the villagers. The two combatants chased one another around the bazaar, uttering bloodcurdling threats; but the affair ended without bloodshed, for each one was too cowardly to risk a blow.

When the entertainment thus provided had begun to pall upon me, I jerked the two apart and sent Satan on ahead. Nothing was settled, of course, but then the matter had already run on for more than three years, and undoubted settlement would have been attended with dissatisfaction, for whenever the two happened to be in the same neighborhood they took the opportunity to repeat to one another the old arguments, obtaining, I feel sure, a deal of satisfaction in the renewal of the ancient quarrel.

We arrived in Namtse about noon, but the horses and mules were already tired, and we decided to halt for the day. In Tibet, with its great plains, a single stage is at least fourteen or fifteen miles, and one expects, if in good condition, to be able to cover two stages a day;

but the rugged nature of the Sikkim country renders such journeys impossible. Two miles an hour is a good average and ten miles a good day's march, particularly if one has not a change of mounts. In the present instance, I was particularly anxious to keep my animals fresh for the trying time we were sure to have in the passes.

We pitched camp just above the bazaar, and as I was still traveling as a European, we attracted a good deal of attention. In the afternoon the local *kazi,* or lord of the manor, accompanied by his son, paid a call. During this time the *kazi* and his son managed to consume of my tea and sugar, the equal of a week's rations.

The *kazi,* his household, and his immediate retainers were all pure Sikkimese of Tibetan origin, but the majority of the villagers, especially the bazaar-keepers, were Nepalese. This holds true of nearly all the villages of Sikkim. The Sikkimese, being Tibetans, are incurably lazy and lacking in the power of sustained application, so that the bee-like immigrants from Nepal are steadily ousting them from all competitive positions, such as those of traders, coolies, and, to a certain extent, agricultural laborers. It is only the fact that the lands are entailed in the families of the Sikkimese *kazis* that prevents the Nepalese from becoming the landowners as well. At present the Sikkimese are becoming more and more the drones in their own country, and but for the power of the British Government the Nepalese would not be prevented from invading the country and ousting the Sikkimese from their territorial rights

The next day, January 12, we continued our ascent of the mountain until we came to the elevated plateau of Damtang. Twice on my way I was asked for my pass—a very unusual occurrence in the old days—which shows that the road to Lhasa becomes every year more, instead of less, difficult. Fortunately, I was still within the bounds of the law, and so was able to proceed without further trouble. But these signs of interest in traveling parties augured ill for later events.

It was on this day that I began my first active cinematography. As we rose higher and higher on our way to Damtang, we came upon a magnificent view of Kanchendzonga—far surpassing that which one gets from Darjeeling—and this I filmed. Kanchendzonga is the third highest mountain in the world, its summit being well over twenty-eight thousand feet above sea-level, and it is even more impressive to look at than Mount Everest, which is nearly a thousand feet higher. Its outlying ranges run, for the most part, north and south and form a good portion of the boundary line between Nepal and Sikkim.

Kanchendzonga occupies a curiously isolated position. It lies several miles south of the true Himalaya range, which tends to run in a general west-to-east line, so that from the Tibetan plateau Kanchendzonga forms no part of the magnificent Himalaya panorama. For this reason it is in some ways the most easily accessible of the major Himalaya mountains, but it will probably be a very long time before its ascent is made, since to the climber it presents far greater difficulties than does Mount Everest. It has already claimed its toll of human life, and many attempts to scale its summit have met with disaster.

Kanchendzonga, which means the great glacier treasure house of the five precious substances, is the object of great worship in Sikkim, and it plays an important part in Sikkimese Buddhism. Special ceremonies and sacred dances are held in its honor, some of them very old, dating from a long time prior to the introduction of Buddhism into Sikkim, and there are dark stories that in the olden days these ceremonies were accompanied by human sacrifices made to the spirit of the mountain.

Arrived in Damtang, we came to the parting of the ways. On the left a road led to the great monastery of Pemayangtse, while on the right a road led to Gantok, the capital of Sikkim. Up to this time all my servants supposed that I was aiming for Pemayangtse, but it was necessary for me here to follow for a bit the Gantok road. As I did not wish to reveal to my underlings all of my plans, I informed them merely that, as Knight was not likely to get to Pemayangtse for another ten days, I intended to take the road to the right and travel a few days seeing something of the unknown parts of Central Sikkim.

Although our day's journey was but half accomplished, the mules already showed signs of exhaustion, and we had great difficulty in getting them to go on. Whereupon the syce gave each of the animals a large bowl of strong tea, the usual Sikkimese expedient in such cases. To my surprise they drank this eagerly and under its stimulus condescended to return to work. In fact, the senior mule, a female dubbed Paris, became so exhilarated that she tried to run away and, in her skittish attempt to imitate a playful kitten, broke a box she was carrying containing our scanty provender. The precious provisions were carefully retrieved to the accompaniment of curses on dame Paris.

Soon after turning to the right the road became a steep descent. As we stumbled down and always down we passed the villages of Temi and Tarko, from which, to the distant north, we could see the passes leading into Tibet, until eventually we came near to the bottom of the valley through which runs the Tista River. The pass, which was our immediate goal, lies very near to the source of the Tista, but it was a long and arduous journey from the point on the river where we were to its source.

We continued our descent next day, January 13, down to the water's edge and then definitely departed from the road, turning to our left in order to follow the river-bed up to its source. The road itself crosses the river and goes on to Gantok, many miles beyond. From Gantok there is another road which returns to the Tista some twenty-five miles further on and then follows the river in its northerly course to the passes, so that ordinarily we should have gone on to Gantok and then come back to the Tista. But in Gantok dwelt the native officials who were in many cases spies of the Tibetan Government. A visit there consequently was to be avoided at all costs, or Lhasa, my objective, could never be attained. The fact that we were compelled to leave the road imposed upon us the problem of making a direct pathway for ourselves from our present point to the village of Drikchu, further up the stream, where the road from Gantok rejoins the Tista. For the most part there was not even the pretense of a path, and for the rest there was a trail fit only for coolies passing in single file. It was quite impossible to use this trail for animals, especially when loaded; that is, impossible to use it in the condition in which we found it, as the pathway on either side was hemmed in by thick jungle growth. The journey of only some twenty-five miles was destined to occupy us for several days, as it was necessary for us to go ahead of the caravan and, with our huge knives of Nepalese and Bhutanese make, the only ones used in Tibet, cut away enough of the ferns, bamboo sprouts, and other wild vegetation to afford passage for our pack-animals.

I am certain that the portion of the country we covered in this way is destined to be opened up eventually and through communication between India and Tibet insured along this route. After cutting through the jungle for some miles, we came across, here and there, an isolated hut, and once or twice a tiny village almost dissociated from communication with the outer world. In many cases these were inhabited neither by Nepalese nor Sikkimese but by the Lepchas, the childlike, nature-loving, timid, and spiritless primitive inhabitants of Sikkim, who were conquered by the invaders from Tibet who constitute the present so-called Sikkimese. These primitive Lepchas still continue to live an almost unaltered existence in the more isolated portions of the country such as the one through which we were traveling. The people do a little cultivation and are expert fishers in the river pools. Sometimes they take the fish to market. Where cultivation is more extensive than usual, the peasants have trouble with the monkeys and kill them wholesale with poison. The Lepchas appear to have no definite religion, though in their beliefs they recognize spirits of good and evil. As a general rule they practise monogamy, and they burn or bury their dead. A simple folk, they are a dying race without energy enough to carry on a strenuous fight for existence.

In the daytime the heat was sweltering; and as the sweat poured down from our faces and bodies, especially when we were working at the cutting of the path, it seemed impossible to believe that in a short time—another week or ten days—we were destined to be among the glaciers we could see far away and buried deep in snow.

That first day in the wilds we halted at the tiny hamlet of Nampak, and I spent the rest of the day in studying the details of Lepcha life, as compared with that of the Sikkimese. A difficult task it proved to be, for the Lepchas have a language of their own, utterly different from all other languages, and understand almost no Sikkimese. They were frightened, too, at the sight of my Sikkimese servants, whom they considered to belong to the conquering race, and I had to get them alone before they would answer my questions.

The next day (January 14) provided us with our most difficult march so far. Up to Nampak there had been vague suggestions of a trail, but beyond that there was nothing. Moreover, the ground became very rocky, strewn with giant boulders, and at one point we had a sheer slide of rock for forty feet, tipped at an angle of fifty degrees. For us, of course, this presented no great difficulty, but we were forced to construct a sort of rope brake for the animals. As usual, the mules kept a much firmer hold than the ponies, though at the last moment Paris slipped and rolled over, an accident that very nearly cost her own life and that of Satan.

Up to this time we had kept to the left bank of the river, but it now became necessary to cross to the other side. This could only be done at a place called Shamdong, where there was a shaky bridge connecting two microscopic villages on each side of the river. The Tista was still completely unfordable by reason of its swift current and of the rocks forming cataracts in its stream.

I had no great love for villages, however, and preferred to camp in the open, even without our tent, under the natural arches of a beautiful grove about half a mile before reaching the bridge. By this time we had almost entirely broken away from the three-meals-a-day habit. In the morning, before starting, we consumed enormous quantities of strong tea but had nothing to eat and made the whole of our march on an empty stomach; such is Sikkimese custom. We halted about three, and it was four o'clock before our one and only meal of the day was ready; but what a meal this was! I have only a moderate appetite as a rule. The thought of having to consume three eggs at a sitting is enough to turn me away from even one. But here I was pushing down six, seven, and even eight eggs at a time, mixed with a heaped bowl of rice. The others ate to match.

This development of healthy appetites necessitated the frequent replenishing of our larder, and later on in the evening I was forced to send Satan and Lhaten into the village to purchase supplies. By a curious coincidence one of Lhaten's old friends had managed to find his way to the village on the other side of the river, being one of the men whom an enterprising landlord imported into the wilderness in an effort to form a new community. This meeting resulted in a convivial evening for them, for the friend insisted on both servants remaining and organized for them a drunken spree that lasted until dawn. They came reeling home just after I had got up and was trying to get started.

This was on the morning of January 15. I insisted on setting out immediately, and so they had to buckle down to the day's work without a moment of sleep. On the other side of the river, however, beyond the Shamdong village—one which is also called Manka—the road improved very considerably because of the activities of this same landlord, who had tried to cut a path between his village and Drikchu, our immediate destination. Successive seasonal rains had washed much of it away, and the jungle undergrowth was sprouting again, but in places we could even ride instead of having to walk ahead of the ponies and hew a way for them.

On passing through the village I found another instance of the landlord's progressiveness. In the marketplace he had dug a well, over which he had erected a stone covering. In one of the sides of this well-covering

Group at Yatung, Tibet: the British trade-agent and family, Bhutanese visitors and members of first expedition: Dr. McGovern in lama dress standing third from right

Inspection of coolies selected for the first expedition

Dr. W. Montgomery McGovern on his return

Dr. McGovern on a voyage to India

had been placed a stone tablet inscribed in *English* with a eulogy of the landlord's deeds and merits. No one in the village, of course, knows a word of English, and he himself was equally ignorant. I was, in fact, the only person who had ever come to the village who could read the tablet; but there, nevertheless, was the stone, imported at great expense from Calcutta, proclaiming to the wilds, with polysyllabic pomposity, the virtues and excellencies of the local magnate.

Yet, absurd as this story may sound, one could not but feel that this local Cæsar had made better use of his money than the plutocrats of Tibet. In spite of the great poverty of Tibet as a whole, the aristocratic families are enormously wealthy, but all of them make a display of their wealth in ways that are completely non-productive and ephemeral. A thousand pounds will be spent in providing butter fuel for the temple lamps. The cost of a single evening's display of this kind is extraordinary, and the next day there is nothing to show for it. Temples and monasteries are allowed to fall into decay while money is poured out in entertaining the monks with a sumptuous banquet. Even if the Sikkimese gentry are becoming enamored of seeing their own names inscribed on stone tablets, at least they must erect something enduring, a building, a well, or a bridge to which the tablet shall be attached. The great poverty which strikes the eye in Tibet is the result not of the lack of money but rather of the misuse of it.

To return to our own adventures, both Satan and Lhaten started off in great spirits after their night's debauch.

Satan indeed managed to get into a fight with a Nepalese boy we met on the way and sent him flying for his life into the jungle. It always surprised me to find what terror the Sikkimese inspired in the Indians and Nepalese, excepting of course the Ghurkas. The Indians, though vastly superior to the Sikkimese and Tibetans in intelligence and industry, are easily bullied by any Sikkimese or Tibetan swash-buckler, though to a European both Sikkimese and Tibetans appear to be arrant cowards.

Lhaten, to do him justice, had acquired such a hard head that he remained impervious to fatigue, in spite of his spree of the preceding night; but Satan began to surrender to slumber shortly after the fight, when we had gone only two or three miles, and three times, while riding, fell so fast asleep that he rolled out of the saddle, the third time sliding gracelessly under his pony's legs.

The need to press on with utmost speed caused me moments of acute anxiety; the weather had been fine for some time past; and I felt that, if we could only get to the pass before another snow-storm, we would have a chance to get through. Every moment's delay was dangerous. But the last time Satan fell, which was after we had traveled only about seven miles, he was in such a stupor that it was with the greatest difficulty we could raise him. In the circumstances, I thought it necessary to halt for the day, much as I disliked the idea of losing a few hours. A short march did not seem to decrease my appetite, and for our single meal I managed to consume a whole chicken and six eggs. The extra free time available on account of our early halt

I determined to employ in getting ready with my disguise. So far I had been traveling as an Englishman, and there was no valid reason why I should not continue as such until we reached the passes, still several days away, except that I was very anxious now not to excite too much attention when passing through villages. A European in this locality is such a rare phenomenon that his existence would certainly be marked. If I were seen going up in the direction of the passes, and then failed to come back, rumors would quickly be spread that I had entered Tibet. This I was most anxious to avoid. On the other hand, I did not wish to disguise myself definitely as yet, as it needlessly increased the chances of detection, for though I was entitled to go as far as the passes, had any of the village officials discovered me traveling as a Tibetan they would certainly have stopped me until full inquiries had been made.

After some mental gymnastics, I decided on a compromise. I would henceforth keep away from all villages and only send the servants in for supplies. I should dress in Sikkimese costume and stain my hair, so that should I be seen from a little distance away I would appear as a native and hence excite no comment. On the other hand, I would not dye my face nor darken my eyes and would admit being English in case any one were to insist on coming to our camp and asking awkward questions.

This preliminary masquerade did not seem to excite the suspicions of my servants, strangely enough, probably because they had always considered me half mad when in Gyangtse. I had then frequently gone so far as to wear Tibetan costume, and they only thought that I was up to my old trick of studying natives by "going native." Up to this time the servants had always expected me at any moment to turn back and carry out the journey to Pemayangtse, but that same afternoon I informed them that, as we had come so far, I intended to go on to Lachen and see the very famous meditative lama there and, after having a metaphysical discussion with him, return to Pemayangtse by way of Gantok. My real intentions they never fathomed, as they all knew that the passes were supposed to be closed; and while they had doubts of my sanity, their slow wits could not conceive that I even would be mad enough to attempt to push through.

After I had finished staining my hair I noticed that Satan continued to lie in his drunken stupor right under the blazing sun, and so I had two of the other coolies pick him up and throw him into the tent, as otherwise he would probably have had sunstroke and thus have added to our troubles. I have never seen a man so oblivious of the world, so literally *dead* drunk.

The next morning, January 16, we were able to continue our northerly journey. After another four or five miles of unusually bad road, we came to the village of Drikchu, where the road from Gantok to the passes once more joins the banks of the Tista River. For the time being our work of road-making was over, but we were once again on the government highway and liable to be stopped.

In accordance with my new plan I did not stop in Drikchu but rushed on ahead, leaving the servants behind to buy provisions for the next few days. I had impressed upon them the necessity of saying nothing about me to the villagers, but merely to state, if asked, that we were a party going on pilgrimage to Lachen.

As I went on alone another six or seven miles brought me to the curious natural elevated plain of Akatang, where I decided we might camp for the night. So I waited for the servants to come up. This place was formerly the site of the village of Drikchu, but for certain political reasons the village had been moved several miles down the river. On the map, however, the changed position is not noted. In several similar instances the Government of India maps of Sikkim are hopelessly incorrect.

As regards this place, even after the village had been moved away, its former site continued to be frequented on account of certain natural hot springs to which are ascribed marvelous curative powers, but about two years previously a large landslide destroyed the springs. The people, being Sikkimese, never thought of digging them out again, and so the site is now completely deserted.

This part of Sikkim is very sparsely inhabited and is devoid of thriving villages such as one meets elsewhere. This is due to the absence of Nepalese and Indians, who are the foundation of Sikkim's prosperity. When left to themselves the Sikkimese do not thrive, nor do they of their own accord develop the natural resources of their own country. The cause of the exclusion of Nepalese is curious. This part of Sikkim is dominated by the Pedang monastery, the largest temple, after Pemayangtse, in Sikkim. Its former abbot was a very powerful person politically, being a past master of intrigue. He inherited the Tibetan dislike of outsiders; and at the time, some forty-five years ago, when the Sikkimese Government, pressed by the English, was importing Nepalese as laborers, he managed to secure a ruling that none of the new settlers were to be allowed to reside in that part of Sikkim which came under the influence of his own monastery. To his diplomatic success is due the economic failure of his province.

The paucity of villages and the poverty of the few that we found along our line of march rendered it increasingly urgent to secure supplies without delay. Fortunately we were becoming expert in "scrounging" from the country itself. The animals had for fodder the bamboo shoots which grew in abundance by the roadside, and the greens for the servants' stew were supplied by three or four varieties of ferns which were always clogging our footsteps. In place of marwa beer or milk we had to be content with pure mountain-stream water.

Eggs and fresh meat were scarce, but on this day we bought from a party coming down from Lachen some of the naturally frozen meat of Tibet, which the Tibetan peasants eat raw (I was to become more than accustomed to it later), but which in Sikkim we cooked. I ate mine grilled, though it had always a nasty putrid flavor. The servants, as usual, chopped and boiled it along with the ferns. The natives of this part of the world have a prejudice against meat cooked in any way except by boiling. They believe that roasted or grilled meat impedes the breathing when climbing mountains. The same notion in regard to roasted meats obtains in Tibet, I found out later, the nomads in particular having a prejudice against meat cooked in any other way than boiling.

The following day, January 17, only took us another ten miles along the road, and we camped between the two tiny hamlets of Singtam (called Singhik, for some reason, on the maps) and Tong. The semi-disguise turned out to be very successful, and as we passed three or four persons on the road they did not turn around, as I expected, to stare as they always do when a European appears. The road all the way was a gentle uphill incline, scarcely noticeable, but we were already seven thousand feet above sea-level and no longer felt the heat. In the best of weather we should have been cool, but to my dismay the spell of good weather was broken. It became cloudy and drizzly, and it was obvious that snow was falling on the mountain-tops. As we heard in Singtam that the snow already lay deep in the passes, my heart was in my boots.

The country hereabouts showed signs of gradual decay. We passed several deserted houses rapidly crumbling away. Unlike the situation in Tibet, where stone and sun-dried brick are employed, the Sikkimese houses are for the most part constructed entirely from bamboo. Under the best of circumstances they last for only eight or nine years, after which they have to be rebuilt.

On this particular day we had great difficulty in

selecting a camping ground, especially as I was anxious to keep well away from villages and out of sight, while at the same time in touch with the road. Eventually we decided on a leaf-filled grotto. The selection of this seemingly satisfactory den, however, resulted in a very unpleasant experience. We woke up in the night to find our bodies covered with leeches which were already half gorged. In the summer leeches constitute one of the scourges of Sikkim, but in the winter, because of the great night cold, they are seldom seen. These had been hibernating under the bed of leaves and had been re-awakened into activity by the heat of our bodies.

Unfortunately they attach themselves to the skin without causing the slightest pain—the pain of an open wound which refuses to heal comes later—so that all of us were drained of a good deal of blood before sufficient sensation had been created to awaken us. As to attempt to pull leeches off makes matters worse, we resorted to the expedient of applying wet salt to the loathsome creatures, whereupon they immediately dropped off and shriveled into apparent nothingness. Even after this, the pain of the sores and the fear of further invasion kept us awake nearly the whole night.

There are several kinds of leeches in Sikkim which are found in all parts up to ten thousand feet of altitude. In the higher elevations a voracious black species is common, smaller than the yellowish-brown creature which abounds lower down. Their activities are one of the worst nuisances travelers have to contend with. Their appetites for blood of man or beast are insatiable, and they will attack in such numbers and gorge so much blood that serious loss of strength may result. In summer travelers have noticed that with an extraordinary instinct these vile pests on the approach of any living creature in their neighborhood will deliberately make for it from some distance. Ordinary clothing is no obstacle for them, for they will suck right through trousers or thick stockings. Watching them at work, one can see the blood they draw dilating their skins, and when full they drop off and roll up into balls. The sores which result from dealing carelessly with leeches which have attached themselves to the body are very obstinate and, unless given close attention, may lead to blood-poisoning or other ills. Animals when attacked have little means of getting rid of the bloodsuckers, and we had to be very careful about our mules and ponies.

The next day, January 18, was to be a long march, and so, for a change, we had something to eat with our tea before we started. At sunrise we saw the beautiful sight of snow falling on the top of the Kanchendzonga range. This mountain is such an important part of the western horizon of so many parts of Sikkim that there is little wonder it is regarded as the guardian spirit of the country.

The road was good and interesting, but already we began to see something of the treeless mountains which characterize Tibet. In some cases trees have been planted along the roadside by the Sikkimese Government. We found later that the timberline on the north or Tibetan side of the mountains was much lower than on the south. On the approach through Sikkim there was quite a lot of timber at fourteen thousand feet elevation, which gradually changed from deciduous to evergreens, the trees between this height and sixteen thousand feet growing scantier and more stunted till they disappeared entirely. On the other side of the passes we had to descend much lower before we met any very definite signs of vegetation, and what there was seemed half-hearted in growth.

Half-way along the line of our day's march we crossed again to the left-hand side of the river by a tiny but quite respectable suspension-bridge. A little further along we could see an old Sikkim-fashion bridge. Such a bridge consists of only three long bamboo poles, one for a footing, and two higher in the air for hand-rails. It requires a tight-rope walker to cross one with any ease, and of course it is entirely useless for animals.

I was more than ever struck by the absence of the industrious Nepalese, and the few people we did meet were for the most part Lepchas and not Sikkimese. In the afternoon we camped in a charming little dell, invisible from the road, about a mile from the well-known village of Tsöntang (called Cheuntang on the maps), to the dismay of Lhaten, who yearned for the marwa beer procurable only in the villages. He could not understand my aversion to staying in an inhabited spot.

We fell to arguing on the subject, and while we were still forcibly discussing the point we heard a mystifying noise in the surrounding bushes. Thoughts of spies and secret agents were chasing through my head when to our astonishment a cow appeared in our camp circle, stood for an instant breathing heavily, and then fell dead. She was frothing horribly at the mouth, and further investigation showed that she had all the other symptoms of the last stages of the dread foot-and-mouth disease. Evidently she had been left behind by some herdsmen because of her illness, and, when hearing our voices, she had come in a last spasm hoping to receive human assistance—a pathetic reminder of man's dominance over brute creation.

The servants were anxious to eat the corpse, but this I forbade, and so we spent some time carting our would-be friend away from our night's abode.

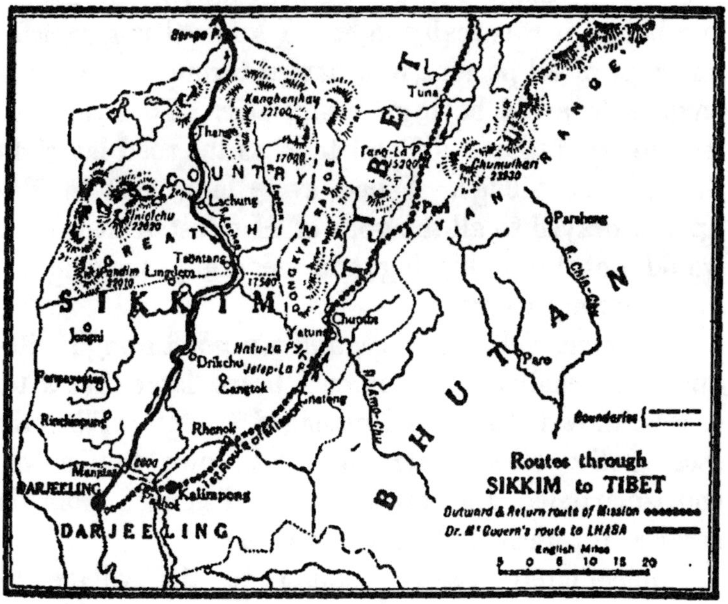

CHAPTER IV

TRAPPED IN THE PASSES

WE started very early next morning, January 19, as I was anxious to pass through the village and government outpost of Tsöntang before it was really light. I knew that a register was kept of all persons who passed through, and I was anxious to avoid having to sign this. To escape attention was rather a difficult task, as the road lay right through the village. I had everything well muffled up and prayed to all the gods of Hindustan that Paris would not begin kicking and generally showing off at the wrong moment.

All went well, however, and we got through without being challenged, though I heard later that after it was known that I had managed to enter Tibet the local police officers were brought down to Gantok, court-martialed, and ignominiously dismissed from the service, for their failure to stop me.

Immediately before coming to the village we passed over the river again at a place very famous historically. Just under the bridge the waters of the river churn and boil in a series of rapids. Until a short time ago prisoners were thrown over the bridge to perish in the turmoil below, and the peasants claim to hear still, in the moaning of the waters, the shrieks of the drowning men.

Although politically Sikkim at present extends several miles north of Tsöntang, in every other way this village marks the boundary line. North of it for the next fifty miles lies what is known as the Pass Country, consisting of gigantic mountains with a few narrow valleys forming passes leading to Tibet. It is in fact a transition land between Tibet and Sikkim with a geography akin to neither. Its inhabitants also form a people apart, differing both from the Tibetans to the north and the Sikkimese to the south. They are known as La-pa, or men of the passes, speaking their own dialect, and observing their own customs. For the most part they are herdsmen living from the produce of their herds of cattle and yaks, the latter an animal unknown in Sikkim proper. In common with the Tibetans they prefer barley to rice. Neither rice nor barley will grow here, but the people find it easier to import barley from Tibet than rice from Sikkim.

At Tsöntang the Tista River breaks up into two branches. On the right it becomes the Lachung, or the river of the Little Pass; and on the left it becomes Lachen River, or the river of the Great Pass. These two river valleys constitute the habitable portion of the Pass Country; but as lofty mountains permanently separate the two systems, the people of the two valleys, though both La-pa, differ considerably one from another. Each valley possesses but one village of importance, called respectively Lachung and Lachen.

It suited my purpose much better to follow up the Lachen Valley, and so we turned to the left and continued our march until late in the afternoon, steadily rising all the time. For the most part the valley was very narrow, and once a single wooden gate barred the way. This was erected to prevent the Lachen Valley cattle wandering down into Sikkim—the only fence needed to wall in a district more than fifty miles long.

Soon we began to get a foretaste of conditions we might expect in the Pass Country. Patches of ice and snow crossed our path and made progress more difficult. In places the road itself was incrusted for long distances with frozen snow a foot deep, a very slippery footing; so we had to dismount and walk. Beautiful scenery abounded. Every twist in the valley brought a new surprise, but the road was tiring, and we were glad to camp at last about half a mile before reaching the village of Lachen, where we had to spread our tent on the snow.

Though the rest was very necessary, I was anxious to push on, as the weather was more than ever threatening. Though the passes might be impenetrable already, they would certainly be so after another storm, and in the morning, January 20, I was much annoyed to find it was impossible to make any move. The animals were exhausted and needed a day's respite. Our boxes were broken and needed to be repaired. Our provisions were completely exhausted, and it would be days before we could reach another village, that which lay on the other side of the passes, in Tibet; so it became necessary to lay in a supply of food at Lachen, and all this work would require time. It was all very exasperating, and, further, it now became necessary for me to inform the servants of my intention to go on to the pass itself. They were still under the impression that Lachen was my destination and a talk with the old lama my goal. I dared not mention anything about Lhasa as yet but determined to inform them that I wanted to go as far as Kampa Dzong, just inside of Tibet. When I called them round and explained my desire, they were horror-struck at the idea of pushing on and kept repeating that the passes were completely blocked. I insisted that we go on for a bit and then turn back if necessary. The servants looked on the prospect in a none too friendly way but eventually, after some persuasion, consented to go forward, though they tried to insist that I make a substantial money offering to the Lachen lama and solicit his indulgence to keep back the snow.

All the natives of this part of the world firmly believe that a life of ascetic contemplation brings with it magical powers, including the ability to control the elements. The Lachen lama is particularly famous all over Sikkim for his regulation of rain and snow. Even villages in the south dominated by other temples send petitions to him with huge gifts, asking that rain be stopped or made to fall, as is desirable.

When they brought forth their stipulation, which

did not at all accord with my desires, I told the servants that in a case like this I was keen on getting value for my money. If I was to pay the money, I wished to be certain that no snow would fall, and as no guarantee would be forthcoming, this could only be assured by paying the lama afterward, when we saw what the weather turned out to be as the result of his devotions. With this they had to be content.

The early afternoon was destined to give us another fright. The animals had been left to graze at will on the patches of earth still free from snow. We later discovered them lathering at the mouth like our friend the cow of the previous day. It seems that they had been eating a poisonous weed which grows in the Pass Country and which constitutes the bane of the native herdsmen. The herb is known as duk-shing and is more prevalent in some valleys than others; it is deadly to yaks and sheep. The places where it is more common the herdsmen generally avoid. My servants assured me cheerfully that unless something was done quickly the effect on our pack-animals would be fatal but suggested that I give the beasts my little hoard of sugar, as it was supposed to act as an antidote. Very sadly I handed over the sugar-bag, for though I was skeptical of its curative powers I could not afford to run any risks. At least the creatures did not grow any worse as the result of this novel medicine, and when they did later drop off one by one it was as a result chiefly of exhaustion.

I then sent the servants into Lachen to buy supplies but impressed upon them the necessity of keep-

A typical Sikkimese village

The takin: the rarest animal in the world, found only in the mountains of Tibet; it is a mixture of many species, goat, cow and bear, etc., breeding now as a distinct species; less than a hundred exist.

Dr. McGovern in mountain kit

The Depön Kusho: Tibetan trade-agent, who is also a general in the Tibetan army

ing absolute silence in regard to me and my movements. Had they followed my orders the course of subsequent events would have been very different, but on their return I found, first, that no sugar could be found in Lachen, which meant months of discomfort for one with a sweet tooth, as the Tibetans eat no sugar in any form and it would be impossible to buy any in Tibet, and, second (and more important), that Satan had met an old bosom friend from Pemayangtse to whom, under the seal of secrecy, he had confided who I was and the fact that we were bound for the Tibetan passes.

I became livid with fury at hearing this. I knew enough about the Oriental manner of keeping secrets to be convinced that in no time the matter would become public property, that all my precautions for secrecy in Sikkim had been in vain, and that in a few weeks' time at the outside the news of my stay in Lachen would leak down to Gantok, the capital of Sikkim where there are numerous agents of the Tibetan Government who would doubtless communicate to Lhasa the news of my suspicious movements.

I was so upset at the news that I refused to eat anything and had a twenty-four hours' fast—a tantrum habit inherited from nursery days. Furthermore, I ordered a start to be made very early the next morning before people were about, lest the news should have already leaked out and a local official arrive at our camp and order us to remain there pending inquiry.

It was, in all ways, a disagreeable day, but it had

enabled us to put our things in order and prepare ourselves for possible calamities later on, a fact which was, as events turned out, destined to save our lives.

To make things even more dismal, the next morning, January 21, saw the beginning of a wretched misty day, with every now and then a few flakes of snow. It was obvious that a snow-storm was impending, and my one hope was that we should be over the pass before it came on. Once on the table-land of Tibet, I cared not a straw for snow, but that promised land lay beyond the mountain, which loomed threateningly before us. The mules had recovered from the poison herb troubles of the previous day, but the ponies still seemed to be very shaky, and so we had to walk the whole day in the desire to give them a further recuperative period.

On the way we had to plow a path through a good deal of snow-drift, so that our progress was very slow, but by early afternoon we were about twelve miles above Lachen and had risen to a height of twelve thousand feet above sea-level. This, I have learned by experience, is the critical height. It is very seldom that a healthy person gets mountain sickness under that height, but once that level is reached he may begin to suffer, and further ascent may prove dangerous. If, on the other hand, having risen so far he experiences no pain, he need have no fear of going on to twenty thousand feet. He is, in fact, practically immune.

I was, therefore, interested to observe that it was just at this point that Satan began to complain of racking headache and ringing in the ears. But he was the only one to suffer, and after I had given him a few cloves to chew he began to feel better. The others and myself felt nothing more than the exertion of the climb.

Another two miles brought us past Tangu, the last village in Sikkim, and even this is a village in name rather than in fact. There are a few La-pa huts inhabited only in summer: in winter it contains only two petty officials, who serve as outpost guardians and as keepers of the government rest-house. By departing from the road I managed to get my little caravan past this point unobserved and heaved a sigh of relief, thinking my troubles were over; but we were not yet out of the woods.

Still another two miles brought us to a point where, for a quarter of a mile, the road and the whole hillside was a smooth sheet of ice, upon which at first we found it impossible to walk. The animals had even more trouble and slithered all over the place. Our loads suffered serious damage in the frequent falls. To add to the confusion, the servants lost their heads completely and began shrieking contradictory orders to one another. Two of them, Satan and Diogenes, improved matters by weeping.

I had to take a strong hand in matters myself before some sort of order was restored, and we then began to throw gravel on the glacial surface and cut out occasional steps in the ice with our knives, the same knives we had used in the jungle a few days previously. By these methods we got our caravan across, but this one job had taken an hour, and we were all so exhausted that we had to camp almost immediately afterward.

In the meantime, Gyangtse, Lhaten's pony, a timeworn nag, showed signs of succumbing. He leaned in a very dissolute fashion against a tree (there were still a few trees about) and refused to eat or drink. Under such circumstances the Sikkimese always resort to some new concoction, and so we brewed strong tea and added to it a half-bottle of raw spirit which Lhaten had purchased in Lachen. The major portion of this we managed to pour down the poor pony's throat, though not without a struggle, for he marshaled all his waning strength in an attempt to hunger-strike, for evidently he had strong convictions on the question of forcible feeding. In the end he managed to break our one and only bottle with which we had been feeding him. Temporarily he revived, but I felt that sooner or later we should no longer have the pleasure of his company.

By this time we were so fatigued that we no longer had strength or energy enough to put our camp in order. Rather than have the trouble of hoisting the tent, I decided to sleep in the open. The servants picked a spot under a tree, one of the sparse sentinels of the timber-line, while I preferred to be without such protection. Our bags and boxes, moreover, were left scattered about, but we were quite satisfied with our day's efforts and too tired to worry about orderliness. Despite the weather conditions we soon fell asleep when we laid ourselves down on the ground.

It is not difficult to imagine the horror which I felt

a couple of hours later when I woke from a doze to find that snow was beginning to fall. Obviously there was nothing to be done, and I could only hope that this was merely the result of a passing cloud and not the beginning of a serious snow-storm. I was soon undeceived. The snow began to settle over me inch by inch. In a way it was a delicious feeling, because it had been bitterly cold, and the new snow acted as a gradually thickening blanket. Consequently I felt not the slightest inclination to get up and seek protection under the tree. Only, in order to keep a supply of air, I occasionally thrust a tiny hole through the snow above me with my riding-crop. The snow fell continuously, but the servants, somewhat under cover, remained asleep the whole night through; early the next morning, January 22, when they awoke and perceived the snow for the first time, they began to yell with dismay, thinking themselves forever lost. Their scare was doubled when they failed to see me, for by this time I was quite hidden from sight by more than three feet of snow, and there was no sign to show where I lay. The servants thought, of course, that I had been smothered to death. I let them howl for a while without moving, for I dreaded to leave the protection of my warm natural blanket, but eventually I set up, the top of my head just appearing above the snow. This seemed to them to savor of the miraculous; something of their fright abated, and for a while I was something of a tin god to them.

We were able to discuss seriously what next was to be done; rather glad we were still to be alive. It would have been death to push on for the moment. The snow was falling faster and faster, and it was certain to lie much deeper higher up in the mountain gullies. There was no hut or village this side of the pass in which we could take refuge. To stay on where we were was equally out of the question. In fact, the delay of another hour appeared dangerous. It was difficult to get back even now, and with more snow to contend with it would be quite impossible. Being unable either to go forward or to go back, we would perish miserably in our present post.

It was, therefore, our obvious duty to fight our way back immediately, but because of the increasing difficulty caused by the snow, it was inconceivable that we could get to Lachen in one day. The servants thought that we would be lucky to get back to Tangu, where we could throw ourselves on the mercies of the two officials there.

Tangu, was however, absolutely taboo, as I knew that once we stopped there our chances of getting to Lhasa would be gone forever. But I remembered that between Tangu and Lachen there were one or two groups of cattle-sheds, or huts, used by the herdsmen only in the summer when their cattle were brought up this far to graze. These huts were deserted now, of course, but we could probably break into one of them and find there some kind of shelter in which we could await further developments.

The nearest such shelter lay six miles back, and I gave orders that we make for it immediately. It was hard work to make headway through three feet or more of freshly fallen snow, particularly as the path had been completely obliterated. It took us all day to cover the six miles, but the sense of danger and the urgent need of finding shelter made us oblivious to the feeling of fatigue, though I had a little difficulty in getting the servants past Tangu. The snow was falling so heavily that we could scarcely see a yard in front of us. Consequently there was no longer need for concealment when we passed that outpost.

In the afternoon, curiously enough, Satan began to suffer from snow-blindness. It is well known that freshly fallen snow is much more irritating to the eyes than snow which has lain for some time, but it is rare to find snow-blindness coming on during a snow-storm. It is usually only the reflection of the sun's rays on the eye that brings about injury to the eyesight, and the sun was then completely invisible. Satan had, foolishly enough, forgotten to bring his dark glasses; so I was forced to lend him mine, and contented myself with pulling my fur cap down over my eyes. In other ways I, also, was feeling far from well, and in fact was experiencing the first symptoms of that illness which was later to develop into dysentery. The result of eating Tibetan meat was already beginning to be felt. We were all, therefore, delighted when we got to our destination late in the afternoon.

The door of the first hut we tried yielded to a push, and we found ourselves inside its one and only room. The hut was built on American log-cabin lines, except that there was a great smoke-hole in the roof. There were huge chinks between the logs of the walls; these let in a good deal of snow, and the wind played in and out as it listed. Our abode was far from ideal, as can be imagined, but we were more than satisfied, particularly as we found inside two or three dry pieces of wood which could be used to kindle a fire. But while unloading the animals I was annoyed to discover that in their morning's fright the servants had been unable to find several of the smaller packages, which we had foolishly left scattered about the preceding night, and which, of course, had been covered by the snow.

The next morning, January 23, we held a council of war. Though the weather had improved, a little snow was still falling; and it was impossible for us to attempt to get to the passes. I was anxious to stay where we were. But the horses were without fodder, and there was still danger that we might be snowbound for an indefinite period, during which time the chances were that the animals, and possibly we ourselves, would die from starvation. The servants were clamorous to retire, and at last I agreed to do so, though secretly I determined to put as many brakes on our backward journey as possible. I still had faint hopes, which, however, I dared not express, that once the snow stopped we might be able to force our way through to Tibet.

The rearward march proved terribly exhausting. By the time we were on the way the snow was breast-high, and each of us had to take his turn to act as a plow to make a furrow through the snow in which the animals might follow, for they were helpless otherwise. Fortunately for all of them, even the invalid pony seemed to be in fairly good condition to-day. When, after three miles, we came to another group of deserted huts, we were, as my diary has it, "almost dead from fatigue," so that I had little difficulty in persuading the servants to go no further for the day. It was a wearying business. With every step on this retreat my hopes drooped a little lower, and I think only a natural obstinacy held me up under this dispiriting reverse. The night's repose stiffened me in my purpose, and next day, January 24, our march had only covered a little over a mile when I purposely went on strike and refused to travel another inch. For here we found another couple of huts, and I remembered that there were no more until we got to Lachen, still some six or seven miles further back. I knew that we must avoid returning to Lachen at all costs.

It was a beautiful day. The sun was shining brilliantly, and the snow was already beginning to melt. Moreover, a curious bend in the valley had sheltered a little patch on the hillside where it was almost free from snow. Here the animals could get a few mouthfuls of coarse winter grass. This solved the fodder question temporarily. Our own food store was running dangerously low, but as we had enough to last us a few days longer I decided to form a little winter camp and wait for a new opportunity to push on to the pass. Under ordinary circumstances I should have returned to Sikkim and waited another two months before renewing our attempt to enter Tibet, but I was convinced it was now or never and preferred to hang on desperately.

From the afternoon of the twenty-fourth to the afternoon of the twenty-sixth we stayed in our little camp on the spot. Personally I enjoyed this short time of rest, but I was careful to arrange little jobs for the servants, for their morale would have been completely destroyed in a few hours' idle brooding. Fortunately we were entertained in a very unexpected fashion. A huge cat began to prowl round our hut and disturb us by its noises. It was in looks and manner much more like a wildcat than one of a domestic breed. It had started its life probably as a kitten in some herdsman's house, and then, being deserted, had "reverted to type." The deep snow had destroyed its food supply; so, sniffing our presence, it had decided to blackmail us into giving it free board and lodgings.

We did, indeed, donate a small piece of meat, but when we ourselves were so near starvation it was impossible to be over-generous. It waxed angry at our miserliness and began a vigorous physical attack on our larder, and later on us, which we had to repulse with our riding-crops. After a fierce battle lasting for half an hour, the cat retired, though not until we bore marks of the fray in the way of scratches so serious that they required first-aid attention. During the remainder of our stay the cat continued in the neighborhood and gave a full solo rendering of what it thought of us.

On the twenty-sixth I decided to go forward again. The snow had been melting steadily in our part of the valley. In a very high altitude such as this, where the air is rarefied, the sun's rays during the daytime have an overpowering effect, however cold the nights may be, and under these scorching rays the snow had begun to shrink, and, though it was still deep, I thought we had a chance to get through. The food question was becoming so pressing that no further delay was to be brooked. A move had to be made one way or the other, but we only got off in the afternoon, as I had to spend the whole morning coaxing and persuading the servants into accompanying me, sometimes even bullying them. It frequently happened that bullying was the best policy with these men, for they took coaxing as a sign of weakness and became awkward and obstinate.

Because of the late start, we were able to cover only four miles. This brought us to the hut in which we had first taken refuge after the commencement of the snow-storm. Soon after arriving we saw a snow-leopard prowling about, and this so frightened the animals that Diogenes had to sleep outside with them to act as guard.

It is extraordinary how these animals can walk over the snow without sinking into it. The natives explain this peculiarity by giving the snow-leopards supernatural powers.

The next day, January 27, was, to quote my diary, "the most awful day I have ever spent." The memory of the miseries we had to endure remains very keen. Because of the more protected nature of this part of the valley, we found that the snow had hardly melted at all, and for a great part of the way it lay between four and five feet deep. The further we went the deeper we sank. Soon after this the valley began to narrow down to a gorge which was literally choked with snow.

For me, the desperate plowing through the snow was absolute misery. My illness had been growing worse these last two days and had sapped me of all strength. I was afraid to show my weakness before the servants and so sent my caravan on ahead while I staggered along after it. Every fifty yards or so I would get quite confused in the snow and fall. Where I fell I was forced to lie and rest for a minute or two before I could summon my energies to struggle up and press on. Fear overtook me that I was being left miles behind, but afterward I found that the servants were faring nearly as badly. Blundering on in my anxiety I caught up with the party at sunset, and we plowed on for another two hours, not in the least knowing where we were, for the road lay deep buried in snow and we had only the general contour of the valley by which to go. The vagueness of our position and direction demoralized the whole caravan, and the animals seemed to be as much in a maze as the men.

Frequently we thought that we were on safe ground, when suddenly the man ahead would disappear from sight down some gully or water-hole rendered invisible by the snow. We had used up all our spirits in a vain attempt to secure extra stimulation, but by half-past eight we were still far from our objective, the plateau of Sitang. Our day's march had been only eight or nine miles, but it had taken us more than fourteen hours to cover even this distance. We were lost. Our strength was failing, and our hearts were in our boots. Where the roadway might be we had not the faintest idea, and we were wallowing in a long snow-drift. It was pitch-dark, although the moon should have been visible. Suddenly, while we were in this state, it began to snow again. I was long past all feeling by now, but Lhaten broke down and wept. Later his weeping changed into hysterical sobbing which could not be stopped; the others were bordering on the same state.

It was absolutely impossible to go any further that night, and so I looked about for shelter. We had long passed the region of houses or huts; but, even more serious, I could see no place where we could possibly erect a tent. Hunting around we espied among the great rocks overhanging the river one with a flat top from which most of the snow had been driven by the wind, and it was upon this that we decided to hoist our tent, for under such conditions to sleep in the open would have meant certain death.

In our exhausted condition the work of hoisting the tent required an effort of will. Snow and wind beat against us and nearly caused a catastrophe even before we had erected the canvas, which we had to hold down by placing boxes on its sides and ends, for of course the rock was impervious to tent-pegs. Into this small tent all five of us had to squeeze, although it was meant for only one person, or at the most for two. For the animals a hole was burrowed in the snow by the side of the rock. There was nothing else we could do for them, but we were afraid that they would be frozen to death during the night.

I deemed it fortunate for our food supply that we were too tired to feel hungry and were content with a small piece of meat apiece. This we had to eat raw in true Tibetan fashion, for we had no means of lighting a fire.

An hour later the wind dropped, but the short comparative calm was succeeded by one of the terrific wind-storms which are known only in Tibet and in the passes. In a very short time the tent had been blown in on us, and we lay huddled together in one tight heap, with the canvas beating on our heads. Still the gale increased, and at last one terrific blast carried our whole huddled mass off the rock and into the snow beyond, where we all landed, badly frightened but unhurt. Satan now suddenly remembered that he had been brought up a priest and began a long invocation to all the Tibetan saints, being particularly vociferous in his appeal to the polygamous, wine-bibbing Padma Sambhava, dead these thousand years and more. He confessed among other things how foolish he had been to come with me and asked pardon therefor.

The wind eventually died down about three in the morning, and until then sleep was impossible. Satan kept up his lugubrious prayers till, with the decline of the storm, immediate annihilation seemed averted; then he fell into a doze like the rest of the worn-out and apprehensive party.

When I awoke again a few hours later, January 28, I found the servants were already packing up.

They were firmly of mind to dash back to Sikkim. They took it for granted that even I could not possibly want to go on. And I must confess that they were very nearly right. All my fine hopes had evaporated, and had I been asked for my vote on the subject it would have been cast in favor of return. But their cool assumption that I had abandoned the enterprise was too much for me. Fearing that argument would be useless, I rushed for the food-bag, already nearly empty, and, holding it over the great river ravine, I swore that if they went back I would throw their food away, which meant that they would starve before they could arrive once more at the inhabited part of Sikkim. I then pointed out that they were more than half-way through the snow and that to turn back would be as difficult as to go on. Letting this argument sink in, I rushed on as fast as I could, leaving them to follow. The strategy had effect: they came sheepishly after me. When I say I rushed on, it must not be imagined it was with any great speed, for the snow was deeper and more clogging and troublesome than ever.

We had a very curious bit of luck that morning. Our friend the snow-leopard had passed us in the night and seemed to be heading for the pass, for we could see his footprints in the snow. There seemed to be a striking regularity about his path, and it occurred to me that he might be traveling over the line of the road. Investigation proved that this idea was correct. By following in his footsteps we saved ourselves a good deal of road-seeking. It was amazing to me how the leopard knew the road, buried as it was beneath several feet of snow and, of course, level with the wide white expanse on every side. I could only suppose that it was by means of a sense of smell, effective through the deep snow, though why he should have kept to the road with all its zigzags, when he could easily have made cross cuts impossible for us, was a mystery which I did not attempt to solve.

The servants looked upon the footprints as a very suspicious omen, or even as a miraculous intervention on the part of the blessed buddhas and bodhisattvas—a notion that I was careful not to contradict.

About four hours later we had an even greater stroke of fortune. The valley continued to narrow more and more. The mountains on either side closed down to form precipitous cliffs, and it seemed as if we were crawling through a funnel. When the snow was at its deepest and further progress seemed impossible, the valley suddenly twisted and once more widened out, and we came into an entirely different type of country. It seemed as if some ghostly wizard had waved his magic wand and a mysterious transformation had taken place.

Not a tree, bush, or scrub was visible. There were only three or four inches of snow on the ground, and here and there were great patches of bare earth, earth of that sandy and desolate kind peculiar to the Tibetan plateau. A few miles further on the valley swept to the right and became a broad plain running in an east-to-west direction, bounded on the north and south by overshadowing mountain ranges. Techni-

Tibetan official and wife watching a lama dance

The road to Gyangtse

Glacier from Mount Chumolhari

cally we were still in Sikkim; the northern range of mountains marked the political boundary line. But geographically and geologically we were already in Tibet. The scarcity of the snow was an evidence of this. The Indian side of the Himalayas is deluged by rain in the summer and by snow in the winter. The rain- and snow-bearing clouds wafted by the ocean do not rise high enough to cross the Himalayan heights, against which they break and precipitate their contents, so that on the Tibetan side there is a notable absence of moisture. In summer the rain is scanty, in some parts almost unknown. In winter, except on the mountain peaks, the snow seldom lies more than a few inches deep, and this is soon melted by the terrific rays of the midday sun, which are so powerful that there is always danger of sunstroke in exposed places if one is careless.

On the other hand, the night cold is intense, far greater than anything known on the south side of the Himalayas, and the terrible Tibetan winds bite through the skin into the very bones. In these conditions death and desolation reigns. There is no country which appears so bleak and dreary as the lifeless plains of Tibet. Even the Tista River, as we neared its source, seemed devoid of life, for here it was but one sheet of rigid ice.

In greatly improved spirits we continued our way until evening and eventually camped just under the Chumiomo Glacier. Here the ground was frozen so hard that we broke several wooden tent-pegs trying to drive them into the soil, and finally we had to discard these and use only giant iron nails. Even these were badly bent by the frost-bound earth.

The next day, January 29, I had hoped to be over the actual pass, but because of the gross inaccuracy of the existing maps we missed our way and went eight miles out of our course. The result was that evening found us still in the upper Tista Valley. By this time I had discovered our mistake, but it was too late to retrace our steps that day.

This event was, to us, a great calamity, for we had completely exhausted our food stock and were well nigh starving. All the animals, too, had reached the danger-mark of fatigue. The previous two nights in the open had, in fact, proved too much for the ailing pony Gyangtse. His lungs had caught a chill, and I saw that at the best he could only last two or three days longer.

In these circumstances, I decided to end, by one stroke, both his miseries and ours. All my servants had very strict Buddhist religious scruples, however scampish they might be in their private life, and refused to kill any living thing, though they were quite willing to eat any animal killed by some one else. Consequently, I had to do the necessary work myself with my huge knife. I slit the poor beast's throat. We waited a few minutes, and then, being unable to restrain our hunger longer, we sliced off the choicer portions of his carcass and set to work to devour the still warm meat. Fuel being more than ever unprocurable, we were forced to eat this raw. To a gourmet the raw and still quivering flesh of a horse may not appear appetizing, but I had long lost all sense of squeamishness, and all of us sat down to the meal with relish. To one regarding this incident from a place of moderate comfort, the whole thing may seem revolting, but it was the wisest thing we could do, in fact the only thing to do to save our lives and end quickly the poor pony's miseries which could not be mitigated.

For eight weary miles we retraced our steps the next morning, January 30. In this part of the valley the road had long since disappeared, but after scouting around in several directions I eventually managed to light on the proper course. This proved to be along a narrow side valley stretching for several miles which climbed up almost due north. This soon became a difficult ascent, for not only were we forced to walk but the weakened state of the remaining animals necessitated our carrying on our own shoulders a good deal of their loads. We trudged stolidly up till we were at an altitude of seventeen thousand feet. During this climb we were often compelled to halt and rest, for at such an altitude any form of exertion brings on a torturing fatigue, and the steady climb seemed to tear the very lungs out of us. The next thousand-foot rise was torture, and it was not until sunset that we reached the path of the pass, some eighteen thousand feet above sea-level, and could shout with joy, "Lha-gyal-lo! Lha-gyal-lo!"—literally, "Victory! Victory! to the gods!"

CHAPTER V

FIRST DAYS IN TIBET

WE turned back to catch our last glimpse of India. For miles and miles on either side of us we could see the Himalayan peaks soaring up to meet and penetrate a huge blank of cloud and mist. It seemed as if a shroud of fear and despondency lay over the high places of the world. For me, with the long and dangerous journey through the Forbidden Land still ahead, it seemed like a message of doom.

We had exhausted all our energies in our battle with the snow and starvation in the passes, and now that we had come through it was as if we were not at the end but at the very beginning of our difficulties. We had still the great winds and the biting cold of the bleak Tibetan plains to contend with, no small matter if that only were our obstacle; but in addition we had from now onward not nature alone but man also to encounter. We were now in the Forbidden Land itself, and every step that took us nearer to the Sacred City brought with it greater danger of detection; for the watch against foreign intrusion, which is sometimes slack on the outer and more sparsely inhabited parts, becomes the stricter the nearer the capital is approached. Knowing all the difficulties which lay in our way, it seemed to us impossible ever to reach our goal; and supposing that by some miracle we attained our objective and reached Lhasa, we would still be faced with our greatest danger, an attack on the part of the fanatical monks of the great central monasteries; for as a result of their threats we had not only been forbidden to come to Lhasa but had not even been permitted to remain in Gyangtse. When they should discover that in spite of their threats I had come to the capital, there was no telling to what length their fury might lead them.

In spite of these despondent broodings, there was nothing to do but to push on with the undertaking. We had not only crossed the Rubicon, we had also burned our bridges behind us, for the prospect of having to return through the passes was even more terrible than to go on. There was nothing to do but to steel myself against anything that might occur.

That night, however, nothing more could be done. The animals refused to go any further, and we ourselves were at the end of our tether, so that we were forced to camp on the broad, even-surfaced summit of the pass, a formation which is peculiar so far as is known to this particular pass. Natives have a great fear of sleeping on the tops of passes. They believe them to be inhabited by dark and terrible demons who bring disaster upon any one who stops there, but in the present instance they had no choice, and we set about looking for a camping-place. An almost ideal spot was found in a tiny ravine hollowed out by a stream which forms in summer from the melting of the winter snows of the pass and the near-by Chumiomo Peak. Soon we were tucked away inside our tent. It was perishing cold, but I feared more for the less protected animals than for ourselves; and so I commanded the servants to take some of our own blankets and tie them around our beasts, for we at least could obtain a precarious warmth by snuggling close to one another, and I had a great dread of losing our principal means of transport.

For food we had nothing but the hunks of horse-meat which we had brought with us, but we were fortunate enough to find a small quantity of yak- and mule-dung, the aftermath of the small native caravans which in summer go over the passes, and we could make a pretense of cooking our flesh, and, what was more, were able to prepare some tea, the best of stimulants. We were, all of us, possessed of a weird and eery feeling, and soon the servants began to recite tales of the hill demons and then equally fantastic stories of the wild men who are supposed to live in the mountains. I had already heard brief mention of these and listened with curiosity to what my men had to say on the subject.

In nearly all parts of Tibet one finds the tradition of the existence of a primitive race of men, former inhabitants of the land who have been driven out of the plains by the Tibetans and who now dwell only in the passes and in inaccessible mountain crags. My own servants referred to them as snow men. They are said to be great, hairy creatures, huge in size, and possessed of incredible physical strength. Although having a certain low cunning, they are deficient in intelligence, and it is the intellectual superiority of the Tibetans that has enabled them to oust the primitive snow men from the plains. These men of the mountains brood upon their wrongs and wreak their vengeance upon any casual herdsmen who may be found straying in their domain. So runs the legend, and many attempts have been made to ascertain what facts may have given rise to it; for it has been permitted to no white man to meet these snow men, and even a Tibetan, when pinned down to it, will admit that he has never seen one but that he "has heard of a man who has"—sometimes it comes to as near as a cousin, or at least a cousin by marriage, who has been pursued by the snow men and just escaped with his life. And after all, they will add, do not every year a number of herdsmen away in the mountains fail to return to their native villages? Sure proof, they will add, that they have been devoured by the wild men!

Rockhill, who came across this tradition in the extreme eastern part of Tibet, suggests, in his "Land of the Lamas," that the wild men may be nothing other than bears! For other parts of Tibet this explanation could scarcely be valid, since in many parts of Tibet, as, for example, in Kampa Dzong, Pari, and the surrounding district, bears are unknown.

Others have suggested that the snow man may be some form of ape. Only one thing can be said in favor of this theory: the many tales told about the imitative habits of the monkey family bear a striking resemblance to some of the native fables related by the Tibetan peasantry with relation to the snow men. As examples

I might quote two anecdotes, crude in the extreme, as told me by my servants that evening.

Lhaten related how a friend of his escaped from the wild men through his acuteness. He was chased by one of the monsters and noticed that when he stopped for a second to look back the mountain man also stopped and glanced back over his shoulder, and this went on for some time, the savage, however, gradually drawing nearer. Eventually the Tibetan threw himself down and pretended to go to sleep, whereupon the pursuer again followed his example and indeed did fall asleep, so that the poor peasant, taking advantage of the fact, escaped.

Satan, not to be outdone in the story-telling business, now chimed in and related an even more thrilling event, which was supposed to have occurred in Lachen, where occasional tins of petroleum are imported to furnish lights for the Lepchas during their long nights. A certain peasant discovered one afternoon that a wild man had entered his hut, at the door of which stood an open tin of oil. The peasant picked up a small tub of water in order to throw it at his adversary, but noticing that the wild man imitated his action by picking up the tin of oil, the man poured the water over himself and was delighted to find that the savage, in imitation, emptied the petroleum over his body. The man then seized a blazing stick on the open fire, and, upon the savage's doing the same, the petroleum caught fire and the wild man was burned to death.

As an anthropologist I had been interested in the wild man discussion, but I soon found out that the information acquired belonged by right more to the folklorist than to the serious scientist, and I proceeded to divert the conversation into other channels, viz., our plans for the immediate future. At this point I revealed the whole of my plans to my men.

Up to that time they knew merely of my desire to reach Tibet. I now told them that my goal was not only Tibet but Lhasa itself, and that to succeed in getting there I should be forced to go in disguise. To each of them I assigned his new rôle and insisted then and there upon a careful rehearsal of it. From the baggage I got out a gala costume, such as is worn by the Sikkimese nobility, and gave it to Satan to try on. Hereafter he was to be the master, posing as a small landed proprietor going on pilgrimage to Lhasa, taking the rest of us along in his suite. Except for this change of masters, the other servants were to continue their present duties, while I was degraded to the status of Lhaten's assistant, and was to act as general cook and bottle-washer. I must admit that the servants entered into the project with unexpected gusto. They regarded it as a game, for the dangers which were before us in case of detection had not yet occurred to their slow intellects.

In fact, they wanted me to diverge the next day to the right and attempt to go directly to Lhasa, but I insisted upon going to Shigatse first. This is the second city of Tibet and the seat of the Trashi-lama, and I thought it might prove easier to get there than to Lhasa, so that in case we were turned back before reaching the Forbidden City itself I should at least have seen that city of Tibet which ranks after it in importance.

The actual process of disguise I postponed until the next morning. This turned out a peculiarly painful business. My hair was already done and required only a few finishing touches, but in order to stain my skin I had to strip and stand stark naked in that bitter morning wind of the pass while Lhaten daubed on me my special concoction of walnut-juice and iodine. I considered it necessary to stain my whole body, and not merely the ordinarily visible parts, as I feared that later on I might have to undergo a detailed physical examination. Finally came the question of eyes, for my blue eyes were likely to prove the weakest point in my disguise. For this I had a twofold remedy. In the first place I sliced open the lemon specially brought for this purpose and squeezed the juice into my eyes. Though sharply painful and likely to irritate the eyeball, lemon-juice serves to give the eyes, temporarily at least, a much darker hue. For further security, however, I employed the glue and dark goggles. I pretended to have contracted a sharp attack of snow-blindness and dabbed copious amounts of glue under the eyelids in imitation of the secretions which customarily result from this trouble, and, furthermore, added the dark goggles as a pretended protection against the glare of the sun. The next thing to be done was to wrap up all my European clothes and other such incriminating articles and secrete them under a rock. It may be that some future traveler to Tibet will find them in years to come and wonder how such things came to be placed in this far-away corner of the world.

About nine o'clock we started on our first day's

march inside of Tibet itself. Needless to say, I was full of very mixed emotions. That day we were due to come in contact with the Tibetan outposts and were to have a chance of proving whether or not my carefully thought-out plans of disguise were to be effective; much depended upon their effectiveness. After a short descent the path gradually rose again until we were on top of a second pass, only a few feet lower than the pass which we had crossed the preceding day. From this point the road, if it could be dignified by this name, gradually descended over a gently sloping plain, which stretched for miles ahead of us and which led down to the Kampa Basin. So gradual is the descent and so even the surface of the plain that almost any part of it could be used for motor traffic. I thought of the extensive use which is now being made on the Mongolian plains of light cars going from Kalgan, only a few miles north of Peking, to Urga, the Mongolian capital, where also resides a living Buddha, directly connected with the Tibetan hierarchy, and I wondered whether, in the not far-distant future, some use could not be made of the ubiquitous Ford across the very plains of Tibet itself. Because of the difficulties of my own situation, it struck me as grotesquely comical that perhaps in future years, when the fanaticism of the ecclesiastical part of the population had been appeased, a party of tourists, shepherded by Messrs. Thomas Cook & Son, might motor their way from the pass to the threshold of the Potala, where the Dalai-lama sits enthroned. Only let me advise such future travelers never to try the journey in winter, when the thermometer hovers between thirty and forty below zero, and the cutting winds slice their way to one's bones.

As I had come to expect, we found only sparse patches of snow upon the plain, but this absence of snow only served to accentuate the bleak and desolate nature of the country. There, stretching mile after mile, was to be found no sign of trees or brushes or human habitation. The constant alternation of midday heat with night cold had broken up even the rocks into a sandy soil, with a sprinkling of small pebbles, and had eaten away the angles of occasional low-lying hills into an even, monotonous, down-like formation. There was only one color to everything, a dark and dirty yellow, alleviated only by the brilliant snowy peaks of the Himalaya ranges, which now lay safely behind us.

At first it seemed as if the plain was completely lifeless, devoid of both fauna and flora. Soon we began to meet with occasional herds of antelope which seemed to be grazing upon nothing but the sand and pebbles of the plain, but I then noticed that here and there almost hidden in the soil was a tiny tuft of coarse grass, almost invisible by reason of its smallness, its scarcity, and its drabness of color, as if the grass were ashamed of its very existence, or desirous of deflecting notice from its weary struggle to live.

So cleverly designed was the coating of the antelopes, so much were they in harmony with their surroundings, that they, too, were almost invisible until we were practically upon them and they turned to flee, showing us a tiny tuft of white hair at the tail like a vanishing wisp of snow. It was possible for us to get a good look at these dainty animals because of their astonishing fearlessness. In Tibet firearms are scarce, and the clumsy bows and arrows of the natives are useful only at very short range, so that the wild animals of Tibet have not yet learned to flee at the distant sight of man. In addition, hunting is strictly forbidden on religious grounds by the Tibetan Government, as being inconsonant with the mercy inculcated by the Buddha, and this prohibition is on the whole fairly well observed, so that the herds of antelope and other wild animals are both fairly numerous and surprisingly lacking in timidity. Several times that morning the graceful animals were within a stone's throw, until suddenly Satan broke into a pilgrim's song. The antelopes seemed to have regarded his voice as a most deadly missile, for they soon scattered. On the whole I was inclined to agree with them.

We went along fairly leisurely. The animals were so weakened by their long privations that I was afraid of driving them too hard, and as they had been without proper food for so long, we halted now and then to allow them to graze on the poor stunted wisps of grass which the antelope-herds had shown us. Both ponies were tottering, and we were forced to walk the whole way.

We were going on our way quite unconcernedly, having seen no signs of human habitations, when suddenly a narrow dip in the broad plain, the bed of a long dried-up and forgotten river, brought to view a little village. We were only a hundred yards away when we saw it, and at the same time some of its inhabitants espied and called out to us, so that it was impossible to make a detour.

I quickly whispered to Satan and Lhaten to lead the way, while I and the others came on with the transport. The village in question turned out to be what is called the Chinese outpost, for during the period of Chinese influence in Tibet, which only ended in 1912, it was the custom of the Chinese governors to keep at this point a small detachment of soldiers to act as a sort of pass guard. The Chinese have departed, and their fort has partly fallen into ruin. In the summer-time the Tibetans themselves always place an official or two here to examine any traveler who may come over the passes. But the passes are only supposed to be open in the summer months. In winter all traffic between Sikkim and Tibet, certainly along this route, is closed, and the officials and their underlings are withdrawn to the great castle of Kampa Dzong, still several miles away.

On arriving at the village, therefore, we were lucky enough to have no one deputed to examine us officially. Nevertheless, I was in great fright lest some one should detect something unusual in my appearance, and so I hid myself among our animals as much as I could, and we stopped only long enough to purchase a small supply of food.

It was a poor, meager little village, hardly able to support itself, and could provide us with very little, so that it was necessary for us to push on to Kampa Dzong that same evening. Because of my whispered orders, we did not even stop to eat our food in this village, but, placing it in our wallets, we started off once more, making an excuse that we wished to get to Kampa Dzong as soon as possible.

Curiously enough, we learned from the head-men, who sold us our tsampa, or barley-flour, that there were in this same village two Tibetan peasants who, having urgent business in Lachen, had attempted to cross the pass into Sikkim a few days previously, but because of the snow-storm had been forced to turn back. One of them had contracted pneumonia and was then in a dying condition. This fact impressed upon us more forcibly the great danger which we had run and the almost miraculous nature of our escape from death while laboring in the passes.

The inhabitants of this village were even dirtier than the average run of Tibetans, and there was a thick coating of grime on every one of their faces, but considering the cold and the misery of their lives, one could scarcely blame them. Since leaving Lachen we, also, had not deigned to wash, and we seemed on a fair way to equal these natives in the extent of dirtiness, given time enough. The dirt, the cold, and the misery seemed to have eaten into the very souls of these poor beings, and they all had that dead, dull, sodden look of a yeomanry long since in their decline; but since it prevented their noticing anything unusual in my appearance, I was quite satisfied to find them as they were.

The village itself, with its twenty or thirty straggling houses, was of typically Tibetan design, forming a violent contrast to the Sikkim villages we had passed en route. In the lower, which is the inhabited, part of Sikkim most of the houses are made of bamboo or wood, the roof being sometimes of thatch. In the Pass Country, one sometimes finds semi-log cabins, through in Lachen most of the houses were made of stone; but in all cases in Sikkim and the Pass Country the roofs have a marked slant in order to enable then to throw off the summer rain and the winter snow.

In Tibet itself, where trees of any sort are a rarity and bamboo completely unknown, there are no houses built in the Sikkimese fashion. The buildings in this first little village were typically Tibetan, inasmuch as they were all built of sun-dried brick. Tibet has sufficient clay soil to render brick-making fairly easy, but because of the absence of coal, oil, and wood, which would serve as fuel for brick-kilns, the Tibetan peasants are forced to rely upon the heat of sun-rays to give their roughly formed bricks sufficient hardness to use for building purposes. In a rainy climate, such as is found on the south side of the Himalayas, these bricks would quickly wash away, but in the dry, rarefied air of Tibet they last indefinitely.

Another striking evidence of the dryness of the Tibetan climate is to be found in the flatness of the roofs. In contrast with the sloping roofs of Sikkim, which are in keeping with the hill and valley formation of the country, the flat, even formation of the Tibetan housetops seem but a continuation or imitation of the broad Tibetan plains, save that they are rendered picturesque by having placed at each corner the prayer-tufts and prayer-flags which flutter in the wind: each

Gyangtse, the third city of Tibet and capital of the province. Castle on hill; Golden Chorten (shrine) on right. Here the first expedition awaited permission (which was refused) to proceed to Lhasa.

Gyangtse plain with castle on hill

Abbots' gallery at Gyangtse cathedral; these effigies of departed abbots of the cathedral exhibit exceptional workmanship

Two of the gods, guardians of the four quarters of the world at the doors of Tibetan cathedral; there are four gods to defend the cathedral against evil spirits.

flutter is as a prayer which rises to the gods and brings supernatural protection to the house and its inhabitants.

We stopped as I have said only long enough to buy provisions, but the whole village had by now assembled around our little caravan, and showed such a lively curiosity in the travelers who had been able to get through the dreaded winter passes that I left Satan and Lhaten to conclude the bargaining and with the rest of the party and the transport started at once in the direction of Kampa Dzong. We moved slowly. Half an hour later we were joined by the other two. A mile or two beyond the village we again halted and sat down to enjoy the first good meal we had had for some considerable time; good, that is, as regards quantity.

While we were still sitting over the remains, we were overtaken by one or two of our villager friends, who were going to the monastery which lay on the way to Kampa Dzong. They came over to continue the conversation of the morning, and I was still fearfully self-conscious and could not believe that my disguise would hold good. As they approached, I immediately rushed away, pretending to attend to the animals, which in their attempt at grazing had wandered a little bit away. I did not dare return until our new acquaintances had safely departed. We learned they were carrying a new flag to present to the monastery on behalf of the poor man who was dying of pneumonia, as he hoped that this present might enable him to acquire enough merit to secure a longer span in life, or if fate was against him and he was destined for death, that he might have a felicitous rebirth, for it seemed he had led a somewhat merry life and had dreamed that he was, in punishment, to be reborn as a louse. I pitied the poor man but could not help feeling that in Tibet the lice—and there are plenty of them—lead a happier existence than human beings.

We had now to decide upon our own further plans for the day. Lack of provisions and insufficient knowledge of the road made it necessary for us to go on to Kampa Dzong, but this necessary visit filled me with uneasy forebodings. Kampa Dzong is not only the capital of a large district, but it is also the official gateway to this part of Tibet. There are placed the governors of the district and all of their official underlings. Trouble to us might arise from any or all of these people, particularly as the Kampa Dzong officials had several times been brought in touch with white men and knew a good deal of their ways. In years back Kampa Dzong officials had turned back several would-be explorers, but on two occasions they had been forced to organize a reception committee on a large scale.

The first was in 1903, when the British Indian Government, anxious to enter into diplomatic negotiations with Tibet and bring about a peaceful conclusion to the points of dispute between the two countries, organized a special commission headed by Major (now Colonel Sir Francis) Younghusband with orders to proceed to the Tibetan frontier and get into touch with some special envoys sent from Lhasa.

Escorted by about two hundred native soldiers, the commission came up to Tibet through Lachen and, brushing aside the few Tibetan soldiers who attempted to bar their way, crossed the boundary pass and in July camped just before Kampa Dzong.

Four weary months were spent by this party, waiting for the arrival of some responsible Tibetan official from Lhasa with whom negotiations could be conducted; but these failed to appear, and in their place some nine thousand Tibetan soldiers were hurried to the neighborhood and threatened to attack the British party unless it withdrew.

Eventually the commission was recalled, but in its place there was organized the more elaborate Younghusband expedition of 1904, whose actions have already been summarized. The 1904 mission did not continue the march from Kampa Dzong but entered Tibet through the Chumbi Valley, and from there marched on to Gyangtse.

The second occasion was the friendly reception the Tibetans were forced to give the two Everest expeditions. Since 1912, when Tibet threw off Chinese overlordship and claimed absolute independence, the Tibetan court has stood under several obligations to the Indian Government, the nature of which will be discussed more at length hereafter. In return, the Tibetans have been forced to make several concessions. One of these was to permit a climbing party to skirt the northern base of the Himalayas from Pari to the foot of Mount Everest. While engaged in their interesting and valuable scientific work, they were not permitted to strike into the interior, but in the course of their progress along the southern fringe of Tibet they stopped for several days in Kampa Dzong and even used it as a sort of base.

Unfortunately the fact that Kampa Dzong had thus been brought into contact with Europeans hindered rather than aided me. The Everest expedition had been armed with special passports from the Dalai-lama, and the local officials had been forced to concede them hospitality. Not only had such passports been refused to me, but I had been especially ordered out of the country, and as there was a shrewd suspicion that I would make some such venture as I was actually making, the officials had been told to keep "an eye open." In the interior, where the simple villagers had only a vague idea of what a European looked like other than that his skin was white, I felt that disguise might not be so difficult, but in Kampa Dzong the officials were acquainted with European features, in which cast, in spite of my disguise, my own features run.

Our sudden arrival in the depth of winter was sure to cause some comment, and I wanted to have any inquiry which might be made over and done with before I arrived. Consequently I sent Satan and Lhaten on to the town in advance, to purchase supplies and to hire a room in a rest-house for the night. Satan was to say that his baggage-animals and the remainder of his servants would come on later. The syce, Diogenes, and I were to stay hidden by the roadside until sunset and thus be able to enter the town after dark.

Accordingly Satan and Lhaten set off, Satan riding Lhasa, the youngest pony, which was still reasonably strong, as he wished to arrive in Kampa Dzong attended by a little state, while we sat down for our long wait. Before long we were troubled by the rising of one of the wild Tibetan winds. The Tibetan winds have become famous from the stories which every Tibetan explorer has brought back concerning them. The bare open formation of the country offers these winds great opportunity for sweeping along unchecked, and gales blowing a hundred miles an hour are by no means uncommon.

They are generally regarded as the most terrible and devastating steady winds known anywhere in the world. These cutting gales penetrate every form of clothing and remove the little layer of warm air which ordinarily surrounds the body, rendering frost-bite a constant and a very real danger. It is to counteract this that the Tibetan retains on his skin the layer of dirt and grease which renders him so obnoxious but which is really the finest natural clothing he could secure.

From some curious meteorological reason unknown to me, these winds become much stronger in the afternoon. Sometimes the whole morning will be absolutely calm, and about one thirty a breeze will set in which by three thirty or four o'clock will have developed into a hurricane. The winds have a tendency to die down soon after sunset but sometimes continue until far in the night.

On this particular afternoon, situated as we were on the great plain without any protection, the wind caused us great discomfort, and we felt perishingly cold. We arranged our luggage in a little semicircle and then crawled into this and curled up. This arrangement offered us partial protection. The syce and Diogenes fell fast asleep, while I got out a Tibetan text or two and began to read—something quite out of keeping with my new rôle of coolie, for it is only the higher priests in Tibet who can even attempt to read and write.

My literary activities very nearly led me into serious trouble. A small party making its way from Kampa Dzong to the outpost village saw our little camp and came over to find out who we were. Because of the wind, they were right over us before we became aware of their existence, and they at once began asking questions. I did not dare answer, and began chanting the text, as if I were carrying on a religious service which could not be interrupted. At the same time I kicked the syce awake, so that he could carry on the necessary conversation, which he did. A very fine tale indeed he spun. The interview must have proved entertaining to both parties, for to me at least it seemed to last interminably, and while it lasted I did not dare to relax my chanting for a single minute. Fortunately the text proved wearisomely long and, in common with most Buddhist Sutras, or religious discourses, full of repetitions, so that I could continue with my bellowing until the small party was once more safely on its way.

In accordance with our plan, toward sunset we started on our way to the fortress-town, but we had several weary hours before we reached it. In the first place, we had underestimated the distance covered, and, secondly, we were considerably delayed by the collapse of Shigatse, our second pony. He had fought the good fight well, but starvation and piercing cold had mortally weakened him, and at last he had refused to go a step further. I was very loath to lose him, and I thought that if we could get him to Kampa Dzong, where shelter and good food awaited, he might yet recover. By alternate pushings and pullings we managed to get him another half-mile on the way, but in the end he died under our eyes despite all our efforts. Already overloaded as we were, it was impossible to add another pound to the weight carried by the other animals, and so I was forced to abandon, with the dead pony, his saddle and one of our saddle-bags, which he was carrying. Our traveling equipment had been reduced to what seemed an absolute minimum, but bit by bit we were being forced to dispense with a good part of even this minimum. The discarded saddle, incidentally, was a good English make and had cost a pretty penny. In Tibet, for the most part, in spite of the abundance of yak-hides, which can be made into excellent leather, the saddles are constructed of wood. The wooden saddles of the richer classes are inlaid with coral and turquoise, the favorite jewels of the Tibetan, and some are of really pretty workmanship, though insufferably hard, so that it is the custom to lay a number of carpets of native make on top of the saddle to ease the rider's seat. When saddled, a Tibetan pony therefore appears to have imitated a camel and grown a huge hump on its back.

In recent years, because of their greater lightness and compactness, a number of leather saddles have been imported from India by the Tibetan gentry, and they are frequently used by the Sikkimese, so that the fact that we had such a saddle would not necessarily lead to exposure, but at the same time I did not dare take the spare saddle on to Kampa Dzong in order to sell it there, for by attracting attention to it suspicion might have been aroused.

Once the pony had been left behind, our journey became easier, and I was able to appreciate more fully the marvelous beauty of the night. The moon had arisen, its light casting a magic spell over the land. The desolation of the place seemed softened and far off in the distance; the indistinct mass of the mighty Himalayas reflected from their many snowy crests a soft yellow sapphire radiance, while the moaning of the wind seemed like the eery voices of goblins hovering above us.

About a mile or so outside the town we were met by Lhaten. He had become frightened by our failure to arrive and had come back along the roadway to see if he could trace us, and at the same time to tell us how he and Satan had fared during the day. The officials had heard of their arrival, and they had been interrogated as to who they were and what they were doing, but they had allowed nothing to leak out about me; and as it seemed perfectly natural that transport-animals, exhausted by their efforts in the snow, should not arrive until later, my two servants were dismissed by the officials and allowed to go on with the purchase of provisions in the little market of Kampa.

Here a little difficulty presented itself. I had exhausted my ten rupee and smaller notes in Lachen and had given Lhaten a hundred-rupee note (approximately thirty-five dollars) with which to purchase our supplies. Some difficulty was found in securing change for this amount.

Rupees, of course, are Indian currency, but as Sikkim has no currency of its own, rupees have gradually become the standard medium of exchange. A considerable number of Tibetan traders go down to India to sell Tibetan wool and bring back cheap goods to Tibet, and the Tibetan merchants have also become accustomed to the handling of rupees. In some cases even they prefer them to their own currency; but generally transactions are carried out with the ten-rupee note, which is remarkably like the note of one hundred rupees in size and in appearance. To an Oriental the addition of a cipher or so means nothing, as any one acquainted with Indian chronology well knows, so that Lhaten had great difficulty in getting the Kampa merchants to believe that there really was a difference between his note and the more usual ten-rupee note. Even when this was done, he discovered that none of the merchants was rich enough to change this stupendous amount. In the end, three or four of the wealthiest had to club together and buy the note, giving an equivalent heap of Tibetan coins in exchange.

The basis of money in Tibet is the trangka, approximately five of which, according to present rates of exchange, make a rupee, or one shilling threepence, so that a trangka is about a fourth of a shilling. These are supposedly made of silver, but of silver so debased that I wondered if empty tin cans did not form a large item in the purchases of the Lhasa mint, where these and all other Tibetan coins are made. Even trangkas are fairly rare, and most of the peasants concern themselves only with the smaller divisions of the trangka. These smaller denominations are coined from various copper alloys. The most important are:

1. The kakang or one sixth of a trangka.
2. The karmanga, or one third of a trangka.
3. The chegye, or one half of a trangka.
4. The shokang, or two thirds of a trangka.

This curious division of the unit results in a good deal of extraordinary calculation in Tibet, where the peasants are completely lacking in a mathematical sense, and I wondered why it had not been changed; but until Great Britain and the United States have adopted the metric system and Great Britain the decimal system, these countries can scarcely say anything about Tibetan backwardness in this regard.

Lhaten kept me shivering in the cold for some time explaining how things had gone, but once I found that everything was safe I insisted on pushing on; and not long afterward we came under the great gloomy castle and entered the little town which lies at its foot. In accordance with instructions, Satan and Lhaten had found lodgings in a little rest-house on the outskirts of the Kampa Dzong, so that once arrived there we had not far to go.

By chance we had come to this town at the time when a small local fair was held, which was largely attended by the small traders and peasantry of the surrounding villages. The local rest-houses were all completely full. Satan, indeed, as master, was allowed to share a room in the house itself with one or two petty merchants, but I and the other servants were forced to spend the night on the roof. This being of course flat, we suffered no great inconvenience, except that we were exposed to the terrible night cold. Although sleeping inside, Satan took advantage of his position to procure all of our best blankets, so that we were forced to face the night with but a single blanket apiece, no small matter when the thermometer registered thirty degrees below zero.

Lhaten and the other two servants prepared themselves for this ordeal by going down to the communal room—used as a kitchen—underneath, and taking a hot and stupendous supper, washed down by huge drafts of chang, or Tibetan beer, which they also drank hot. I had not yet acquired enough courage to face the crowd that gathers in every Tibetan inn and remained on the cold roof, telling Lhaten to say that I was ill and had to go to bed immediately. On this excuse he managed to bring some food up to me. Any one who noticed must have thought that for an invalid I ate surprisingly well, but it must not be forgotten that we came very near starvation in the passes and that in my joy at seeing food again I wanted to devour everything in sight.

The festivities continued for some time down-stairs, and as I lay on the roof shivering with cold I was fearful every moment that in their bibulous merriment the servants might let fall some words of the true nature of things. I had given orders for an early start the next morning, however, and so before long the party came up the rickety ladder and settled down to sleep. Soon their snores told me that for the next few hours, at least, they were not likely to get into mischief.

I was less fortunate in my attempts at repose. The cold, which increased hour by hour, was so insistent that every time I dozed off it seemed to claw me awake again. Besides the nervous excitement of the venture, the responsibility which it entailed prevented that relaxation which was necessary for sleep; and at last, giving up the job as hopeless, I sat up and surveyed the moonlight panorama. The kindly night hid the dirtiness of the streets and made the castle which loomed on the hill appear very impressive.

These castles ("dzong" is the word in Tibetan; hence the name "Kampa Dzong,") fill such a prominent place in the landscape and life of Tibet that a special word must be said about them. A great deal of Tibet is inhabited by nomads who make no attempt at agriculture and who eke out a scanty existence by moving along with their flocks of sheep and yaks. Over such people the central Lhasa Government has a scanty and only indirect control. Where, however, the nomads have given way to small settled communities engaged in trade or agriculture, an attempt has been made to set up a definite system of government, partially modeled on the old bureaucratic régime of China, but very largely modified to suit the ecclesiastical nature of the whole of the Tibetan political organization.

At the present time Tibet is divided into fifty-three administrative districts, of which fifty are ordinary and three are extraordinary; and each such district has some town or village which has been chosen to serve as the local capital, or center of administration. In nearly every such case the governor resides in a great fortress castle, built, as far as possible, of stone, and placed on the summit of a small hill commanding a view of the surrounding plains. At the base of this hill is situated the village itself. These castles are for the most part really imposing-looking places, and although, as the events of 1904 showed, incapable of withstanding bombardment by modern artillery, they are, or should be, practically impregnable against any attack by men armed with only bows and arrows or even rifles. But their massiveness is not only designed to protect them against attack from an invading army but also to inspire awe in the hearts of the peasantry of the district, making them the more willing to obey all orders issued by the officials appointed from Lhasa.

In many cases, these castles owe their origin to conditions similar to those which brought about the erection of the castles on the Rhine and other parts of Europe, and were constructed by local chieftains who had a close resemblance to the robber barons of the European Middle Ages. The local chieftains have been gradually ousted by the centralized Lhasa Government, and the seats of former semi-independent overlords transformed into residences for the centrally appointed governors. A few castles are comparatively modern in origin and have been built for their present purpose by the Government but in close imitation of the older robber fortresses, while, on the other hand, one finds all over Tibet ruins of former stately castles and prosperous villages which have gradually fallen into decay.

The interiors of these castles, as I found out afterward, are dirty, dark, ill shaped, and in many cases, because of structural defects, really unsafe, but their exteriors, especially when viewed from a distance, strike one as magnificent, and display a talent and a taste for architecture which seems entirely out of keeping with the degraded and barbarous state of the Tibetans. I had wondered whether these buildings might not reflect a former period of culture which has since been lost. But in this connection the recent history of Gyangtse and Pari deserves to be brought to mind. As the results of the Younghusband expedition, both Gyangtse and Pari dzongs, or castles, were razed to the ground, and it was a provision of the treaty signed by Tibet that neither of these citadels should be rebuilt.

Strict observances of treaties is by no means a strong point in Tibetan character, and a few years later the authorities set about rebuilding them. The English Government, being then in the hands of the Liberals, did nothing to stop this proceeding, and both the castles have now been completely rebuilt and on quite as grand a scale as previously, so that at one stroke the Tibetans have once more justified their reputation as architects and as treaty-breakers.

An excellent instance of the double nature of the Tibetan Government is to be found in the fact that each administrative district is governed by two governors, one of them a monk and the other a layman. Needless to say, the monk governor ranks higher than his lay brother official, although the power is divided pretty equally between them. In Tibet it is only the priesthood who are taught to read and write, and although the lay governor may have picked up the rudiments of writing, it is the monk governor who has charge of all official correspondence, while the layman is charged with the supervision of purely business affairs.

The salaries of both officials are small, but both become enormously wealthy during their terms of office, for bribery and corruption are rampant in every part of Tibetan public life. The officials have practically unlimited powers of extortion, powers which they are by no means loath to use; and huge monetary bribes are made to the higher officials in Lhasa in order to secure the post of governor in a particularly wealthy district. Ordinarily the governors are appointed for a period of five years, although this period of office may be shortened or prolonged, and it is quite customary for governors to be transferred from one district to another at the expiry of their term of office, from the fear lest one man, by residing too long in any one place and gaining too great control over it, should be tempted to break away from the Central Government and form a little principality of his own. In fact, the governors possess enormous powers of local self-government and, especially in the outlying districts, have very little to do with the higher Lhasa authorities except to send once a year a small fixed tribute to the capital, a tribute which is chiefly paid in kind—barley, butter, or wool.

By good fortune, just at the time when I came to Kampa Dzong, one of the governors, by far the more active of the two, was away in Shigatse on a visit, and his absence probably influenced the slovenly way in which my servants had been questioned by the officials that afternoon. Life is indeed deadly dull in the outlying Tibetan towns, and when the winter months come, suspending all agricultural work, and thereby all chances of monetary gain on the part of the officials, it is not uncommon for one or another of the governors of the smaller districts to discover some urgent business or a dying relative which takes him to the gayer life of Shigatse or Lhasa. Later on, I came across several cases where a young governor, who had powerful connections in Lhasa, practically never saw the district over which he was supposed to rule. He appointed some retainer to act as deputy to collect the moneys, while the young aristocrat enjoyed his amusements in the capital.

Too much landscape, whether in literature or in life, is apt to prove very wearying and sleep-inducing, and so, after I had gazed my full at the castle, the sleeping village, and the broad plain around, I once more lay down to sleep and this time with more success. But my night's rest was very short; for, according to plan, I got up very early next morning and, accompanied by Lhaten, left the village before it was light, being still afraid that if the Tibetans got too good a look at me they would penetrate my disguise. The syce, Diogenes, and Satan were left behind to see that the animals were loaded, to pay the rest-house charges, and to start as soon as it was dawn. Such an early start is by no means unusual in Tibet, and I found that, early as we were, one or two of our fellow-lodgers had already

William Dederich, F.R.C.S. (organizer)

Tibetan lama devil-dancers in masks

Devil-dancing at a small monastery

departed. We crossed over the little stream from which the Kampa Dzong inhabitants get their water, but which at this time of year is practically one block of ice, and went on for another mile and a half, then halted for a moment to get a last backward look at Kampa Dzong, over which the sun was just rising. The day was remarkably fine in contrast to the cloudy weather we had experienced the last several days, and the young, fresh rays of the sun cast a pink radiance over the peaks of the Himalayas, which now stretched in perfect visibility to the south on both sides to seeming infinity. It was far and away the finest view I had ever seen, and even so stolid and humdrum a person as myself had to pause to drink in its grandeur. Here at last the Himalayas were no mere geographical name but a living reality, seemingly aware of its own serene greatness. From no part of India is it possible to gain so general a view of the mighty range, for the great altitudes of the higher peaks are rendered apparently less than they actually are by the gradually ascending foothills, and it is impossible to see more than a few miles on either side. Furthermore, the constant humidity of the southern slopes brings about cloud-caps which more often than not render the topmost peaks invisible. Here, on the other hand, the great mountains rose sharp and clear from the dead level of the Kampa plain to their greatest height. The dry crystal Tibetan atmosphere brought out every detail into relief, and it almost seemed as if at one glance one could see the whole of the long stretch of mountains. To the east was Chumolhari, under whose base we had passed on our journey to Gyangtse; to the south Kanchenjao and Chumiomo, between which we had battled with the snow; and to the west Mount Everest, the highest mountain in the world.

It is curious to note that even the great ocean tides pay their tribute to the massiveness of the Himalayas. Colonel Waddell was the first to point out that the stupendous projecting mass of the Himalayas was so great that it disturbs the symmetry of the earth's attraction and pulls the sea-level of the Bay of Bengal some distance up its sides so that in sailing to Calcutta one is actually sailing up-hill.

It is probably known generally that, geologically speaking, the Himalayas are of very recent formation, being the last great range of mountains to be formed. Whereas we ourselves belong to the Quaternary period of the earth's history, the Himalayas rose about the middle of the preceding or Tertiary period, while to an earlier portion of the same period are ascribed the Alps, the Pyrenees, and the great range of mountains in the west of both North and South America which are known in different parts by widely differing names. To a far earlier period, the Primary, belong the low-lying mountains of Wales, Scotland, and Scandinavia and the mountains of the eastern portion of America.

We halted for some time here waiting for our main party to come up, but as they appeared to be delayed, Lhaten and I went on our way across the Kampa plain. Running diagonally across it, we could see the streak of silver which marked the frozen river. This ran for several miles to the west before it turned south and, passing through a gap in the Himalayas, poured down through Nepal to India and the sea. It was very interesting to me to note that, high and stupendous as the Himalayas are, they form no true watershed, and that the waters of the Kampa and its allied plains, finding no other outlet, have eaten a way through even that massive wall of rock. Our road, however, now turned to the north, and we soon left the river behind us.

Needless to say, the Tibetan officials never dream of spending a penny on roads, and the so-called roads are nothing more than tracks on the plains, which have been made by the passage of the mules and yaks of the small caravans which are constantly going to and fro all over Tibet. Were it not for the terrible climate, the cold, biting winds and the absence of fertilizing moisture, these great plains would be ideal spots for agricultural cultivation. The soil itself is excellent and practically virgin. But Lhaten, who, though a Tibetan, had traveled extensively in India, expressed his interest in the great contrast there was between the life on the Indian plains and here on the Tibetan plateau. In India one would see such a flat country teeming with life, cut into paddy-fields, with a cozy village every few miles, half hidden behind a clump of bushes; while here there was neither field nor village nor any sign of life, for now even Kampa Dzong was safely hidden from sight.

Soon we came to a place where the road broke into three, all of which would in the end lead us to Shigatse, but as I had no idea which one was most direct, and as I was afraid that our main party would not know which track to follow, I sat down to await its arrival. We had not long to wait, for soon I caught sight of our animals, with Satan, of course, riding our one remaining pony, but I was very much puzzled to see not two but four men following behind. On catching sight of us, Satan spurred his pony on ahead, and as soon as he was within speaking distance I asked him who the two strangers were.

To my utter astonishment, he told me that they were two Kampa Dzong peasants whom he had hired to act as coolies to carry the food supplies he had bought the preceding day, as he did not wish to overload the mules. This news was completely staggering, and for the first and only time while on the way to Lhasa I lost my temper. I explained very forcibly, and with frequent reference to his genealogical table, according to the immemorial custom of the East, how many kinds of a fool he was, and in what great danger he had brought the whole venture. I had ordered a large supply of food and grain to be purchased in Kampa Dzong, expressly in order that we might be able to keep away from all villages until we came to Shigatse. I thought my disguise might be good enough to pass muster with any chance travelers we met on the road but was afraid of the close contact that halting among Tibetans might entail, and now here was Satan actually bringing Tibetans along with us, men with whom I should have to carry on long conversations—far worse than merely halting at towns each evening and starting early the next morning before sunrise.

It was even impossible to stay where we were and

talk the matter over, for our new servants were almost up with us. I ordered Lhaten to stay behind and halt the caravan for a few minutes on the excuse of shifting the loads on the mules, while I went on with Satan and argued out what was to be done. The mules were indeed overloaded, but it was better that they and we carry a few extra pounds until we got to Shigatse, a noted train-animal market, than that we should needlessly run chances of detection—little did I guess of the many more serious chances with which we were later to meet; in fact, I would rather leave some of our older equipment behind than carry along two spies with us. Having thus decided to rid myself of the two new servants who had been thrust upon me, I had next to decide how this should be done. It would undoubtedly seem strange to them to be arbitrarily dismissed a few hours after they had been hired, particularly after the master had been seen in an animated conversation with his mysterious servant, and so I told Satan to go back and tell them that they had only been hired because two of his servants, Lhaten and myself, had been so ill in the passes that it was thought to be impossible for us to carry any heavy loads for the next few days, but that the good food and rest we had had in Kampa Dzong had completely restored us, and consequently there was no longer any need for outside help; at the same time, they were to be paid the whole of their first day's wages.

Satan took my remarks in no very gracious manner and attempted to argue, but I was very emphatic about the matter; and as I began to finger my Bhutanese dagger in a very noticeable way, he went back and carried out the necessary order. Lhaten, always true and faithful, backed up his story, and the Kampa coolies took their dismissal surprisingly mildly—partly, no doubt, because they were by no means loath to return to the local festivities which were then taking place in the district capital—and before long I was again joined by the whole of my original party.

The disagreeable scene, however, was destined to have lasting and unfortunate effects. My vocabulary of unpleasant Tibetan words was fairly large, and I had made very full and effective use of them towards Satan in explaining my attitude with regard to his action; they very obviously rankled in his devious soul. I had deeply injured his pride, and from that time on he was practically my declared enemy. To serve his own purposes and to fill his own purse, he consented to continue to play his part, but he was only waiting for an opportunity to humiliate me and to wreak his revenge. I was fortunate, however, in having all the other servants against him. Tibetan servants have curiously little loyalty to one another, and in the present instance there was positive rancor on each side. Generally speaking, Lhaten and the syce stood together against Satan. The half-idiotic Diogenes formed a third party, but the petty quips and persecutions to which Satan subjected him gradually began to fill his slow, stupid mind with a burning hatred that was likely to prove terrible in the end.

We now had to skirt a low-lying group of hills set in the center of the plain, and, rounding these hills, we suddenly came in sight of no less than six villages, so that my impressions of the absolute lifelessness of Tibet had to be revised, particularly as all of these villages appeared to be in a thriving condition.

It was impossible to avoid them, as the road led through four of them; and as we were not quite sure of our way, we had even to stop once or twice in order to find out first which tracks we were to follow. Putting on a bold face, we marched right into their midst, though I insisted on changing loads with Diogenes, who was carrying the biggest pack, as it was a fixed point in my creed that no Tibetan would suspect the humblest and seemingly the most oppressed member of a party of being a European—such is the prestige which the English have acquired even in this Forbidden Land—and subsequent events turned out to justify my belief.

As we stopped for a moment at one or two of the houses, I was able to inspect them more carefully. Although equally filthy, they were certainly better built than those of the first village we struck in Tibet. Nearly all of the houses were two-storied and quite a number three-storied; for the Tibetan peasant is no great advocate of the bungalow type of architecture, and as it is customary for all the branches of a family to live together they can afford to have fairly large dwellings. The houses appear to be even larger than they really are, as they are built around a courtyard. Most of them have verandas running around the first or second floors, looking down into the courtyard, and in many instances the staircases connecting the floors ran from veranda to veranda, there being no connection between the various stories on the inside of the house. These staircases were very rickety affairs, generally mere step-ladders, with small, round rings made of unplaned, smaller tree branches. In nearly all cases the ground floor of the house was used only for stables or ware-houses, with occasionally a room set aside as servants' quarters, the residential part being on the first or second floor. Most frequently, I was told, the head of the family had the highest room, as it was considered injurious to his dignity to have any one standing or sleeping above him; think of having the feet of a servant just over the master's head! The houses of the poorer villages are uncolored, retaining the natural mud-color of the sun-dried bricks, but, in these more prosperous communities the dwellings had been color-washed, either white or red, with also an occasional blue.

Our inquiries as to the way were answered very satisfactorily, and though we were asked who we were and where we were going, no suspicion seemed to be aroused. In accordance with my instructions, we always gave our destination as being merely Shigatse, as I wished to avoid any mention of Lhasa. Our experience in these villages gave me a great deal of confidence. The villagers obviously noticed nothing peculiar in my appearance, so that I was emboldened to think that after all the mad venture we were on might meet with success, though the attitude of Satan worried me considerably. In any case, I intended taking no risks, and we halted for lunch not in any of the villages but a little beyond them in an open space, where ran a little stream which, much lower down, joined the river we had seen earlier in the morning. Here, in this more protected part of the plain, the ice was very thin, and I was able to break through it and quench my thirst with the chill water flowing beneath.

My servants preferred to drink some chang, or Tibetan barley-beer, which we had brought with us from Kampa Dzong. This is really a very refreshing drink and very mild, seldom containing as much as four per cent of alcohol, and I would very willingly have shared it with them, but for politic reasons I thought it better to content myself with water.

Because of the great difficulty I found in persuading my Tibetan servants to accompany me, a barbarian, to Lhasa, the Holy of Holies, I found it very convenient to employ as much as possible the honorary Buddhist priesthood which had been granted me, several years previously in Japan, as the result of certain scholastic studies carried on there into Buddhist literature and philosophy; and it was only by emphasizing my lamaistic qualifications that I got my poor superstitious servants to follow me as faithfully as they did. In theory a good Buddhist priest does not drink any form of alcohol, and it behooved me to play the part of lama to my own servants quite as perfectly as the part of coolie to the general Tibetan populace. Satan, indeed, though a priest, drank anything that came his way, as does nearly every Sikkimese monk, as well as those lamas in Tibet itself who belong to the older red-hat or unreformed sect; but such wine-bibbing is despised even by the most drunken of the Sikkimese or Tibetan peasantry, who always want their priests to be something better than they are themselves. I am therefore led to think that a great deal of the loyalty which my servants (with the exception of Satan) showed toward me was the result of the little ecclesiasticism I was always careful to throw in from time to time.

On the present occasion, I was able to get my own back with a little irony. A tiny vest-pocket edition of Omar Khayyam was one of the two English books I had with me; and while sipping my water, I took out old Omar and chanted two or three of his particularly bibulous verses, while the servants, who, of course, understood not a word, took it as part of some religious service.

Once on our way again, we rapidly neared the northern limit of the Kampa plain and soon came upon another fork in the road. To the left ran the road to the Sakya monastery, while to the right lay the more direct route to Shigatse.

The Sakya monastery is one of the oldest existing Tibetan monasteries and more than usually famous historically. Sakya is renowned not only for its monastery and temple buildings but also for its great library with its ancient manuscripts. The town is built on the eastern slopes of a hill, around the foot of which the river Tom flows. It is the home of the royal Kön family of Sakya, but, apart from its temples and abbots, is not held in very high repute in Tibet, being notorious for its thieves and bandits and its immorality.

Lhaten had once been to Sakya, and told me a good deal about it. According to him the buildings of Sakya are striking, being painted red with clay obtained on the near-by mountains, and with black and blue perpendicular stripes. There are four temples with Chinese-style roofs, the many spires being gilded, and these in days gone by were ruled over by four abbots of hereditary rank who were allowed to marry.

The books and manuscripts are on shelves along the walls of the great hall, the volumes being six feet in depth and eighteen inches broad. They are bound with iron, and on the cardboard covers of some are innumerable images of Buddhas. On the margin the pages are illuminated, the first four volumes having illustrations of the thousand Buddhas. Some are written in gold. There are also books in Chinese and Sanskrit.

Another interesting relic is a conch-shell, the whorls of which turn from left to right. Lamas alone may blow it, and they do so only on receiving seven ounces of silver. One acquires great merit by blowing or inducing a lama to blow this shell.

Sakya Monastery is chiefly famous, however, for the fact that for many centuries it was the headquarters of the Tibetan Government.

When Tibet emerged from absolute savagery in the seventh century A.D. it was ruled by a line of hereditary kings. It was these kings who introduced Buddhism and established the earlier monasteries. As the number and power of the monks increased they became jealous of the temporal authority and eventually overthrew it. After this there followed a long period of anarchy. The country was split up among a large number of petty rulers, some of them laymen, though more of them were ecclesiastics, for the larger monasteries tended to secure absolute domination over the surrounding districts.

At this time one of the most important monasteries was the Sakya monastery, which belonged to what is known as the semi-reformed branch of Tibetan Buddhism. In the middle of the thirteenth century the abbot, an astute and ambitious man, managed to convert to Lamaism, or Tibetan Buddhism, Kublai Khan, the great mongol emperor of China, the son of the even more famous Genghis Khan. Not only did the whole of Kublai's court embrace Lamaism but the abbot of Sakya was recognized as the head of all spiritual matters. Even more important was the fact that he was established by Kublai as the temporal sovereign of all Tibet.

The downfall of the Mongol dynasty in China deprived the Sakya pontiffs of this powerful support, but for nearly four centuries thereafter the abbots of Sakya continued to reign over the greater portion of Tibet, though the new Chinese dynasty, anxious to increase its influence in Tibet, gave encouragement, jade seals, and even royal titles to the abbots of several other monasteries belonging to rival orders.

This muddled state of affairs continued down to 1641, when the fifth Dalai-lama of Lhasa secured the aid of some marauding Tartar tribes, overthrew the temporal power of Sakya, and established himself as the absolute ruler of the whole country. Since this time Lhasa has remained the center of authority, and now Sakya is nothing more than a relic of former glory.

I had it in my mind to visit this famous place and

then double back to Shigatse, but careful thought convinced me that I had better push on to Shigatse directly. Sooner or later my prolonged absence from Darjeeling would arouse suspicion that I had gone to Tibet, and if I was to get to Lhasa it was necessary to get there quickly before too many rumors about me had got about. And so, taking the road to the right, we soon began to climb the mountain range which forms the boundary of the Kampa plain. Although called a table-land, Tibet is intersected by a number of mountain ranges, many of them of considerable height, which break up its vast level expanse into a number of flat-bottomed basins of various sizes. These basins also differ considerably as regards elevation. In the great Changtang, the desert wilderness which lies to the northwest of Shigatse, only a small part of which is inhabited, the beds of some of these basins lie more then seventeen thousand feet above sea-level. The Lhasa plain is, for Tibet, comparatively low, being only about twelve thousand feet high. The Kampa plain, which is one of the largest single basins, is about fifteen thousand feet above sea-level, on a level with the summit of Mont Blanc, the highest peak in Europe. Occasionally, as between Tuna and Shigatse, these plains are connected by valleys which make traveling comparatively simple, but for the most part traveling in Tibet consists of long marches along level plains interspersed with steep ascents and descents of mountains, which may be said to act as the walls or sides of the basins.

This particular divide proved very steep and very sandy, and we found its ascent even more difficult than that of the pass over which we had entered Tibet. All the morning I had insisted on Satan, as the master, mounting our one remaining riding-pony, but now even he had to dismount and help us get the struggling pack-animals through the huge sand-drifts in which they were hopelessly struggling. Nearer the top we came across some long-lying snow which had become frozen into a single icy block. For the animals this proved still more difficult, and so we had to go back to our old custom and hack out steps and footholds for them. All this took a good deal of time, and it was already 3 P.M., before we got to the top. Here we found another gyatse, or shrine; and though no one was around we carefully followed Tibetan custom and added a stone to the little heap in front of the mountain shrine and called on the gods for protection.

From here we could see below us another plain, similar to the one from which we had just come, but on a smaller scale. No villages were in sight, but grazing on the plain were several herds of yak and sheep, with a number of herdsmen looking after them.

It took us some time to get from our mountain pass down to the bed of the plain, but once this task was accomplished I decided to halt for the night and to pitch our camp by the side of a tiny little frozen lake we found just at the base of the mountain. Although it was invisible, I knew that a few miles further on, on the other side of the plain, lay a large village, the village of Kuma; but I felt that the further away we camped from every village the safer we were.

We were still in contact with the herdsmen, but this

I did not mind. The herdsmen belonged to one of the nomad tribes, a simple and kindly people, though many of them, especially in the north, are given to brigandage. The townsmen and the nomads are never on particularly friendly terms, and the latter tend to look on the government officials who dwell in the towns with a certain amount of suspicion. We stopped one of the men in charge of a yak herd and purchased from him some yak's milk, which I drank with great relish, for, though possessing a slightly peculiar taste, it is very rich in cream, and in this bitterly cold climate everything of a fatty nature is very palatable. In taste the quality of yak's milk lies somewhere between cow's milk and goat's milk.

Strangely enough, notwithstanding the enormous number of yaks to be found in Tibet and the great amount of milk which they produce, the Tibetans themselves are very loath to drink it or to use it in any way in cooking. Most Tibetans regard milk as filthy as being a different form of urine; and when drunk it is regarded as a kind of medicine which must be taken, however unpleasant it may be; so that when we purchased our supply from the herdsmen we had to explain that one of us was ill and required it on medical grounds.

The repugnance which the Tibetans feel against milk is more than counteracted by their fondness for butter. Curiously enough, while milk is regarded as filthy, butter is considered clean, and incredible quantities of butter are consumed every year. It is chiefly used in the preparation of tea, as we shall see hereafter.

Quite apart from its food-value, butter is largely used in two other ways as a fuel for lamps and as a decoration.

Nearly every one of the older religions reveals a fondness for having some light burning before its sacred images, and in Tibetan Buddhism this practice has been carried to extraordinary lengths. At all times the principal idols have two or three sacred lamps burning in front of them, and at festival periods the number of such lamps set alight in a temple will be increased by hundreds and even thousands. It is a common form of piety to bestow a sum of money on a temple to have a special display of such lights. In all such cases the only fuel used is butter. The lamp itself is a wide, shallow bowl, the wick being a twisted cord made of wool placed in the middle of a lump of butter. The flame is a rich and creamy yellow and is rather pretty but gives out little light, for which reason, and also because of the expense of the fuel, these butter lamps are chiefly used in religious buildings and are but sparsely employed by laymen. The Tibetan believes in going to bed with the sun, and in an ordinary household artificial light is seldom required. During the last few years wax candles of European design have been imported into the larger centers, such as Shigatse and Lhasa, and the townsmen are taking to the use of them; but they remain entirely secular, and it would be considered blasphemous to burn a candle before a sacred image.

As a decoration for the temple or family shrine butter is also in great demand. The butter is molded into various shapes, having some more or less geometrical form and frequently having some bas-relief design—an animal or, more frequently, a flower. Although made entirely of butter, these *torma,* as they are called, are usually dyed in various different colors, reds and greens being the popular shades. Some of these *torma* are made for a special occasion and then ceremonially destroyed, but many of the larger ones, on which a great deal of sculptural effort has been expended, are expected to last a year, and are solemnly replaced at some annual festival. Although I enjoyed yak's milk, Tibetan butter I always found particularly unpleasant. The Tibetans never think of preparing it with salt, and because of the peculiar nature of yak's milk, it very soon becomes rancid. Even a few days after its preparation it acquires a smell and a taste which is to Europeans extremely repulsive. Consequently, although Tibet is a land overflowing with butter, every Englishman, such, e.g., as the officers stationed at the military outposts at Gyangtse and Yatung, are forced to import tins of butter from Australia. The Tibetans not only find nothing wrong with their butter but actually appreciate it more the older and riper it is, and the same nomad who sold us the milk offered us some butter which he proudly declared was forty years old. The one whiff which I got of it made me readily believe in the antiquity claimed for it. At this moment Lhaten came to my aid and declared that though our master (Satan) was of excellent family, he could not afford such a costly luxury and would prefer to buy some butter which was fresher and cheaper.

De gustibus non est disputandum, to use Frederick

the Great's one Latin quotation: in Tibet it is butter; in China it is eggs. A Chinese gentleman considers an egg which is literally black with age a peculiar delicacy, but until we have rid ourselves of our taste for game and cheese which is more than "high" we shall hardly be in a position to criticize Oriental preferences.

As dusk drew on, the herdsmen gradually began to lead off their flocks to a point some distance away, where their encampment lay. These yaks seem to have an ear for music, for their herdsmen always whistle in a peculiar way through their teeth to keep the flocks together and on the march; but the Tibetan sheep appear impervious to melody, for in their case the men employ slings with which they throw small stones with really remarkable accuracy. It was very interesting to see huge herds of sheep guided along their way by a small hail of pebbles which assailed them on every side.

Soon we were once more alone and I could again take an active part in the proceedings. While the herdsmen were around, I had curled myself up near our unloaded baggage and had pretended to go to sleep, while Satan and Lhaten carried on negotiations, though I was gradually losing my timidity as to my disguise. The great cold, which had lessened at midday, once more came on, and as it gradually soaked into our pores we became nearly paralyzed and stupefied both as regards body and brain. I longed for the partial protection which the erection of our tent would bring us, but that tried and faithful friend was of too obviously European design, and I was afraid that the herdsmen, or some chance traveler, might see it and wonder as to the nature of its occupants; and so, to the great dissatisfaction of my servants, I gave orders that we were not to use it. Instead we made a semicircle of our bags and boxes and crept inside this with nothing but heaven above us.

We were partly consoled by being able to light a fire. We had not seen a single tree for several days past, but we found on the plain some old yak-dung, which we collected and used for fuel. Incidentally it may be noted that this is the only fuel used over the greater part of Tibet, which is barren of both trees and coal. It is collected by the village children, and specially dried before being burned. It gives a quick, hot fire but has to be frequently replenished. Unfortunately, because of the ammonia contained in it, it emits a very acrid smell, which even flavors any food cooked over it. Strangely enough, one becomes accustomed to this taste and subsequently finds for a time that food cooked in an ordinary way seems almost tasteless.

On this particular evening the yak-dung was worse than usual, for we had to use what we could find. None we recovered had been properly dried. Some of it was so fresh that it refused to burn, and as the bitter acrid smoke got into our eyes it became very painful. To a certain extent I was glad of this. The weak point in my disguise was my eyes, and if they were obviously swollen and bloodshot I should have all the better excuse for wearing my dark goggles, which served not only to hide the color but also the European formation of my eyes.

Our nightly camp-fire conversation was shortened that evening by the increasing cold, and all of us were anxious to tuck ourselves in as soon as possible. In the absence of the tent, the only thing to do was to sleep as close to one another as possible. I never thought I should enjoy sleeping huddled up among filthy natives; but then all other thoughts save that of warmth were banished, and so we piled all the blankets together and crept under them. Even so, we could only find sleep by lying so close together as to feel the warmth of one another's bodies. Social distinctions were only to be seen from the fact that Satan and I were in the middle and therefore protected on both sides, while the others were arranged on the outside, Diogenes sleeping at our feet. He, poor boy, was destined to have a bad time. The shoes he had brought with him from Sikkim had fallen to pieces, and we had purchased for him a new pair of boots in Kampa Dzong. Unlike most Tibetan boots, which are made entirely of wool, these Kampa Dzong boots were made of very badly treated yak leather and were insufferably stiff. During the later part of the day Diogenes preferred the cold of bare feet to the torture of the boots and had exposed his toes to frozen soil and the biting night cold.

We were so tired from the previous day's exertions, and our night's rest had been so miserable, that we slept longer than was intended. It was nearly eight o'clock before we were on the move again. I was glad to see that a good feed had improved the spirits of our animals: they looked fresher than they had done for some time past. On the other hand, all three of the mules had been developing very sore backs.

Our packs were modeled on native Tibetan lines

and were very difficult to balance, so that they had always a tendency to drag on one side or the other, which, of course, served to irritate any saddle-sores. The Tibetans are notoriously callous in their treatment of their animals and, so long as it does not interfere with the efficiency of the animals, do not seem to care what horrible sights the saddle and blanket may cover. It was always a trial to my patience to see at each rest-house the cruel way in which the transport-animals were loaded and unloaded. With other people's affairs I had nothing to do, but I was determined to make the lot of our own creatures as easy as possible; and when the others were engaged in packing up our things, the syce and I always did what we could for the mules. I had ordered the servants to purchase in Kampa Dzong whatever local remedies for saddle-sores might be used in Tibet, and on this morning I found that they had purchased for the purpose a tin of a well-known English make of black shoe-polish! shoe-cream being one of the things the Tibetan merchants bring back with them from Kalimpong. The Tibetan boots being made, for the most part, entirely of wool and colored red, the natives have no need for any kind of shoe-cream for its ordinary purpose, but the superstition has grown up that it is useful for saddle-sores, and in the larger Tibetan towns it is occasionally to be found in the market for this reason.

I must confess that I had grave doubts as to its efficacy and would have preferred ordinary vaseline, but there was nothing else available, and after washing out the sores we dabbed them over with the blacking. This was destined to give us one further inconvenience. What in the daytime served as saddle-blankets were used as blankets for ourselves at night, so that the blacking which came off on the blankets was bound to transfer itself to our clothes as time went on. But in Tibet, the paradise of filth, a little extra black makes a very trifling difference one way or the other.

Now that we were alone, I thought of washing my face and hands at least before starting on the day's journey, but even this prudence forbade. We were likely to touch another village later in the day, and in case the peasants were to see me without that grime which comes only with a long abstinence from ablutions, their suspicions might be aroused, and so, following my servants' example, I set out though reluctantly in all my accumulation of filth.

As our track lay across the open plain, the first part of our march proved fairly easy, though I noticed the bed of the plain was not as even as that of the Kampa or Tuna plains. It rolled slightly up and down hill, and was occasionally eaten away into ravines by some long extinct rivers. Judging by the number of such dry river-beds which I saw in this land, one is compelled to believe that at some time the climate of Tibet was much moister than at present; for I later found, after careful inquiry and observation, that even in summer, which is the wet season of Tibet, the rainfall is so scanty that hardly a trickle passes over the river-beds, which look as if they were hollowed out by some mighty stream.

Under the influence of the desolate plains and the

dry river-beds, I waxed very pessimistic that morning and called to mind the many other places in which man seems to be fighting a losing battle with nature. All the great deserts seem to be gradually widening their boundaries. In Africa, in America, and in Australia, the deserts are slowly eating into the pasture-land. In the highlands of Asia this devastation appears to be encroaching even more rapidly. Just north of Tibet, in Chinese Turkestan and in Mongolia, this transformation presents itself as a tragedy of civilization. There the explorer everywhere comes across ruins which show that here, only a few hundred years ago, flourished prosperous kingdoms endowed with magnificent palaces and sparkling fountains; phantom civilizations they were, for now not only are the palaces deserted but for the most part they are also covered and obliviated with the sands carried on the death-bearing winds of the ever-encroaching desert.

In one of the depressions in the plain we found the main camp of our nomad friends of the preceding day. This consisted of four or five tents, colored black and made out of yak skins. These tents are very picturesque, and I was very anxious to purchase one, more particularly as I should not have had any hesitation in erecting one for the use of our party every night, for it would have attracted no particular attention from the casual observer, while our white canvas tent, of course, would be at once an object of curious inquiry. The nomads were very much surprised at our request for a tent and refused on any consideration to sell us one.

It was interesting to contrast these primitive tent-dwellers with the more sophisticated dwellers in the villages. Their communities are particularly important in certain circumscribed areas, however; and they live a freer, more open life than the townsmen or villagers. Out on the hillsides and over the moors they pasture great flocks and herds, their live stock including yaks, sheep, goats, and ponies. In the Rudro, Ngari Korsum, and Dro-tö districts of Western Tibet, practically the whole of the inhabitants belong to the nomad tribes of herdsmen, the only exceptions being monks and government officials. Some live in villages during the winter, and in Western Tibet the herdsmen retire to their stone-built huts for shelter when the hard weather begins. In places these winter encampments, however, consist of encircling walls and stone defenses against wind and snow, inside which the tents are erected in deep excavations; elsewhere certain tribes have hewn large galleries in the rocky hillsides. These are entered by narrow holes, but inside it is roomy, lofty, and warm.

In summer one comes across the Dro-pas in all parts of the country on the higher plateaus, where pasturage is to be found for the cattle. Their picturesque encampments of black tents, decorated with yaks' tails and prayer-flags, are very interesting. Each tribe clings to a particular district or *de*, and each tent houses a separate family. These tents are made of black canvas, very coarse in texture, which is spun from yak's hair; hides are sometimes used. Along the centre, at the top, runs a six-inch aperture through which the smoke escapes; at the entrance of the tent a more or less rude shrine is placed, and inside there is room for twenty or more persons to sleep. The clay-built stove and oven occupies the center, and round this assembles the whole family. The chieftain's tent in comparison with the others is well appointed, and one may find imported wares, tobacco, and tea inside.

The nomads live pretty well, for their flocks supply them with ample food and material for clothing. Yak-flesh and mutton, always boiled, are in plentiful supply; and butter and cheese are available. Parched barley made up into balls in tea is a staple food-stuff. Far better off are these nomads than the average urban dweller, for even the poorest has a small flock, while ofttimes a family tent will own up to fifteen hundred head of cattle, goats, sheep, yaks, and ponies.

The dress is a sheepskin robe with the wool on, bound round the waist by a yak-hair girdle; the women in addition wearing woolen petticoats and striped shawls, with traditional head-dress (the form depending on the district), which is profusely bedecked with coral and turquoise. The women, too, have an advantage over their village sisters in that they do very little field-work and attend to their homes; the heavy labor is the sphere of the men.

Throughout Central Tibet, covering the provinces of Yu and Tsang, the nomads wander between town and village, encamping wherever possible, probably on a ledge up the hillside, where, from their tents, they can command a view of their pasturing flock and at the same time be somewhat free from molestation. They cover the land south of Lake Yamdro, the districts adjoining the frontiers of Nepal and Bhutan, and far away in the extensive pastoral area east of Lhasa, a hundred or two hundred miles northeast, where the whole country is covered by the herds of these folk.

While within its district the tribe is an entity, the families split up and roam about independently; but rarely, except in the case of the marauding nomads, do they overstep the confines of their territory. Some of these families do not retire to special fastnesses during the winter months but merely strengthen their tents and dig themselves in. Taxes on their flocks are paid by the Dro-pas in cattle and ponies, and also in butter and coin, while they must provide transport-animals for the monasteries and government officials. But some of the wilder tribes ignore these tax claims.

The Horpa tribes northeast of Lhasa sometimes leave their pastoral pursuits and go off on mounted raids into neighboring territories and along the highways. Sometimes a gang, which may number up to a hundred or two, will range over hundreds of miles of country, raiding and carrying off flocks and pillaging villages and travelers.

The Rong-po Dro-pas, who live in the territory contiguous to Yu on the east, are a race of giants, who have proved themselves of sturdy character in the wars. Of an athletic bent, they add hunting to their occupations of agriculture and horse-breeding, while the Gya-de tribes of the Eastern and East-Central districts, who practise polygamy and not polyandry, by the way, and raise large families, live in permanent tent encampments, raising large flocks of sheep and milch yaks.

Altogether the Dro-pas tribes, as a people and for their peculiar customs and habits, provide one of the most interesting features of Tibetan life.

After a few minutes' conversation with these interesting nomad folk we went on our way across the plain. About noon we came to a small lake, which, being very shallow, had completely frozen over.

Earlier in the day I had been rendered sorrowful by the absence of water. I was now to find the presence of water in the form of ice even more troublesome, for the glassy surface of the lake at which we had arrived presented a serious obstacle. The path lay directly over the ice, and so, sillily enough, instead of skirting the lake we embarked with all our animals upon the unstable footing of the slippery ice. One of our mules fell and badly sprained a leg. This was London, the most gallant and hard-working of the three mules. I at first feared she had broken her leg and that we should have to cut her throat, but only a tendon had been strained, and a few minutes later she was pluckily limping on again. Poor faithful little old London, how brave you were, exhausting all your strength struggling to keep up with the others, until a few days later having come to the end of your tether you lay down and died without a sign of complaint!

London, who was the first to cross, taught us a lesson; as the other animals made their journey, Lhaten stood at the head and I at the tail of each, and whenever one slipped we held it up until it could find a footing again.

At last, when we thought all was well, Satan slipped and had rather a nasty fall on the ice. His cumbersome attempts to get up were really so comical that all of the others, including myself, had to laugh. A man of very quick temper, he was rendered perfectly furious, and, once on the other side, I had the greatest difficulty in restraining him from physical violence. It is an interesting commentary upon human nature that ridicule seems to be the cause of more deep-seated anger than anything else.

Warmed by our attempts to bring the animals safely over the ice, we stopped for a few minutes on the other side of the lake and took our midday meal. While we were resting there a merchant caravan with some twenty yaks came up to the lake on their way to Kampa Dzong. The merchants gave us but scant attention and after a brief hail to us started across the ice. It was interesting to see the slow, sure, and perfectly poised way in which the yaks managed to get across. Great, clumsy, awkward-looking brutes they are, but they seemed quite unconcerned at crossing the glassy surface and lumbered across without the slightest suggestion of falling, though the ponies which the merchants were riding experienced the same difficulties as those undergone by our own animals a short time earlier.

The yak is indeed in many ways a remarkable animal, and a whole book could be written about it. This beast is found wild as well as in domestic service. There are several species and crosses. The cross between the yak bull and the Indian cow is the beast in largest demand, being found throughout Tibet in domestic service, farm work, and transport.

The wild yak is a sturdy beast rather like the American bison, with a large heavy head which the beast bears close to the ground. The back slopes down to the tail, and the flanks are draped with long thick wool which reaches to the ground, the under part of the belly, which is practically bare, being protected from the cold in this way. The hoofs are large and cleft as suitable for climbing, while the strange tongue is armed with barbs, enabling the beast to tear off and masticate the coarse herbage on which it feeds—lichens, camel's-thorn, mosses, and such like. A bull will measure eleven feet from head to tail-root and stand five feet high at the shoulders. Horns, points forward, will measure more than thirty inches. The tame yaks and cross-breeds are smaller.

This splendid beast is very sure-footed, though slow, and will climb the roughest way like a goat. It roams about in herds, sometimes with wild ass and antelope, over vast tracks; in the winter it scrambles up the mountain-side far above the snow-line, rooting out mosses and such food-stuffs from under the snow.

Once we had recovered our breath and had disposed of our meal, we hastened on again, for the wind began to blow in an alarming fashion, the sky, which in the morning had been so clear, became murky, and evil-looking clouds seemed to threaten some kind of storm. We wanted to get on as far as possible before any radical change in the weather might hinder our march.

Satan continued in a bad temper the whole afternoon. He had been rendered irritable by the hardships of the last several days. The ridicule he had suffered as the result of his slip was the last straw, and he continued to make numerous insolent remarks. I could not afford to break with him and so was forced to keep the peace in spite of the fact that he was already talking of giving information to the authorities.

Before long we came to the other side of the plain, and it looked as if we had another mountain range to cross before dusk should come upon us, when suddenly we saw a narrow opening in the mountains divide ahead of us, which led directly into another plain a few hundred feet higher than the one on which we were standing and which instead of being level was tilted slightly, forming a long, shelving upward slope.

More or less at the junction of these two plains we found the important village of Kuma, seemingly a thriving community; and though without a castle, it was the largest settlement which we had yet come across. Seing that we had with us sufficient supplies for the future and had therefore no need for further purchases, I wished to pass by this village unnoticed, as I had heard it was the residence of several government officials, but though we did not stop we were not lucky enough to escape attention.

The dogs alone on seeing us made enough noise to awaken the dead. Tibet abounds with dogs. The natives have no conception of breeding or racial purity as regards their animals, so that the dogs are weird mongrels of a hundred known and unknown breeds.

Apart from a few pet dogs kept by the aristocratic families in Shigatse and Lhasa, all Tibetan dogs fall under two main categories, scavengers and watch-dogs, both of which are found in great numbers in every village.

The scavengers are all hopelessly hungry-looking animals, usually of a light-brown color. They are left free to prowl about at will but seem to have been divested of every form of moral or physical courage and with furtive eye and drooping tail slink around the family courtyard. They are really despicable curs. The only thing one can find to say in their favor is that as scavengers they are really effective, as there is nothing, no matter how filthy, which they refuse to eat.

The watch-dogs are of an entirely different build, larger and stronger, with a much longer coat, generally black. They are always chained up in front of the great gateway, which leads into the courtyard, and thus lead a life of perpetual captivity. They bark vigorously at the approach of any stranger and generally make a blood-curdling attempt to bite as well. These dogs are purposely underfed in order to keep them in a savage temper.

Kuma is a trade-center which depends a good deal upon catering to the Tibetan merchants passing to and fro on their journeys; and as in winter times are slack, a number of rest-house keepers came out to secure our custom when the dogs warned them of our approach. These touts were by no means pleased when we told them that we were not stopping. They told us there was no other village for many miles further on, for which I was not sorry, and we persisted in our story that we had to push on to Shigatse because of urgent business. This did not seem to satisfy them, and one or two uncomplimentary phrases were hurled at us. Not that we minded this greatly; much more unpleasant was the fact that a shepherd fell in with us and said he would accompany our party until he came to his hut, a mile or so further on. His unsolicited company proved more disquieting, as he insisted on carrying on a lengthy conversation with me personally. A man of very humble origin, he did not presume to address any remarks to Satan, the supposed master, and both Lhaten and the syce exhibited a coldness which he could only imagine came from a dislike to exchanging pleasantries with a poor shepherd. So he turned his attentions to Diogenes and me, as obviously the humblest members of the party. Poor Diogenes was never very brilliant at conversation, and so, very unwillingly, I had to shoulder the responsibility of the dialogue, though I made frantic signs to Satan to come back and relieve me of my task—signs which he completely ignored.

I had long since reached a point in my Tibetan studies where practically every word which I heard was intelligible to me, and my own Tibetan was always understandable and comparatively fluent, but I was afraid that the misuse of some word or a false intonation might betray me.

The intonation was the important point, because, unlike any so-called Aryan language, Tibetan, in common with other South Mongolian languages such as Burmese and Siamese, and also with Chinese (a Central Mongolian language), makes constant use of various tones to indicate changes of meaning. In Chinese, as is generally well known, several words can be phonetically spelled and pronounced exactly alike, but can have widely different meanings according to whether they have a rising or falling intonation. The Tibetan tones are somewhat differently arranged. In conversation the pitch of the voice varies, each word having a tone in which it should be pronounced, but it is the initial letter, or sometimes the silent prefixed letter, which governs the tone. Grammarians distinguish six tones, but for practical purposes these may be reduced to three, the high, the medium, and the low tones. Thus, for example, Tibetan has three letters (ཀ ཁ, and ག), which in the modern colloquial sound like our letter k (all three are so rendered in the present book), but the first is given a high pitch and is pronounced with the tongue between the teeth, the second is given a medium pitch and is strongly asperated, and the third is given a low pitch and is pronounced through the throat. Similarly there are in Tibetan three kinds of p's, of t's, and ch's and ts's, two kinds of s's, and two kinds of sh's. In speaking Tibetan it is very important that all these distinctions be observed.

Not wishing to show our shepherd friend too many of my tone exercises, I was as laconic in my replies as possible and assumed my rôle of a dull, stupid, vacant-minded peasant, to whom any great conversational effort was a serious mental strain. He seemed quite content to find a good listener, chattering gaily on, scarcely waiting for an answer, and any divergences on my part from his conception of standard Tibetan vocabulary or accent he put down to dialectical peculiarity.

All the time he was with us he busied himself spinning yarns, both metaphorically and literally, for he occupied his hands spinning a large wad of wool into a coarse thread, which his wife would later weave into cloth. This yarn was spun with the aid of a curious little bobbin which kept swinging round and round like a pendulum.

This is a favorite occupation of the Tibetan peasant men when they are on tramp or with their herds. It serves a useful economic purpose and at the same time gives them some way of occupying their minds during the long idle hours when tending their flocks, which require so little supervision.

Our companion, whose presence had proved so unacceptable at first, really amused me with his guileless chatter, and I felt genuinely sorry when we came to his hut and he left us with his "Kale pe a" (please go slowly), the usual polite parting phrase in Tibet.

We had felt so sure of being able to follow the track that we had neglected to ask him for directions and found ourselves puzzled when we came to a place where the trail split into three, leading in widely different directions. Not knowing which to choose, we at length took the usual Buddhist course and chose "the middle way," following it for several miles, with ever-increasing difficulty and discomfort, for the day had grown murkier and colder than ever and the devastating afternoon gale drove straight against us. At length we met a small party of peasants bringing some yaks into Kuma. Their information told us we had battled several hours with the wind quite uselessly, because for once the middle way was not the right way, and we should have taken the way to the right.

Kindly, simple souls, these peasants became excited over our troubles and told us how we might cut across the sloping plain and get back on to our road without having to retrace our steps. One, a toothless old grandmother, who was perched on top of a yak, took pity on Diogenes and me, who were obviously not only the humblest but also the most miserable members of our party, and offered us a drink of the chang or barley-beer she was carrying. For once, in spite of my teetotal intentions, I accepted the offer with alacrity.

Another hour's weary trudging brought us back to our road, and we continued along it until we were ready to drop from utter weariness and misery, eventually halting at a dreary, desolate spot only some ten miles beyond Kuma, so much time had we lost in taking the false direction. A few flakes of snow fell, and, looking back from our elevated position, we could see that a real snow-storm was taking place on the pass by which we had entered Tibet. Had we been but three days longer in the mountains we should certainly have perished in the snow. I was thankful for our deliverance from the danger of the pass, but certainly our present position was heartbreaking enough.

Not daring to pitch our tent, we were exposed to the full fury of the wind-storm, which brought with it the greatest cold we had yet experienced. Worst of all we could not find even yak-dung and were unable to light a fire, so that we were even without that Tibetan tea which cheers the soul. We had become frightfully thirsty, and though we had encamped by a tiny rivulet, the water of this was frozen fast, so that the only way we could quench our thirst was by chipping off pieces of ice and letting these melt in our mouths. The night was even more miserable. We tried desperately to get to sleep, but after every few minutes' uneasy dozing we would be awakened by an extra gust of icy wind, which penetrated right through the blankets. Poor Diogenes moaned the whole night because of the agony he suffered from his frost-bitten feet.

CHAPTER VI

WE JOIN A TIBETAN CARAVAN

IT was too much to expect human nature to stand such misery, and I was not surprised when shortly after midnight Satan announced his intention of abandoning the project. The other servants unfortunately were awake and for once joined their voices in favor of Satan's declaration. Considering our obvious discomfort, it was a bad time to attempt to argue with them, and so in the end I was forced to compromise. I pointed out that their physical suffering originated only from the fact that they were sleeping out in the open and that if they were to spend each night in a village, where they could find food, drink, fire, and shelter, they would have nothing to fear, and that even if we gave up the project it would be impossible to return to Sikkim immediately, as the passes were now definitely closed.

After some argument they agreed to carry on, if the plan of halting each stage at some village were carried out. This, of course, would enormously increase the chances of detection. Each day I would come under the surveillance of the villagers, but I felt that I could no longer expose my servants to such privations as we had endured. Furthermore, I felt emboldened by the success of my disguise. Already I had met and talked with numerous Tibetans, who seemed to notice nothing unusual about my appearance or speech. Peace and unanimity were thus once more restored to our party. By a curious coincidence the bitter wind, the immediate cause of our misery, died down very shortly after that, and we were able to get a little real slumber.

We had made most excellent plans to start early on our journey, but all of us were still sound asleep when the sun arose, and I was awakened to find a strange Tibetan face peering into mine. I was astounded and thought that through some treachery we were discovered, yet I still had enough presence of mind to pretend to go back to sleep again, for in the night I had taken off my dark goggles, and I was therefore afraid to let any one get too close a view of my eyes without this protection.

My sudden alarm proved groundless. The strangers were an old man and his son who were on their way to Shigatse. They had halted the previous night at Kuma and having started early in the morning had caught up with us soon after sunrise. Being surprised to find a party sleeping in the open, they had come up to make inquiries.

Lhaten told them we had lost the way the preceding evening and consequently were so delayed that we had been unable to get to the next village and had slept out. He spoke feelingly of the miserable night we had spent in the open. Our visitors did not stay long, but on leaving said that they were halting a mile or two further on to eat and rest and that we should probably catch up with them.

Half an hour later we had packed everything up and were on our way, though I felt in a very depressed mood. It was impossible to go back on my promise to my servants, but I felt that under the new conditions which were to await us I had very little chance of ever getting to Lhasa. I felt that all the sufferings we had undergone had been in vain, and the only thing to be done was to penetrate as far as possible into the country before I was discovered.

The morning was very misty; often it was impossible to see more than a few paces ahead. Then for a moment the mist suddenly lifted, and we saw coming toward us a number of riders armed with swords and rifles followed by a large caravan of yaks. At first the procession smacked of something official, but the consequent apprehension was misfounded, for the cavalcade turned out to be a peaceful trading-party only, though even so, to be on the safe side, I knelt down and pretended to attend to my boots as they came by, so that my face should be hidden.

The presence of the armed men was easily explained. Whereas the villagers in Tibet are more or less under control, the governmental officials have not yet managed to imbue the outlying nomads with any lively conception of discipline; and they are always prone to turn highway robbers. Consequently when a caravan containing merchandise of any value is destined to go over territory outside the influence of the towns, well-armed guards are always employed to protect it.

The hasty glimpse got of his party showed me that the swords were all of native design. The inhabitants of Central Tibet have never shown any great aptitude for design or craftsmanship, and most of the daggers and knives of Tibet come from Nepal, from Bhutan, or from Kam, the great semi-independent province which lies between Tibet proper and China.

The rifles, on the other hand, were of modern and European design. Of recent years a great many modern rifles have found their way from India into Tibet, some legally and some illegally. In addition, the Tibetans are now busy manufacturing such rifles in Tibet itself. Even before 1904 the Tibetan Government had established a small arsenal in Lhasa where quite creditable imitations of European rifles were made, chiefly based on samples secured from Russia, and such guns were in the hands of some of the soldiers who fought against the Younghusband expedition. Since 1912 the arsenal has been very considerably expanded and now turns out a number of rifles every year. Some of these imitations, which later fell into my hands, I found to be very exact, so exact in fact that they had even copied the name-plate of the original European makers.

I was able to catch only a fleeting glimpse of the loads which the yaks were carrying, but from the size and shapes of the bundles it was pretty obvious that they mostly contained wool, barley, flour, boxes of brick-tea, and salt. The three last articles were probably for consumption in and around Kampa Dzong, for they have little or no export value. Nearly all the tea used by the Tibetans in every part of the country comes from China. It is compressed into bricks, which make the tea much easier to transport, but it was curious to find tea coming to Kampa Dzong from distant China when excellent tea is grown in Darjeeling and many parts of Sikkim. Such is the power of custom that this nearer and far more delicate tea is never imported. The barley was more explicable, for even the villagers in the neighborhood of Kampa Dzong depend largely upon the flocks for their livelihood. Though a certain amount of barley is grown, the climate is too cold and the altitude is too high to make any form of agriculture particularly successful. In some places the barley plant never fully ripens and on the approach of the bad weather has to be plucked green and used merely as fodder for the animals during the winter months.

The environs of Kampa Dzong, being essentially grazing land, produce more than enough wool for all local purposes, but Kampa Dzong itself is one of the places from which wool gathered from every part of Tibet is, in the summer months, sent down to Sikkim and India, where it commands very high prices, for Tibetan wool is very nearly the best in the world; the reason for this is that the terrible cold of Tibet has forced nearly all animals that live there to grow a curious sort of inner coat of a fine and silky nature which lies close to the skin and keeps out a great deal of the biting wind which penetrates the outer coat. Although nearly all animals, including the dog, grow this soft silk wool it is particularly luxuriant on the yaks, the sheep, and the goats, and can be used for commercial purposes. Because of its silk-like texture it is much prized by the natives of the surrounding countries.

Most of the wool caravans go over the Gyangtse-Pari-Yatung-Kalimpong route, but here there is practically a monopoly which kills all competition, and many of the smaller traders prefer to use Kampa Dzong as the export base. Incidentally I was told that a good deal of smuggling has been going on since 1912, when the Chinese-Tibetan customs office was abolished. India and Tibet have established absolute free trade, and there is no import duty levied on either side, but the Tibetan Government, in a desperate attempt to secure money for its new enterprises, levies a tax of five trangka on every bale of wool that is sold; in many cases this tax is only extorted at the frontier stations as a sort of port duty. It is payment of this tax that the smugglers try to avoid.

The salt used in Tibet is derived in nearly all cases from the saline crustations surrounding many of the lakes. In most cases the natives use it exactly as they find it with no attempt at purification. Consequently one frequently finds with it grains of sand and in many cases it contains mixtures of salts other than the common sodium chloride or ordinary table-salt. For this reason Tibetan salt has frequently a peculiarly acrid and bitter taste. Finally one finds it sold in fairly large crystals, which makes it difficult to sprinkle over food, but which does not interfere with the principal Tibetan use of it, viz., boiling it with their tea.

We went on steadily uphill for some time after leaving the caravan which had aroused our fears without seeing any one else, and I began to think that after all we would be spared meeting the two traders who had awakened us that morning. But just as I had come to the conclusion that they had gone on ahead without waiting for us, we came in sight of a deserted and ruined stone house and found that this served as the halting-place of our friends. They hailed us as we came up, and we again stopped for a few minutes' conversation. Learning that we were going to Shigatse on pilgrimage, they suggested that we continue the journey together, Shigatse being their home place, to which they were returning after a visit to a relative in Kampa Dzong.

Such a proposition is not unusual in Tibet, for because of their fear of brigands small parties do not like to make a long journey alone; and where small groups of travelers are unable to hire armed guards such as we had seen that morning, it is usual for them to join together in order to make a show of bigger numbers and thereby frighten away the less bold, or isolated, brigands.

Personally I was not so much afraid of brigands as of the law-abiding Tibetans, but thought that at least if these two friendly travelers were with us we should no longer have any fear of again losing our way. I was still very loath to come into such close personal touch with Tibetans, which would not allow me to relax my disguise for a single minute, even when on the road. Only two days previously I had made a great scene when I found the Kampa Dzong coolies had been added to our party. Much had happened in the short space of time which had elapsed, and I felt much surer of myself and of my disguise. Still I would certainly have rejected our present companions' offer had it been possible to discover a satisfactory excuse. The matter was taken out of my hands, however, by Satan. During the last day or two he had waxed very independent and had found the rôle of master so congenial that he decided to play the part in earnest. Without even so much as a glance at me to see how I wanted things to go, he accepted the Tibetans' proffered companionship; and as it was obviously impossible for me to make an open protest, we waited another few minutes until our new companions had time to reload the horse which they had with them to carry their loads, for they themselves were walking the whole way and pushed on together. I was rather sorry for this, for if they, like Satan, had been riding there would have been less need for me to come into personal contact with them.

While they were thus busy with their loads, I quickly made up my mind as to the best way to meet the new situation. I whispered to Lhaten that I and the syce would go on ahead and try to keep ahead of the main party the whole day. Lhaten was to follow with our new companions and tell them our prearranged story, informing them that I was a little queer in the upper story. Incidentally, I added that he was never to leave Satan alone with them, as I had already suspicions that the scamp might attempt to betray me. By this arrangement I felt that there would be less danger of detection than if I remained in closer contact with the party all the time.

Until about noon, the road continued uphill, though nearly always with the same gentle incline, a formation which I believe to be very rare in Tibet. We came eventually to the apex of the slope, marked, as usual, by a pair of shrines with rags and prayer-flags attached to them. We added our stones to the votive pile, duly invoked the gods, and passed over to the other side, where our descent began.

The pass marks the watershed of this part of Tibet. Up to this time all the streams, when they did not evaporate on the open plains, joined the rivers that pierced the Himalayas and penetrated directly into India. The river which we reached on the other side, a stream of important size, considering how near it was to its source, ran down to the great river of Tibet, the Brahmaputra, which may be called the life-artery of Tibet, for it runs diagonally across the country for many hundreds of miles, and nearly all of Tibet's cities are placed either on it or on one of its tributaries. Shigatse and Gyangtse are on the Nyang and Lhasa on the Kyi River, both of which empty into the Brahmaputra. I felt, therefore, that we had really entered the heart of Tibet once we had crossed the watershed. The portion of the country drained by the Brahmaputra is the most fertile part of Tibet, and I could feel as soon as we began the descent that it was four or five degrees warmer.

We had now come to an entirely different kind of country. Instead of the broad, flat plains, we found a valley, a valley which gradually widened out, but from which the mountains rose sharply on either side, in a more or less parallel direction, contrasting with the plains, which seem to be inclosed on all four sides by mountains.

Geographically the Tibetans divided their country into three principal types. These are known as the *Rong,* or valley type, the *Dro* or the flat pasturage type, and the *Tang* or desert plain type of country. The Rong type naturally is found in the more mountainous part of the country and consists of the narrow but frequently well-cultivated valleys and gorges which lie between Mountain ranges. Both the Dro and Tang types are broad plains or flat-bottomed basins but are distinguished from each other in that the lower plains, which are more fertile and can support a large number of flocks, are called Dro or pasturage country, while the higher and bleaker plains retain the title of Tang.

The change in scenery which we noticed, therefore, indicated that we had emerged from the Tang to the Rong type of country.

The Rong district, particularly between Shigatse and Lhasa, contains numerous villages and monasteries. It is a rugged land of steep ridges, ravines, and wild waterways, difficult to traverse on account of the bare, forbidding mountains which have to be crossed, and the dark narrow gorges. Yet within this seemingly unfriendly tract, the people are industrious and happy, with villages grouped on ledges on the hill-sides, and sometimes along the sides of a valley, particularly at the juncture of one river with another, where the alluvial soil provides profitable cultivation. The abundance of water, and the rich, raised earth beds washed up alongside the rivers, and possibly the protective nature of the broken-up country, make the Rong districts a favorite stretch for village settlements.

The Dro country, the territory of the semi-nomadic Dropas with their herds and flocks, lies chiefly in the southern part of Tibet, but carries away to Drode, northeast of Lhasa, which, in a district from one hundred and fifty to two hundred miles of the capital, is surrounded by a very beautiful country with wide and fertile valleys, fairly intensively cultivated, and watered by large rivers.

The Dro districts are mainly tracts of heath and moorland, sometimes very wild and bleak, with huge mountains which rise up straight from the valleys and run rugged spurs from all angles into the surrounding plains. Bogs and swamp abound in parts, and dangerous gulches and crags. The soil is of a dark, peaty nature, bearing a coarse herbage and some shrubs, and near the rivers willow- and poplar-trees. In favored spots a wealth of beautiful flowers may be seen for four months of the year, between the snow periods, and also juniper and stunted firs. Small towns and villages are dotted about here and there, but are not nearly so frequently met with as in the Rong districts.

Summer lasts for four months. In October the snows come and the whole aspect of the land is changed. Through the winds the snows are driven and frozen hard, and throughout the bleak winter the only life is that of hares and foxes, a few antelope, and here and there the wild ass and yak, which will be seen high upon some rocky ledge rooting round in sheltered nooks for the scant herbage on which they subsist during this drear period. The herdsmen withdraw from the plains and upland pastures to the stone-built huts, or to the villages with the domestic cattle, leaving the land to the wild life and to stray wayfarers.

The great tract of country in the west of Tibet is known as the Tang territory, a region of wide steppes, rising out of which, particularly in the more westerly portion, are formidable mountains. The plains are really wide, shallow valleys bounded by steep hills, the valleys being anything from fifteen to forty miles in length. From the hilltops as far as the eye can reach appear vast bare and desolate-looking even stretches, perhaps broken by a river, and shallow lakes. The lakes are mostly salt, and fringing them are whitish borders where the evaporated water has left deposits of sodas and salts. The soil, broken up by the alternating heat and cold, is usually of a dull-brown, drab, flaky substance, powdering into a light sandy nature, with occasional patches of dirty white, where clay is uncovered. The lakes and swamps between latitude 33° and 82° E. are in the midst of a dry region

Wall-engravings in Tibetan cathedral

Engraving of devil in Tibetan cathedral

Phari rest-house early morning

Yaks transporting wool to Lhasa from Tibetan provinces

where the soil is covered with saltpeter. There is scant vegetation, with slight herbage only in the deeper, damper, valley beds, and in places it is absolutely bare. A course grass south of latitude 33° and at an altitude of fifteen thousand feet supports the tame cattle of the Changpas, as the natives of this region are called, and also provides food for the wild asses and antelope; and there is here also a broad belt of fertile pastures running for about forty miles where thick grasses, wild rhubarb, and other herbs are found. Then again, in the saline valleys to the north, where slabs of salt lie about in the surface, grass of a coarse quality occurs and still further northward somewhat luxuriant herbage serves as efficient pasturage for herds of wild animals.

Here, too, the summer is short, and a severe winter period sets in early, changing entirely the aspect of the land. But the saline lakes do not freeze, even though the surrounding land and fast-flowing rivers are frost-bound in a cold which will descend to forty-five degrees below zero. The appearance of these unfrozen lakes is rendered then even more curious by the fact that the hot springs which occur near the lakes, generally of the gusher type, are frozen into hard crystal columns of ice. In this regard it should be noted, however, that the higher plateaus of Chang-tang (or plains of the north) are at an altitude of anything from 15,000 to 17,300 feet above sea-level.

I was glad that I had not in my fright rushed on ahead alone but had brought the syce with me, as we met several natives on our way down the valley, with whom an occasional word was necessary. I let the syce do most of the talking and contented myself with throwing in a remark when I felt on safe ground.

In the excitement of the morning, I had quite forgotten to get out any food from our common stock, but in the load which I was carrying there was a small sack of barley-flour; and filling our tea-bowls full of water from the icy stream, the syce and I mixed up the barley-flour to form a paste and with this sparse food we had to be satisfied for the rest of the day.

We were fortunate that afternoon in having very little wind and consequently made much quicker progress than had been possible the preceding day. About four o'clock a bend in the valley brought before our eyes a village some three or four miles away. This I knew was the place where we were to halt for the evening.

The syce and I waited until the others came up, as I certainly did not want to have the unpleasant task of searching out a lodging and bargaining over the amount to be paid. We had obviously done our march at a pretty good rate, for it was nearly half an hour before our party arrived. When they did come up I asked the *gyepo,* or old man, the elder of our two companions, where we were to stay for the night. He answered that there was one lodging in the village in which he always stayed, and being known there he could get things cheaper. So he and his son now led the way, and the members of my party followed. I pulled Lhaten aside and with him dropped even further behind, as I wanted to find how things had gone during the day and also to give certain orders as to what I wanted done during the coming evening in the rest-house, where, of course, I could no longer directly issue orders. This took longer than I expected, and when we arrived at the village, whose name I discovered was Yako, I found that our party had already disappeared into some rest-house courtyard. I was very angry that they had not left a rear-guard to tell us where to go, as it meant that Lhaten and I had to wander around the whole village and ask at several places before we came to the rest-house which they had entered. At the entrance to the rest-house there was the usual watch-dog, who sprang out at us in a very threatening way. Being in rather an irritable mood, I raised the whip which I was carrying, but before I delivered a single blow I noticed that the dog cowered down and slunk into his kennel. This struck me as particularly amusing, because it showed that the Tibetan dogs are like the Tibetan men, fierce and threatening creatures, whose main idea is to terrorize all around them, but like most bullies arrant cowards at heart.

On entering the courtyard we found that the syce and Diogenes were busy unloading the mules and that the younger of our companions was helping them, an act of kindness which I had not expected, so that without more ado Lhaten and I went on to the rest-house common room and began preparing the food for that night.

This was my first real experience of a Tibetan rest-house—in Kampa Dzong I had merely slept for an hour or two on the roof—and so I was much interested in observing how such places were run. The Tibetans, strangely enough, are great travelers within the limits of their own country; and nearly every village has at least one rest-house and sometimes two or three, where such travelers can stay for the night and find food and drink. At the same time such places differ a great deal from any European equivalent, having little in common with even the old village tavern or inn which has come down to us from time immemorial. On the great highroads, along which government couriers and officials are constantly being sent, certain places are appointed as official rest-houses and are more elaborately equipped; but along the minor highroads, such as the one on which we were then traveling, the accommodation is very primitive. The house is properly a private dwelling. The male members of the family engage in ordinary occupations such as agriculture; and the hostel side of the business is run by the female department, the chief woman of the family acting as the all important *nemo,* or landlady.

The animals are, of course, cared for in the great courtyard. The travelers are expected to attend to the loading and unloading of their own packs, and must also look after giving the animals food and drink. The water in this house was supplied by a well in the middle of the courtyard, while the fodder was to be purchased from the rest-house stores. This consisted, needless to say, entirely of barley, a small amount of barley grain plus a much larger amount of the dried barley stalks. Any grooming of the animals that is required has to be done by the travelers or their servants. In our case, this business was attended to by the syce aided by Diogenes.

If the traveler is very wealthy or possesses sufficiently high official rank, he and his party are given a private chamber; but in other cases, all the travelers share a large communal room, in which they rest, eat, drink, and sleep. Here we found the common room to be on the first floor, with no window overlooking the village outside, but with a huge opening—to be closed at night with a wooden shutter—overlooking the courtyard below, where therefore we could see how our animals were faring. The shutters were already half closed, so that it was very dark in the room, a fact which I appreciated very much, as it allowed me to go about my duties as Lhaten's assistant without very much fear of detection, and I was able to lay aside my dark goggles.

By good luck we found only one other party in the rest-house, a group of four people, and as they seemed to be occupied with their own affairs, after a biief exchange of greetings, we were able to ignore them.

The room contained no furniture of any kind. Both the walls and floor were void of any covering. The floor consisted of bare ground, though the corners of the room were filled with the bales of the more valuable portion of the loads which we and the other travelers had brought along inside; for petty theft is very common in Tibet, and every traveler wishes to keep his valuables as near to him as possible.

Shortly after our arrival the *nemo,* or landlady, brought in a small iron tripod, and on it an iron brazier with holes in order to secure a draft. Filled with yak-dung intermixed with a few barley-straws, this was lighted by means of a tinder-box, and we were now in a position to proceed with the preparation of our evening meal. Cooking in these rest-houses is left entirely to the travelers themselves, for in no case is the rest-house anything of a restaurant, though it is possible to buy raw supplies from the landlady.

It can be seen that the occupation of a landlady at a Tibetan rest-house is in no way arduous. She has merely to provide the room and sell any general supplies which may be wanted. It is, therefore, quite obvious why every Tibetan traveler who can afford it goes along with a retinue of servants, for the work which would ordinarily be done by the servants of an inn in the West falls on the shoulders of the traveler's personal attendants if he feels it infra dig. to attend to such matters himself.

In addition to servants, moreover, the traveler in Tibet prefers to take the major part of his food supplies along with him, instead of buying them at each rest-house at which he stops. The reason for this I could never fathom, except, perhaps, that, curiously enough, most food supplies can be bought cheaper in the larger cities than in the villages. As we had laid in a fairly large supply in Kampa Dzong, we were also able to follow Tibetan custom in this respect, and I noticed that our party in common with our companions had to purchase only fodder, barley-straw, for the animals, yak-dung for the fire, and chang, or beer, all of which were too bulky to carry conveniently along. If the accommodation in a Tibetan rest-house is poor and service practically non-existent, yet we certainly could not complain as to the amount we had to pay as *nela,* or rent, which, apart from supplies purchased, was only a chegye, or half a trangka, less than two-pence, and this for a party of five people!

Our two companions were too small a party to form a camp-fire of their own and so joined in our circle. This forced me to take a seat behind the others, for now that my goggles were off I was afraid that the light from the brazier might show up my eyes if I came too near. This position also allowed me to hear everything that was said without taking too active a part in the proceedings.

The company sat talking and sipping chang some time after the meal was concluded. There were no chairs, of course, and the travelers sat either on the bare floor or on some of the saddle-carpets which they had brought with them. When the time came to break up, the *nemo* was called in and everything paid for, as we intended to start early the next morning before it was light. We then proceeded to prepare ourselves for the night. Bedclothes are never furnished by the rest-house, so that every traveler in Tibet is forced to bring his own. This, of course, was no difficulty to us, for now that we were indoors and had no longer the cold night winds to contend with, the blankets we had with us sufficed, though, unfortunately, it was necessary to give Satan all of my blankets while I had to take the place he had formerly held and share blankets with Lhaten. In place of a bed, a Tibetan carpet of conventional size—generally five and one half feet by two feet—is spread out on the floor. Sometimes by the richer classes two or three such carpets will be used, so as to counteract the hardness of the floor. Either no pillow at all is used or else one of the saddles or smaller packs will be placed under the head. For covering there is the usual sheepskin blanket, the furry side being laid underneath, or next the body.

Following Tibetan custom all of us slept in our clothes, though the sash which acts as a belt is either loosened or completely discarded, yet I noticed that one or two of the party in the other corner of the room preferred to follow a custom which is not uncommon among certain of the Dropas, or nomads, and stripped themselves stark naked, placing their clothes over them as an additional protection.

The Dropas, as has been mentioned, not infrequently sleep on their stomachs, sometimes with their knees drawn up under them in a curious crouching position, but I noticed that all of our party slept either on their backs or sides but always stretched out straight. This curiously enough proved one of my greatest trials. I had long got into the habit of sleeping more or less curled up so that when lying perfectly straight I found it difficult to get to sleep. But as I heard that sleeping with doubled-up legs was never done in Tibet I was forced to try and accommodate myself to new conditions. Incidentally, as I was in possession of but half a blanket, any attempt at curling up meant that knees or feet were exposed to the bitter night cold.

The next morning our two trader friends initiated us into the routine of true Tibetan traveling. I knew that we had agreed upon an early start, but I was certainly surprised when I woke up at two o'clock the next morning to find that the others were already up and making preparations for getting away. The Tibetans are accustomed to making incredibly long marches every day, and in order to cover the necessary distance they rise long before sunrise in order to get as much as possible of the march over before the afternoon winds set in.

Arrangements for departure proved very short and simple. We had not a mouthful to eat or drink before undertaking our long march. I have long been a convert to the "continental breakfast"—a cup of coffee and a roll instead of the porridge and ham and eggs with which most sturdy Britons load up their stomachs before beginning their work—so that I had no yearning for a heavy meal at that time of day; but I should certainly have welcomed a large bowl of tea as a stimulant. However, when I faintly suggested such a plan, it was at once negatived by our companions, and they were astonished that any one should have thought of the idea.

Needless to say, no time was wasted in washing. There were no facilities for doing so even if we had felt inclined. Most Tibetans never touch their bodies with water during the whole course of their lives, and become practically incased in a layer of fat and dirt which serves the useful function of keeping out the cold. In this connection it may be added that from the time I entered Tibet until I entered Lhasa I found it impossible to wash even my face or my hands. Tibetans find the layer of dirt by no means objectionable, and are even proud of it. They believe that such a layer not only keeps the cold out but also keeps the luck in, and in many parts of the country a young man wants to be sure that his bride-elect has not washed this luck-covering away. Not infrequently the natural layer will be supplemented by smearing the body with butter or sheep's fat.

As a proof that washing brings bad luck, I was once, while in Gyangtse, told the story of a young woman who thought she knew better than her elders and insisted on washing herself. The heavenly buddhas and bodhisattvas were evidently displeased with this unfilial presumption and sent her an attack of pneumonia, from which she died.

As though, however, conscious that some criticism might be leveled against them, the Tibetans have a common proverb, "The Tibetan is black outside but white inside, and the foreigner is white outside but black inside."

On this particular morning, we were greatly helped by the fact that the moon was shining very brightly, because otherwise we should have had the troublesome task of loading our mules in the dark; but at the same time the night cold was so intense that our hands were numbed, and it took some time for us to tie the straps together, for our fingers refused to perform their function.

We then struck out on our journey, which continued down the narrow valley worn out by the Re River on its way down to the Brahmaputra. We had to cross and recross the stream several times, but this offered no great difficulty, for the river was covered with very coarse and corroded ice and was not very slippery.

I did not feel it necessary to separate myself from our Tibetan companions as on the previous day. In the first place, in spite of the moonshine, it was very difficult to see one another's faces, and, secondly, I had now established friendly relations with them, and having heard our story they were quite willing to accept us as they found us. I discovered these travelers to be extraordinarily kindly, simple, naïve people, completely ignorant and grossly superstitious, but quite willing to accept life as it came to them. The old man carried a prayer-wheel in his hand which he kept constantly turning, thereby laying up an enormous store of merit for himself, and he occasionally ejaculated the sacred formula of Tibet: "Om mani peme hung," (spelled "Om mani padme hum,") to make up for any delinquencies which the prayer-wheel might have left untouched.

The younger man, although nearly forty years of age, had not yet reached the stage of piety, and instead of religious exercise occasionally flicked his horse with the whip which he carried and varied this proceeding by now and then bursting into song.

The leather used for all straps and whips is made from yak-hide which the Tibetans have learned to cure in such a way as to make it soft. Most of the whips are only two or three feet long. Many of them have handles between one and two feet in length, made either of wood or more commonly of bamboo. The bamboo and a good deal of the wood is brought in from Sikkim.

The songs which our friend sang were not all pious; in fact, they were distinctly ribald, being chiefly in praise of the merits of chang and pretty ladies. I was surprised that his father did not seem to take any notice of them, but perhaps the old man was of the opinion that his religious exercises were sufficient to cover the sins of the family and so let his son go on unchecked.

Although all my servants were very religious, with the possible exception of Satan, who was too much of a priest to take religion very seriously, I noticed that they gave expression to their ardent admiration of the wit hidden in the songs. One of the worst of these lyrics Satan insisted on learning then and there. In the meantime I was troubled by matters of a different kind. The walnut-juice and iodine I had used for my face and body had proved very satisfactory; but the "hair-restorer" had already shown signs of weakness, the glossy black hue had begun to fade, and I was afraid that any application of water to the hair would wash out the dye and leave the original brown color. That morning because of the cold I had wrapped my face so well in a Tibetan scarf that even my nose and mouth were covered and my breath came directly on my beard. So bitterly cold was it that the moisture from the breath collected on the beard and froze, making a hard icicle of the whole of the beard. I had not minded this at the time, but later on when the sun appeared and it became warmer, the icicle began to melt, and I was afraid that the thaw would also take some of the dye away. Carefully examining as much as I could of my beard, I found to my horror that this was so and that the color had become very streaky. I cursed the well-known makers of the "guaranteed hair-restorer" at great length to myself. In our luggage there was still another bottle of it, but until our next stop I should not be able to get at it and repair the damage. In the meantime it was necessary to bind the scarf even more tightly around the beard so as to hide it from sight.

About nine o'clock we came to a point where the valley widened out considerably, and the river was joined by a tributary which came in from the right and which had its origin not far from Gyantse. A village lay at the junction.

I noticed something strange about this village but could not at first explain what it was that made it seem out of the ordinary. Then I realized that for the first time since entering Tibet we had met with trees. It was only a small clump of trees, a dozen at the outside, bare and bleak in their winter undress, but it was indeed a joy to see them. It is only in the Brahmaputra basin and its connecting valley systems that one sees any trees at all, and here they are only kept alive by attentive cultivation. A wild natural-growing tree is unknown. What trees there are in Tibet, it is interesting to note, are nearly all deciduous, evergreens not being able to stand the bitter winter weather.

I had hoped that we would stop at the pleasant village, for by this time I was ravenously hungry; but our guides kept steadily on for another two hours, during which time we passed two other villages, before at last they stopped in front of a large isolated farmhouse, where they said we were to rest for an hour and eat our first meal.

At last, I thought and prayed, we should be able to go up-stairs to a room which would be somewhat private and also in semi-darkness, but we had to stay in the courtyard under full public gaze, and we were soon surrounded by a host of youngsters, who were anxious to inspect the newcomers, and who passed audible comments upon our appearance. In these circumstances, I was doubly afraid to expose my streaky beard, and instead of unwinding my scarf as the others did, I pretended to have toothache in addition to all my other troubles—toothache, because of lack of dentists, is very common in Tibet—and I resolutely stuck to my wrappings and buried my face in my hands as well, giving vent to occasional short moans. This seemed to amuse the children, who shouted, "The coolie has got toothache; the worms have got at his teeth." But soon their attentions became directed to poor Diogenes's feet, and I was once more left in peace.

The women brought the yak-dung brazier out; this time it was of earthenware, not of iron, and before long our simple meal was ready.

The Tibetan peasants are very irregular in the time of their meals. There are no definite times for eating. Food is prepared whenever they feel particularly hungry, but generally speaking they are content, especially when traveling, with two meals a day; one is eaten shortly before noon and the other at the end of the day's march, which is usually shortly before dusk.

These two meals consist almost invariably of the same food, viz., meat, barley, and tea. The meat eaten in Tibet is either mutton or yak's flesh. A haunch is left outside to freeze, and this preserves it to a certain extent for several months, though the recurrent heat of the day causes it to thaw sufficiently to become putrescent. At night it freezes again, a process which repeats itself as long as the meat lasts. The Tibetans do not object to the semi-putrescent, as they consider that the taste is in this way improved. Occasionally the meat is cooked, but for the most part the peasants prefer to eat it raw. Hacking off small pieces with their great knives, they eat it with their fingers.

The tea is of a very coarse kind. It is all imported, chiefly from China, in the form of compressed bricks. As it is difficult to make the leaves stick together, the tea is mixed with small quantities of moistened yak-dung, which acts as a cement. A portion will be broken off a tea-brick and thrown into the water to boil. After it has bubbled for some time a huge mass of butter will be added, and at the same time smaller quantities of soda and salt. This is thoroughly mixed, and then allowed to boil again for several minutes. Needless to say, the use of milk and sugar is unknown. Sometimes sheep's fat will take the place of butter. In any case, as we have seen, the butter is invariably rancid. This buttered tea is consumed in incredible quantities, and serves as a food as well as a drink.

The barley-grains are first parched and then ground into very fine flour. A handful of this flour is poured into the tea and kneaded with the fingers into dough-balls. These are then eaten without being cooked in any way. The aristocratic families of Tibet have become addicted to certain Chinese dishes, but the peasant is forced to content himself with the above diet all the year round. Fish and fowl are considered too filthy to be eaten. Vegetables are unknown. Raw putrid meat, buttered tea, and barley-flour do not constitute a very appetizing meal, but a march of thirty miles dulls the senses to every feeling except that of hunger, so that I ate these with avidity. Satan, as master, was able to purchase from the rest-house some Chinese delicacy, but as I was forced to eat in company with Tibetan peasants I did not dare to secure any of this for myself.

While Lhaten was getting out our barley and meat, I whispered to him to secure the bottle of hair-dye as well. He did so and managed to hand it to me without any one's noticing the action. I at once hid it away inside of my bosom. Lhaten saw that I wanted a little time in private to use the dye, and while the others were reloading the mules, he ordered me in a loud voice to take up my load and go on ahead as I was so confoundedly slow and he did not wish me to lag behind.

I seized upon the hint and hobbled off as fast as I could. When out of sight of the farm-house, I sat down and quickly repaired the damage my beard had suffered earlier in the day, and at last I was able to discard my scarf.

Not long afterward the river crossed my path again. Coming toward me, on the other side, was a huge peasant accompanied by a tiny wife. The man was easily six feet three inches in height, while his wife must have been under five feet. The contrast was startling. In the central parts of Tibet the inhabitants generally are rather short, an inch or two under the average height in England, and so I judged this fellow or his ancestors must have come from Kam, the great eastern province of Tibet, where most of the inhabitants are extremely tall and many of them attain to even gigantic size. This giant peasant was obviously in a hurry, for he came along at a great pace, but with his gigantic stride he seemed to have no difficulty in covering the ground. Not so his poor wife, who with her short steps had literally to run in order to keep up with her spouse. He seemed little worried by her exertions and occasionally gave her a push to make her go faster, and so I was surprised at the gallantry he showed when he came to the river. The ice was here too thin to bear any weight and broke through at every footstep. Not in the least perturbed by this, and seeing his wife hesitate, he picked her up with one hand in a most casual fashion and, tucking her under his arm as if she were a sack of flour, carried her over and deposited her on dry ground not far from where I was standing.

I wished very much that I could be conveyed across in a similar fashion, but for me there was no help but to wade through the icy stream, the freezing water of which came up to my knees. I was afraid to take off my shoes and stockings, which as they became soaking wet made me feel extremely uncomfortable afterward, and I had to walk very fast to prevent the water which they retained from freezing.

I now began to be overtaken by a number of mounted parties who seemed to be riding to a village in the distance. All the members of these bands of travelers had on their Sunday-go-to-meeting clothes, made of silk imported from China. As they passed me they all stared very inquisitively, and certainly I must have presented a very drab appearance. As many of them obviously belonged to the official class, local headmen and landowners, against whom I had to be especially on my guard, I was afraid that their curiosity might lead them to more active steps of inquiry. I decided to wait till my party came up, when I should have some one who could answer any questions, and so I departed from the road and lay hidden in a ditch until I heard the voices of Lhaten and Satan, engaged, as usual, in a fierce argument.

Thereafter our march continued for some time without further incident, save that before long the river had again to be crossed. Still suffering from the previous crossing, I heartily cursed the Tibetans for making their roads cross streams so frequently, particularly as at no place was there a bridge. Satan, of course, on his pony, had no difficulty, and even the *gyepo* or old Tibetan, who was still with us, mounted his loaded horse long enough to cross the stream with dry feet, but when I attempted to do the same with one of our mules the sinful creature kicked out so lustily and made such a commotion that I was once more forced to wade through the icy water.

Another hour and a half brought us to the village, toward which I had seen the people riding. We found it an insignificant place depending for its existence upon the large monastery of Ragyimpa, which lay stretched up the side of the hill beyond.

There seems to be a curious distribution of territory between castles, monasteries, and villages in Tibet. A village is nearly always placed on a flat plain or in a valley, but whenever possible at the foot of some mountain. A monastery is nearly always built on the slope of a mountain, neither on the top or at the base, while the castles are nearly always placed at the very summit of a low-lying but precipitous hill. The site selected, whenever such can be found, is preferably a hill set in the middle of a plain, so that from the castle ramparts a clear sweep of the horizon may be obtained.

The village we now entered was astir, and we saw a large number of people going up to the monastery. There was obviously some great religious festival taking place, which had attracted people from all over the country-side.

In this connection, the relation that exists between

the villages and the monasteries must not be forgotten. The religious houses of Tibet are not temples, properly speaking, but monasteries, inside the walls of which will be a temple which is indeed the principal college of the monasteries, and where the mysterious Tantrik rites and occult ceremonies of the Tibetan religion are taught and celebrated.

Every morning the monks foregather in the temples for services, but no sermons are preached, except on rare and special occasions. There are one or two minor exceptions to the above, such as, for example, the Cho-Kang, at Lhasa. The religious officials of Tibet, therefore, are not rightly called priests; they are more correctly monks. There is no parochial work, and the monasteries and their temples are not for the inhabitants of neighboring villages or towns, but for the monks themselves and the novitiates. The village will have its shrine or shrines and its prayer-wall, perhaps, but the great religious house is built away from ordinary habitations; and while the sick or dying peasant will call in a holy man to read prayers, and, maybe, administer relic pills, certain herbal medicine, and medieval concoctions, his messenger may have a ten-mile journey to the monastery.

As already mentioned the monasteries are built up hillsides. Sometimes the outer wall of the monastery will reach down to the valley, with the various buildings attained by stone steps, stretching one over the other, high up the mountain-side, the topmost building generally being the storehouse, in which are kept the huge quantities of dried flesh—goat, yak, sheep, and other carcasses, which are for the provisioning of the inmates.

Within the inclosure, a great wall pierced by gates facing the cardinal points of the compass, are the dwelling-houses of the monks, the colleges, and the great hall where worship is practised. This main hall with its carvings and frescos, its roof supported by wooden pillars, carved and decorated, contains images of the buddhas on engraved wooden and metal altars, before which butter lamps are continually burning. Here, too, are the effigies of departed abbots (as at Gyangtse) all along the walls, and the great pictures of Buddhist deities (as at Trashilhumpo), which are brought out in the months of June and November and hung on the outer walls.

The tombs, containing the embalmed bodies of head lamas long passed, are within the walls, the libraries, offices, punishment cells, shrines, and such buildings all going to make up a small thriving township, with lanes and byways, and centrally situated, the great courtyard or square, where takes place the outdoor ceremonies and religious dances.

About the hillside on which the monastery stands are seen small solitary buildings, the isolated cells of contemplative monks, who dislike intrusion and interruption of their vigils, while at the foot, up against the great wall, are built the lodging-houses and club-rooms for monks and pilgrims who may come in from all parts of the country. These club-rooms are curious: the monks form themselves in societies or unions, and each such has its separate and distinct meeting-house. On the wall itself, and sometimes on top of one of the main buildings, may be found *chortens*, or pagodas.

Over the monastery is set the chief lama, who in case of the larger and more important monastic communities is himself an incarnate buddha, a personage of considerable power, and under him a number of assistant chief lamas. The *ge-longs* and other inmates of the monasteries form influential bodies politically and do not refrain from violence in espousing this or that particular cause. Their numbers are extraordinary, the two large monasteries near Lhasa containing about six thousand (Sera) and ten thousand (Drepung) inmates.

While the chief monasteries are largely endowed with lands, and are mainly stone-built—though sometimes sun-dried brick is used in construction—and imposing, the lesser *gompas* are poor, mean, and of no architectural importance, being ofttimes insignificant collections of buildings, or just a square block housing a few monks.

Shortly after passing this point we left the main river course and went up a side valley which led to the right. If we had followed the river to its mouth, we should have reached the Brahmaputra some miles to the west of Shigatse, and so we decided to take a short cut which led over a mountain pass. Once more the road lay gradually uphill, but it was many weary hours before we reached the apex of the slope and the pass itself. On the way I commenced to be beset by new troubles, this time of a physical nature.

So far my constitution had stood up wonderfully

well under the enormous physical strain to which it had been subjected. I had appeared to be able to stand even more than my servants. The early symptoms of dysentery which I had experienced in the passes had worn off, I had hoped for good, but suddenly that afternoon they returned with increased vigor, and each new spasm seemed to sap all my strength. I began to fall behind the others, and only by a terrific effort of will was I able to force myself to go on in the endeavor to keep my party in sight.

To make matters worse, my feet began to suffer fearfully from blisters. The wetting which my shoes and my feet had had earlier in the day was probably responsible for most of the damage, for nothing makes for blisters more than walking in wet shoes. Finally two of the blisters broke, and the agony caused by the shoes' rubbing against the raw flesh was too much for me: I pulled my shoes off and began to walk with bare feet. This scarcely improved matters, as the sharp stones cut my feet badly, and the lacerated soles left bloody footprints behind them. As night drew on and the sun disappeared, the cold nipped at my toes, and I was afraid I should fall into the plight of poor Diogenes. But the terror of being left behind drove me on, and at last I came up with the others, who had waited for me just on the near side of the actual pass.

The last two hundred yards was very precipitous, and we had great difficulty in getting our loaded animals over it. Poor London, the mule which had been limping for several days past, found the task impossible, and so we had to unload her and distribute her burden over our own already overtaxed backs, faithful old Lhaten taking the bulk of it.

After incredible exertion we eventually reached the top of the pass, known as the Nambula. The whole of the Brahmaputra basin lies much lower than any other part of Tibet, so that even this steep pass was only 14,800 feet above sea-level.

Unlike the gradual ascent on the hither or south side, the descent proved extraordinarily steep and very stony. As I was now able to move only very gingerly, I whispered to Lhaten to go on ahead with Satan and our companions, while the syce, Diogenes, and I brought up the rear-guard. This was done, and when at last I got to the bottom of the slope and arrived at the village of Nambudzong I found that the main party had been there some time and that everything was in readiness for our accommodation.

The name Nambudzong implies the existence of a dzong, or castle, but I found that this was only a memory of the distant past, that the fortress had long fallen into decay, and that the place was no longer the center of an administration.

Unlike most Tibetan houses, which are built *around* a courtyard, the rest-house in which we were staying resembled more an English farm-house, in that it was one compact building with the stables and storehouse in a wall-inclosed yard on the outside.

On arriving I found that the house was filled with people and that one of the parties within consisted of a Kampa Dzong official and his suite on his way back from Shigatse. I was so very anxious to avoid any such person and felt so ill and so weary after our journey of over thirty miles, that I was in no mood for carrying on my disguise, and so I decided that, on the excuse of overcrowding, Diogenes and I should spend the next night in one of the stables near to the animals, and this plan was duly carried out. Poor Lhaten must have noticed my disgust for the raw flesh which I was supposed to eat, and he managed, in secret, to grill me some meat, mutton of course, which was so well done that it thoroughly disguised the offensive putrid taste which it otherwise would have had.

Not long afterwards I fell into a long, heavy, but troubled sleep, interspersed with nightmares. I began to cry out in my sleep, and Diogenes, slumbering beside me, was awakened by the noise. In the circumstances, he displayed more sense than I had given him credit for by waking me up lest I should make some sound which might betray my nationality.

The whole party was, I think, exhausted by the endeavor of the previous day, for the next morning we made, for Tibetans, a late start, it being nearly six o'clock before we moved off. Before our departure the syce, to whom I had communicated my troubles, bought for me a new pair of Tibetan boots, as I thought they would be softer than the shoes I had been wearing.

In a few instances the Tibetan boots are made out of leather. Those which Diogenes had bought in Kampa Dzong were of this order; and of a different shape and size but also of leather are the boots which most of the monks around Lhasa wear; but for the most part Tibetan boots are made of closely woven wool, with or without a thin layer of leather on the sole.

They reach to a point a little below the knee, and are held up by two thin woolen bands often prettily embroidered. The major part of these woolen boots is dyed red, but is frequently faced with sections of other colors. Variations in color have in most cases a ceremonial significance. Priests' boots when made of wool are of one pattern and color, those made for laymen of another. In most cases those made for women are faced with green, a color that seems reserved for the fairer sex.

These woolen boots are very comfortable for wear indoors, but are less adequate for outdoor service. They absorb and retain water. The wind seems to penetrate through the pores of the wool, and finally the thinness of the sole makes one feel every stone and pebble over which one walks.

My new boots were indeed an improvement, but even they were so painful that I once more tried the experiment of going barefooted. But not for long. The reopening, by the stones, of the wounds of the preceding day was even more of a misery than the Tibetan boots, and so I pulled them on again.

Diogenes fared even worse than I did. The long journey had told cruelly on his frost-bitten feet, and though he uttered scarcely a murmur and did his utmost to keep up with us, he began to lag behind. This did not please Satan at all, and he turned his pony round and riding back gave the miserable boy several lashes with his whip and threatened even more dire punishments unless he kept up with the party. I felt deeply outraged at this callousness, but with our companions standing by there was nothing which I could do, and so I had to content myself with whispering to him as he came up that however severe his trials might be at present, I would liberally reward him when the adventure had come to an end.

We soon found ourselves in a wide, flat valley, and the country assumed a more prosperous appearance. Another mile or two further on, our road ran into and joined the great highway which runs from Shigatse to the west. Along this rolls the stream of traffic which connects Central Tibet with the upper portions of the Brahmaputra River and the sacred Manasarowar Lakes, where go every year thousands of people on pilgrimage. Still further beyond this Tibetan Mecca the highway runs until it reaches Leh, in Ladak, and even into the dreamy valley of Kashmir.

It is indeed the highroad of enchantment, and once we were on it we met or were passed by a steady stream of traffic. There flew past us a swift government courier carrying messages and orders to far-away governors in the unknown West. We had no fear that he would stop to parley with us, for by a system of relay horses he was bound to cover a hundred miles a day. Buxom matrons, living in some village lying near, were returning from marketing in Shigatse, each covered with cheap trinkets and bright-colored beads, which she had purchased after enormous bargaining in some open stall. Some came riding sedately on ponies and mules, and others trudged sturdily along in twos and threes, and compared trinket with trinket, and talked volubly of the prices they had paid for each, and of the marvelous reductions they had secured as the result of their ready wit and voluble tongue. Then we would overtake a small body of Nepalese workers in metal, who had been sent for by the Grand Lama himself to cast a bell for his monastery, for which the cunning of his own craftsmen was not sufficient; then a body of Kashmiri Mohammedans, taking advantage of their proud privilege to bring rare goods in great mule caravans for sale to the aristocracy of Shigatse and Lhasa; pilgrims galore, going in either direction, spinning their prayer-wheels and telling their rosaries at a dizzy speed, monks and laymen alike. There came also trotting by on a long, lank mare the bursar of a monastery, lean and hard of face, out to collect rents for his establishment and to drive a cruel bargain as a money-lender on his own behalf.

Small caravans of every sort, with yaks, mules, ponies, and donkeys, passed by; donkeys were particularly noticeable, for in this part of Tibet local traffic is largely carried on by means of them. Tiny things they are, but many a peasant went riding by on one, the man twice the size of the animal and only having to stand up to be free of his mount; and last, but exceedingly interesting, a herd of sheep, also used to transport heavy loads, for Tibetan sheep are strong and are frequently used as beasts of burden.

The interest of the highway and its travelers helped to while away the long, dreary hours of the morning march, but I was nearly dropping from fatigue and weakness when at last we stopped at a little village not far from the famous Nartang monastery, which we could see quite clearly from the road.

Nartang owes its fame to its printing-press. Here are printed most of the books which are to be found in every respectable monastery throughout the land. Lhasa has also its printing press, and some Tibetan books are printed in the lama monastery of Peking, but neither of these places can vie with Nartang for fame.

Tibet has a large literature, but almost all of it of a religious character, and a large part of it consists of translations of works originally written in India in Sanskrit. The originals of these works have in most cases been lost, so that the students of ancient Indian literature, history, customs, and thought must turn to the Tibetan canon for purposes of research.

There are a large number of isolated and individual works, but most of the better known and more authoritative works are incorporated in two collections or canons called Kangyur and Tengyur.

The Kangyur (lit. *bkah-gyur,* or the rendering of the word [of the Buddha himself]) consists of one hundred, sometimes printed in 108, volumes of approximately a thousand pages each and comprises 1083 separate works. All of these are translated from Sanskrit, a few indirectly through Chinese, and are supposed to be a record of the actual discourses of the historical Buddha, though higher criticism will not allow this claim for an instant. Thirteen volumes deal with the Vinaya or canon law affecting the discipline and organization of the monks, while the remaining volumes consist of very long-winded discourses upon religion and morals.

The Tengyur (lit. *bstan-gyur* or rendering of the [traditional] teachings) is usually printed in 225 volumes, and is the official commentary and interpretation-giver of the Kangyur. This collection also consists of a large number of separate works. Many of them were composed by Nagarjuna, Asangha, Vasubandhu, and other great Indian Buddhist philosophers, while others consist of original works written by prominent Tibetan worthies. This collection shows us something of the rational and philosophical side of Buddhism. The crudities and absurdities of the Kangyur are softened down. In addition to works of a purely exegetical and philosophical nature, it contains books dealing with music, grammar, rhetoric, prosody, medicine, mechanics and alchemy, all of which formed part of Buddhism in its medieval development.

Most of these works were translated or composed between the ninth and the fourteenth centuries A.D., the period of Tibet's greatest literary achievements. Modern literature is very scrappy and inferior, and consists chiefly of pious tracts and biographies of various important lamas.

As we were halting only for an hour, we had once more to content ourselves with eating in the courtyard, instead of withdrawing to the privacy of a room above. One of the sons of the *nemo,* a youth of about eighteen years of age, hearing that we came from Sikkim, took a lively interest in us but in quite a friendly way. In fact, he was infected with the *Wanderlust* and asked Satan to engage him as an extra servant in order that he might travel along and see the country and eventually return with us to Sikkim. From Sikkim he had even thoughts of going down into India, where the terrible *Chiling kyi mi* (foreigners, i.e., English) live, and he wanted to know if we had met any and whether they were as terrible as all the stories of them represented. I rather liked the boy for his general brightness and interest in life, in contrast to the sodden, sullen stupidity which characterizes most of the population, but to take him along with us was out of the question; even Satan, in spite of his high-handedness, saw this and put him off.

Diogenes, the *gyepo,* and I departed earlier than the others, leaving them to pay the bill and to reload the animals. As we passed down the village street I felt so stupefied by the prospect of another long afternoon's march that I scarcely noticed a *möndang,* or prayer-wall, in the middle of the street and was about to pass to the right of it. I had still my dark goggles on, and the old man, believing implicitly in the story that I was still half blind as the result of the snow, shouted out to me that the prayer-wall existed and that I was passing it on the wrong side. This startled me into my right senses, and I quickly swerved to the left, passing the sacred wall in orthodox fashion.

In Tibet respect to a person or thing is shown by always keeping it on one's right-hand side. In circumambulating any religious edifice, and this is considered an act of great merit, it is proper always to pass round from left to right, "clockwise," which is also the direction in which the prayer-wheel should be turned. Any deviation from this rule is considered an act of outrageous blasphemy.

These prayer-walls are very common in Tibet. They consist of a thick stone or sun-dried brick wall, of varying length, sometimes a few yards long, and sometimes stretching for a quarter of a mile or more. They are frequently placed in the middle of the highroad, so that travelers may acquire merit merely by passing them in the prescribed way. In some cases prayer-wheels are set in the sides, and in nearly all cases, the sides are ornamented with sacred inscriptions, or with bas-relief sculptures representing various buddhas and bodhisattvas.

It is considered an act of great merit to erect such a prayer-wall, so that they are to be seen in the neighborhod of nearly every village.

Thereafter, the course of the afternoon's march went fairly smoothly. The other members of the party caught us up, and we journeyed on and on, though at every moment I thought I would have to give up.

A great sturdy Dropa fell in with us and journeyed with us a good part of the way. Instead of the ordinary clothes made of woven wool which are worn by the townsfolk and the villagers, this fellow's clothes were entirely of sheeps' fur, the skin on the outside and the fur next to his skin. His coat was also much shorter than those worn by the townsmen, only reaching to his hips, so that his trousers, of the same material, were very much in evidence.

He was nearly six feet tall, carried a long sword, and was extremely fierce-looking, and most of our party were much afraid of him, but he soon embarked in amiable conversation and gradually told us his life-story. He confessed that in addition to looking after his flocks on the Chang Tang he had frequently acted as a brigand and had amassed quite a little fortune in that way. Recently he had fallen very ill, and, believing his disease to be a punishment from the gods, he had decided to come on pilgrimage to Shigatse and thereby wipe out his sins, without in any way having to get rid of his illgotten gains.

He kept alongside of us for some time, but as our progress was slow and he wanted to get to the city before nightfall he left us later.

In the middle of the plain we came across another wide, shallow river, but this time, learning by experience, I took off my boots before crossing it, and consequently did not experience the same ill effects as the preceding day. Later in the afternoon, we came to the end of the valley plain and had to ascend another pass. This was not nearly so difficult or so steep, but as the result of the dysentery my weakness had come on me so fast that I had to hold on to the tail of Satan's pony and be almost pulled up the incline.

Once we were over the top, however, I felt rewarded for all the misery I had undergone, for there at the end of the valley, only some five miles away, we could see the huge mass of buildings constituting Trashilhumpo, the famous Shigatse monastery. The city of Shigatse itself was hidden behind a hill a mile or so further on, but I knew then that at last we had come to the end of the first stage of our journey and that even if we never got to Lhasa the adventure would not have been altogether in vain.

CHAPTER VI

SHIGATSE AND BEYOND

AT the foot of the monastery there is a tiny village. In this our two Tibetan companions had a house. By this time we had become such friends that they invited us to make use of it during our stay in Shigatse instead of going to a rest-house in the city proper. The invitation we gladly accepted, and, having covered the intervening five miles, we put up at our new quarters. We decided to spend the whole of the next day in Shigatse in order to give ourselves and the animals a much-needed rest. We thus had the opportunity of looking about the city and entering the monastery, to which so many thousands of pilgrims come every year.

Central Tibet consists of the two provinces of Tsang in the west and U (spelled Dbugs) in the east. The capital of the former is Shigatse, of the latter Lhasa. Not long ago the two provinces were practically independent states, and the abbot of the Trashilhumpo monastery is still the titular king of Tsang, though now the Lhasa officials have managed to secure complete control over this province, as well as the others. Politically, therefore, the Dalai-lama is greater than the Trashi-lama, but religiously the two great abbots rank as equal. On account of the greater spiritual character of the Trashi-lama, many Tibetans regard the Dalai-lama as merely the secular and the Trashi-lama as the spiritual ruler of Tibet. I was therefore delighted to hear that he would pass in procession through the streets that afternoon, and by standing among the worshiping crowd I managed to catch a glimpse of him. He was a man with a very gentle and refined appearance, with a look almost of shyness that fitted in well with his character, as this was reported, and with his post. The Trashilhumpo monastery is generally considered the best conducted in Tibet. It is famous for its learning and attracts numerous monkish students from all parts of the country, who seek to obtain the highly prized degree which it bestows. At present it numbers between four and five thousand monks.

On the same day we purchased an aged donkey in the hope of lightening our load for the remainder of the journey. In the evening our hosts arranged to give us a farewell banquet. The banquet consisted of larger quantities of the same food as heretofore, this being washed down by copious drafts of liquor. The Tibetans have two staple intoxicating drinks. The first is chang, a mild beer brewed from barley, very refreshing after a long journey. The second is arak (not to be confused with spirits of the same name known in other parts of the world), the distilled form of chang. This is frightfully strong and generally proves too much even for hardened drinkers.

The arak very nearly proved our undoing. The evening started in very jovial fashion. Broad jests with hilarious Tibetan folk-songs followed one another in quick succession, and the whole company soon became very maudlin. Both Lhaten and Satan chose to drink only arak, despising the weaker chang. They soon lost control of themselves and, having become hopelessly drunk, chose this moment to start a violent quarrel. From words they came to blows and in the end had to be forcibly separated. In the heat of their anger they forgot their assumed rôles, and both appealed to me as master to settle their dispute. I was nearly wild with terror of being discovered, and if our hosts had not been such simple-minded folk they would soon have grasped the true situation, but in the end everything calmed down.

It was nearly one o'clock before everything was quiet once more, but a calm sleep was impossible. I had no idea how much of the situation the spectators might have understood, and it was possible that they were only waiting for daylight to inform the Shigatse authorities of their suspicions. This fear grew so strong in me that although I was mortally tired, as soon as it began to get light and long before the actual sunrise took place, I got up and whispered to Lhaten that it was imperative for us to get on the move at once. We got the mules and the new donkey loaded and only woke Satan when we were on the point of departure, and then hoisted him into his saddle and were on the road before he was sufficiently awake to expostulate effectively.

Our road led right under the monastery and through

the city. Early as it was, when we passed by the monastery, we could hear the low hum from a service taking place in the great central hall—the services in a properly conducted monastery begin between three and four in the morning—and we constantly met pilgrims making a circumambulation of the whole monastery, in the prescribed "clockwise" fashion. As they did so some turned their prayer-wheels and others told their rosaries, the rosary, generally with 108 beads, being much valued by every branch of Tibetan Buddhism. Some of the devotees were making the round at great speed while others stopped to make frequent prostrations.

We then passed through the heart of the city, once more seeing the great dzong, which towers on high, and then struck to the right down to the Nyang River.

To the right of us lay the Chinese graveyard, where several hundred Chinese lay buried, an apt symbol of the extinct suzerainty of China over Tibet. Some of these graves were old, and covered the bodies of the Chinese who had suffered a natural death during the old days prior to 1912, when there was a garrison of Chinese soldiers and a small body of Chinese traders in Shigatse. An even larger number of graves, however, were filled by the Chinese inhabitants who were killed in the Tibetan revolt of 1912, when Tibet declared her absolute independence of China and gave effect to this declaration by killing as many of the Celestials as possible and forcing the remainder to return immediately to the territory of the new Chinese republic.

For the most part these graves marked the resting-places of middle- and lower-class Chinese. When a high official died his coffin was generally transported back to China, for it is the highest ambition of every Chinaman, however far he may wander during his lifetime, to sleep the long sleep of the dead in his native land.

Curiously enough, there is no Tibetan graveyard in Shigatse or for that matter anywhere else, for the Tibetans do not go in for burials. A few of the very highest lamas are embalmed and are then gilded to be placed in some temple to serve as an object of worship. A few other lamas, of high but lesser rank, are cremated in accordance with the old Indian Buddhist custom, but wood is too scarce in Tibet to allow cremation to be practised extensively, and so the Tibetans have evolved their own methods of disposing of the dead.

In certain instances the flesh is fed to the pigs and dogs; kites and vultures join in the feast. The dogs are pariahs which roam about every Tibetan town and village scavenging. They are far different from the fierce mastiff breed of canine used as guardians and in hunting.

The graveyards are special places set aside for funeral ceremonies. Here the dead bodies are brought out, spread on a large stone slab, face downward, and hacked to pieces, to be fed to the carrion birds and animals. As, to insure a good rebirth, it is considered advisable that the corpse be devoured by birds rather than by quadrupeds, members of a rascally tribe of beggars known as Ragyabas, who haunt the cemeteries, will hire themselves out to keep off the four-footed scavengers till the kites and vultures put in their appearance, which is not tardy, for they sense the dead from afar and foregather quickly.

The first portions hacked off the body are fed to the oldest vulture of the flock, which will waddle forward to receive its reward, when called. The birds are extremely tame and respond individually to the cry of the officiating lama. The Ragyabas complete the dismembering of the body. Sometimes the remains are buried, but this is an expensive business, though more frequently the bones, and the scraps left after the pigs have gorged, will be interred where possible.

Before long we reached the river and crossed the clumsy bridge which spans it. Both Shigatse and Gyangtse stand on the Nyang River; that morning I saw the same stream through which I had waded at Gyangtse, several months earlier.

Shigatse is supposed to be situated at the junction of the Nyang and Brahmaputra Rivers, but really it is placed on the Nyang itself, four miles from its confluence. The Tibetans in spite of their architectural precocity have never arrived at the use of the arch. All their doorways are supported by a single beam, resting on two pillars. This has proved no great handicap in their house-building, but in bridges it means that a single span can never be more than ten yards across, so that supporting mounds have to be placed in the riverbed every few feet. When the stream is rapid these supports are not infrequently washed away and have to be replaced.

This particular bridge is called the Sampa Shar, or eastern bridge, and is some 350 yards in length and seven or eight yards in breadth. Slabs of earth-covered stones are placed on the long wooden boards spanning the earthen supports.

Satan was still in a very bad temper. He must have realized how much he had jeopardized the adventure, for he took refuge in abusing the others. Fortunately he and I were alone at the time and I purposely kept him ahead of the party until such time as every one should have forgotten the events of the preceding night.

I had a very good mind to tell him what I thought of him, but I felt that to lose my temper in the circumstances would be useless, and so I contented myself with a few delicately phrased hints as to how such things should be done in the future.

What particularly angered me was that he decided to change hats with me that morning. Without a word of warning—I was walking beside his pony—he seized my hat and placed his own on my head, saying that as mine was the finer-looking cap it was necessary for him to wear it, and nothing that I could say would make him give it back to me. What made my cap so satisfactory was the fur flaps, which could be pulled down and which, though something of a luxury for a coolie, served very effectively to mask my head and face. Satan's cap was without these flaps, and I felt much less safe in it. It is curious how much of the ostrich there is in man; as long as my head was swathed in leather flaps I felt content.

When at last our transport and the other servants caught up with us, a few Billingsgate compliments were hurled at one another by the two parties; but the long morning walk had dulled the edge of our tempers, and I managed to patch up the peace. Fortunately we were alone. Our two Shigatse friends we had left behind, and we had not yet fallen in with another caravan, so that at least for the time being we did not have to wash our dirty linen in public.

We did, indeed, meet a number of people on the road, but for the most part these were local travelers, and we met no one who was either going to or returning from Lhasa, for we had once more departed from the highway and were taking a short cut. The official roadway from Shigatse to Lhasa makes a long detour. Instead of following the Brahmaputra River, the couriers and most travelers go down from Shigatse to Gyangtse, and then from Gyangtse strike once more northeast to Lhasa. But I had no intention of passing through Gyangtse again, and so we stuck to the short cut, which for some extraordinary reason is very little used.

I had been so busy in Shigatse trying to see and learn as much as possible that my stay there had given me very little real rest, and the excitement of the previous night had done me little good physically. As a result, not many miles after leaving Shigatse, I became so weary that I began to stumble in my tracks. Even Satan noticed how near I was to the end of my resources, and when we came to a long stretch where no one was visible he suggested that I ride the pony for a bit, while he walked. This sudden display of warmheartedness on his part really surprised me, and I took it for an indirect apology for the rumpus he had caused the preceding evening.

I gladly accepted his invitation, but it seemed as if some angry fate was against me, for I had scarcely gone a hundred yards when London, the ailing mule, suddenly succumbed. She had seemed much better for the rest and good food in Shigatse, so that her sudden collapse was very unexpected. We had now lost three out of the six animals with which we had started, and we were still several days away from Lhasa. The load which our new donkey was carrying consisted largely of bundles which the two remaining mules were now too weak to bear, and so there was nothing to be done except for me to climb down from my seat on the pony and to put the mule's load on to his back, while all of us walked. We stood over the fallen mule for some time, trying to find out if anything could be done; but shortly afterward she died, her last act being to launch a vigorous kick at the syce's shins. This had its required effect, and the syce danced around in agony, so that I think the mule must have died happy.

Thereafter our march continued for mile after mile without incident. The feeling that I *had* to get on kept me on my feet. Thick heads and swollen, thirsty tongues made the journey unpleasant for the others as well, but it was noon before we came to a halting-place. This consisted of a small farmer's hut, one-storied and indescribably filthy, but we were allowed to enter the main room of the house adjoining the courtyard instead of remaining outside, as was usual for a midday halt, and I lay down for an hour and rested my weary bones. In the middle of the room there was already a pot of tea boiling, so that we did not even have to light a fire before sitting down to a meal. The mixed cooking of Shigatse was behind us, and we returned once more to a diet of tea, barley-flour, and raw meat.

The tea we drank out of the bowls we brought with us. Every Tibetan carries his own tea-cup with him, along with other articles in his capacious bosom. This is curiously in accord with modern sanitary ideas of individual drinking-cups.

Satan, as the master, drank his tea out of a very elaborate affair. The top or cover and the stand or saucer consisted of finely beaten silver, while the cup itself (without handles, of course, for no Tibetan cups have handles) consisted of earthenware. In some cases the cups of the wealthy are made from porcelain, from glass, or even from precious jade. As a servant I had to be content with a simple wooden bowl with neither top nor stand.

Before leaving we purchased from the good housewife another donkey, thinking thereby to ease our journey. Once more our hopes ran high, but before long we found that we had been badly done. Our new friend became more and more slow in his paces and finally refused to go any further. We lightened his load and applied our whips, but he seemed to remain in a state of meditation on the ineffable. After we had gone only two or three miles, and shortly after we had passed through the village of Pengma, the crisis came; our obstinate purchase refused to be dragged or flogged another step further.

I thought perhaps he had been overworked earlier in the day, before he was sold to us, or that he had not been given sufficient food, and so after a long discussion we agreed to let him have a night's respite, and all of us turned back and halted for the night at the village of Pengma.

The villagers here turned out to be an unusually surly lot. We tried at two or three rest-houses to get lodgings, but they were already crowded, and we were ordered gruffly away. Finally we were taken in at a place which was already housing a number of monks on their way back from Shigatse to their own monastery some miles further down the river. They were drinking very heartily and making such a noise that I thought it better to camp in one of the stalls in the courtyard rather than attempt the common room with them. Once back in their own monastery they would have to lead a much calmer life, where drinking was strictly prohibited, so that they were probably having a last fling before returning to comparative respectability.

Even in their festivities, however, they remained sullen. Each village in Tibet seems to strike a keynote of its own, and certainly that of Pengma was sullenness. I was disturbed to find one embarrassing exception to this rule. The *nemo,* or landlady, of the rest-house, was a portly woman of about forty years of age. In accordance with Tibetan custom she had already five legal husbands, but she seemed, for some extraordinary reason, to find my appearance very pleasing, so that in addition to playing the part of lama to my servants, and that of a servant to the outside world, I had now to take on a new part and play Joseph to Potiphar's wife.

In Tibet winking, the "glad eye," and kissing are unknown. It can be seen from this how backward is the state of Tibetan culture. I had often wondered how flirtation was carried on, but I had no intention of finding out by too much first-hand experience, and so I extricated myself from my difficulty as soon as I could. The filthiness which my lady friend shared with all Tibetan women made it more than easy to resist temptation.

Both polyandry and polygyny are practised in Tibet, and monogamy has but few supporters. The different practices are somewhat affected by conditions in various parts of the country, but the traditional joint ownership of family property is probably the strongest factor in fixing marital relationships.

It is common for the wife taken by the eldest son of the family to become the joint property of all the brothers, who share responsibility. Should a brother leave the family, however, he is not entitled to compensation in respect to his share in the wife. In fact, the relationship of the younger brothers to the wife exists only so long as they remain in the family. There are occasions when the father or uncle of the husband claims to live with the wife; and sometimes, but as a general rule only in higher circles, the father's part possession and marital rights are recognized. It is less frequent that a woman acknowledges husbands of two or more different families, but examples of this form of polyandry are also to be found.

It is said that the origin of the Tibetan form of polyandry, with its desire to preserve family property intact, was with the Kams, and that the natives of the other Tibetan provinces of Tsang and U developed the practice later. This may well be so, for while among the Kams it is to all intents and purposes universal, in the other two provinces it is not so widely general. The women-folk defend polyandry on the ground that it gives the female more importance in the community, and while polygyny is not unknown, the women of the higher grades rather despise the comparatively helpless women of India and the polygamic rule under which they live.

It is not a difficult matter to obtain divorce in Tibet, provided the injured party desiring to sever the matrimonial bond is prepared to pay for the accommodation. The divorce fees vary according to circumstances, but are governed by definite laws. Should the husband desire to rid himself of his wife, and make charges against her which are groundless, and the wife is still content to live with her husband, he must pay to her twelve gold sho (equal to about ninety rupees), and in addition make over to her six pounds of barley for every day, and an equal amount for every night she has been with him since the wedding-day. All presents made to the wife since the wedding-day, or a sum equivalent to their value, must be given to her, and she may retain all jewelry given her by her relatives.

In the event that it is the wife seeking divorce, and the husband is found blameless and prepared to continue living with his wife, to obtain her freedom she must pay an amount of money or goods equal to double her settlement; but should the husband's innocence remain in doubt the wife may pay him only a suit of clothes and a pair of boots, bed-carpet and rug, and a scarf, the husband handing his wife a scarf or some other article agreed on.

The husband takes the male offspring of the marriage and the wife the female offspring; and the man, if well enough off, may be charged to contribute to the upkeep of his daughters; while, should the wife have property she will have to consider the welfare of her sons.

These general arrangements apply more to the upper classes; they are much modified in the lower ranks. Where a man of aristocratic rank has married a woman of meaner grade, but with a distinct understanding as to equal possessions, the property is divided at dissolution of marriage with a regard to the degree of blame on each side. There are, however, so many forms of marriage that these terms are liable to considerable modification. For instance, the master decides the destiny of serfs, and where a female of this class marries she may be cast off with one sixth part of her husband's goods whenever she fails to be an asset in his household. Then there are the temporary, generally pleasure, marriages, which may at any time be dissolved by an equal division of property. Divorce does not invalidate the man or woman's chances of remarriage. The one and the other are facilitated by the circumstances which prevail.

I was now in completely unknown country, unmapped even by the native spies who were sent out during the last century by the Indian Government to make

Sacred *chortens*, or shrines, on the road to Shigatse

Tibetans with the native four-horned ram

Procession with palanquin of Trashi-lama, Shigatse

A typical Tibetan village

secret surveys of Tibet. Consequently I made a great point of noticing as many geographical details as possible. Because of my disguise, a regular survey was out of the question, but as it was a moonlight night, I stayed awake long after the others had fallen asleep in order to make some sketch-maps of the country through which we had passed and to enter up the events of the last few days in my diary. Such things had to be done in this way or not at all. In the daytime I was constantly in the sight of various Tibetans, and at night-time there was no artificial light. Even so, great secrecy was needed and every time any one moved in his sleep I had to hide away my writings under my blankets, fearing lest he wake.

Our journey this day had been so short, only sixteen miles or so, that we were anxious to make up for lost time and once more started off at 2:30 the next morning. We kept on at a steady pace until daybreak, having only the vaguest idea of where we were going except what we got from the murmur of the river to the left of us. Early as we were, we yet met occasional parties on the road, donkey caravans for the most part. The Tibetan seems to be as casual about his time of traveling as about his eating. If he feels in the mood he travels all night and sleeps all day, and there was never a single hour of the night or day in which I could be certain of meeting no one on the road.

Our chief difficulty was with the occasional small streams which run into the Brahmaputra. These were nearly all frozen fast, and we had our usual trouble in getting over the slippery surface, though we had become somewhat expert at the game by now and managed to get our caravan over without accident.

Not long before daylight we ceased to hear the river, but as we seemed to be following a well-beaten track we went straight on. Dawn showed us that we had a low line of hills instead of the Brahmaputra on our left. This worried us, but thinking that we were making a detour we continued our march for another tour. At the end of this time we met a peasant who told us that we had quite lost the way and were going up a side valley, and so we had to retrace our steps some distance, going back to the mouth of the valley.

We lost about seven miles in this way. Satan, as usual, lost his temper and blamed everybody but himself for the misfortune. Finally he decided to vent his spleen on Diogenes and began to beat him unmercifully with his stick. The Tibetan peasant was still about, so that I dared give no vigorous command; but as it was impossible for me to stay there and let the boy be so cruelly beaten, I threw myself in between the pair, and this forced Lhaten and the syce to come to the rescue. They dragged Satan off swearing all sorts of vengeance.

Satan was not the only one who seemed to be upset at the fruitlessness of the early morning journey. The miserable donkey which we had bought the day before had been coaxed to come so far, but of a sudden he recommenced his old tricks and refused to budge one step more. Flogging was of no avail. I thought he must be shamming and twisted his tail to make him show an interest in life but even this proved fruitless, and after literally dragging him along as so much dead weight for another mile we gave it up as a bad job and abandoned him by the roadside, once more adding another load—that which he had been carrying—to our own. Under these circumstances even Satan was forced to walk in order that his pony might carry a portion of our burden, but he was careful to point out that it would be inadvisable for him to bear any load himself, as such a course would be entirely out of keeping with the rôle it was necessary for him to play.

Arrived back at the Brahmaputra, we were able to strike out once more on the right road; our peasant informant stayed with us up to this point. I now discovered why we had gone astray.

For the most part mountain ranges ran parallel to the river-bed on each side some three or four miles away from the water's edge, but occasionally a mountain spur would run out at right angles from the general range and come down near the main stream. This made the country bear a resemblance to the general basin formation, except that we saw only half-basins, as the river had eaten through a gap in the mountain divide between the basins.

Here the hill came right down to the water's edge, and we had actually to wade through the stream in order to get around it.

Not long after rounding the spur we came to another plain, set in which was a large monastery. This was very interesting to me because it was the first monastery I had seen which was not built on the side of a hill. It is also quite a famous place historically, and it is said that its library contains very old and interesting manuscripts.

The ancient manuscripts of Tibet consist of writings in both Sanskrit and Tibetan, very occasionally in Chinese. Contrary to popular supposition there are no Pali manuscripts in the country, as Buddhism had long rid itself of the Pali literary tradition before Tibet came under its influence.

Nearly all of these remains, if of any value, date from the period previously mentioned, the ninth to the fourteenth century A.D. To the scholar they are chiefly of value because many of them were not incorporated in either of the two great canonical collections, the Kangyur and the Tengyur, and are otherwise unknown.

The greatest interest is attached to the Sanskrit manuscripts which were brought from India. In many cases these were the originals from which the canonical translations were made, and as these originals have elsewhere disappeared, they are eagerly sought by bibliophiles in every part of the world.

It was quite impossible to attempt to secure any such manuscripts on the present occasion, and we continued on our way until we came to the little village of Rugu, where we halted for our breakfast-lunch, or "brunch."

I was so tired that instead of stopping in the courtyard I insisted on going to the living-room upstairs, where I lay down while Lhaten prepared the food, for I felt too ill to act in my capacity of assistant cook.

Fortunately there were no other travelers about, but later the nemo, or landlady, came up to talk to us and to tell us all about the local scandal.

She had a good deal to say about the local abbot, who was considered to be an incarnation of deity, and the troubles which he was having.

He had of course been chosen as the true incarnation and appointed abbot when he was still an infant, and during his minority the power had been exercised by one of the senior monks. Even when the young "divine ruler" came of age, the regent was very unwilling to renounce his power, and a bitter enmity sprang up between the two as to who was to have the real control of the affairs of the monastery.

The regent as the older and craftier man had proved successful and in wrath the incarnate abbot had resigned his post and left the temple.

I was very much interested to learn that an incarnate and reincarnate abbot could resign his job, and asked our gossipy informant what had become of him.

She answered that he had received an invitation from another monastery to become its head, and had ordained that thereafter he would be reborn as the abbot of the new temple, rather than as the ruler of the temple from which he had been ejected.

This little incident was of great interest to me, as it threw fresh light on the way in which the Tibetans regard and regulate the institution of reincarnated divine rulers.

Before leaving Rugu we tried to get another donkey, but our bargain of the previous day had warned us to be on our guard, and in this mood we could not find an animal which was to our satisfaction. All really usable and salable country-side animals are sent to the animal market in the near-by large towns, in this case Shigatse, and we found it a hopeless task looking for suitable beasts in the villages.

We had brought with us the wooden pack-saddle of the dead mule, hoping to find another mount on which to use it, and when I realized the unlikelihood of getting another suitable transport-animal I told Lhaten to sell it. We discovered that pack-saddles were a drug on the market, but as ours was of precious wood we finally disposed of it as fire-wood, receiving several trangkas for it. This stretch of Tibetan territory along the banks of the Brahmaputra, however, is much better off for fuel than most parts of the country, although, of course, lacking in trees. We saw along the wayside a quantity of thorn growing, and we found that this was largely used for fuel in place of the more general yak-dung, particularly as yaks were rare in this part of Tibet and the dung of mules, horses, and donkeys was much less serviceable.

After an hour's rest we again took to the road. Once more we had to round a spur of hills which ran down to the river's edge and again found on the other side a broad flat basin. During the afternoon we were much troubled by the heat. The Brahmaputra River valley is the warmest part of Tibet. The nights continued to be bitterly cold, but at midday the direct rays of the sun made it hotter even than India. It was impossible to touch any exposed object with the naked hand, so scorching did it become. Of course, it was only those spots directly exposed to the sun where this great heat prevailed. In sheltered and shady places the cold was almost as great as at night. This great difference in the temperature at the same time and place, according to whether one was in or out of the direct sunshine, was one of the most extraordinary things experienced in Tibet.

On many occasions the temperature would be thirty degrees below zero at night-time and 110 or 120 degrees above at midday.

The heat, however, is felt only under the direct rays of the sun, as the heat in the rarefied atmosphere does not radiate, and in the hottest part of the day we would frequently find that our tea would freeze to a solid block of ice inside of a dwelling.

It was a curious feeling to stand with one foot in the shade and the other in the sun. One foot was in danger of frost-bite and the other of being scorched.

Our way seemed to continue endlessly; I began to feel worse and worse, and it seemed impossible for me to go on. I thought of stopping at a large farm-house we came upon near a large and curious back-water of the Brahmaputra which extended far into the plain; but, being told by a passing peasant that the regular resting-stage of Trangka was only a little distance off, we decided to push on. Keeping on for another two hours without seeing anything of the village, we asked another traveler where Trangka lay and received the same answer as had been given two hours previously. We were, in both instances, led to suppose it was only a stone's throw away, but it took still another hour's tramp to bring us in sight of our goal, and at that Trangka still five miles away.

The Tibetans are, indeed, extraordinarily inexact in their calculation of distance. For calculating distances, I heard mention of only three terms. One of these was *kosatsa,* literally the distance which the voice carries, but which in practice seemed to vary from one hundred to five hundred yards. The second was *tsapo* or *tsasa,* a half-march, ranging from five to ten miles, and finally a *shasa,* a full march, which meant anything from ten to twenty miles.

These were the only methods of computation used or understood by the peasantry. The religious literature employs a method of computation evolved by the ancient Indian Buddhists,[1] and occasionally more sophisticated officials would calculate distances in Chinese *li,* itself a variable quantity, or in English miles. They have learned of the mileage system from the milestones which are placed along the Gyangtse-Yatung road.

As regards time they are equally vague, though they have a larger number of terms. Among the phrases I heard most frequently employed in this connection were:

nyima, day-time.
tsen or *gongmo,* night-time.
chake-chik-pa, first cock-crow.
chake-nyipa, second cock-crow.
torang, just before dawn, "false dawn."
tse shar, sunrise, lit. "peak-shining."
shokke, early morning.

[1] For details *cf.* my "Manual of Buddhist Philosophy," Part One.

tsating, late morning.
nyin-gung, midday.
gongta, afternoon.
sa-rip, dusk.
nam-che, midnight.

Because of the greater exactitude of the European system of the measurement of time, the Tibetans who have come into contact with life in India have learned to understand and even employ European reckoning of the hours. Curiously enough this is quite irrespective of whether they have watches or not. A certain position of the sun in the sky means to them 3 P.M. and so on. I had brought with me a cheap Ingersoll, the only timepiece I had dared to have with the party (one or two Lhasa merchants have acquired such watches), but on entering Tibet I had given it to Satan to wear, as a watch was much more in keeping with his rôle than mine.

Even after, at length, we had caught sight of Trangka, it took a long time for us to reach it on account of my weakness. Lhaten insisted upon my taking a long drink of arak, which, he declared, was good for bowel troubles. Chang, the mild fermented form of barley, is supposed to be a laxative, while arak, the distilled form, has exactly the opposite effect and is, incidentally, supposed to be a sure cure for most internal disorders. A similar view is taken in various parts of Europe in regard to the efficacy of certain alcoholic beverages and spirits. Certainly in my case it worked temporary wonders. The taste of the arak was so vile

I could hardly get it down, and once down it seemed to burn my inside to such an extent that I was spurred into activity and managed to do the last couple of miles in record time. Satan, not troubling about any one else, had gone on ahead, and we found him installed in one of the neatest little rest-houses that I had yet seen.

Trangka is situated about a mile away from the edge of the river at the foot of a curiously isolated hill which rose up in the middle of the broad flat basin. On the top of the hill, instead of a castle, was a shrine, at which every morning and evening incense is burned. The ground around the village was so barren that even by cultivation no trees could be grown, and the population were forced to find their principal support in tourist traffic, with the result that the accommodation was much better than in many of the villages through which we had passed. Each house was only one story high, and the common room was opened directly on the courtyard. But inside the room there were two elevated mud daises to serve as bedsteads for better-class travelers. On these were spread thick, hard cushions, stuffed with wool, which, placed together, served as and looked like mattresses with a carpet thrown over them; one got a very pleasing divan effect. These mattress-cushions (*shuden*) are very common in the richer houses in Tibet, but this was the first time we had met with them, as the rest-houses at which we stayed were off the beaten track.

One of these divans we found occupied by a monk, who was on his way from Lhasa to Shigatse. The other, of course, was occupied by Satan, so that I got a better idea of what the divans looked like than of what they felt like.

The monk was the sole other occupant of the room. We found him busy chanting some religious books, but his tea-bowl was in front of him, and every five minutes he would stop and take a sip. He came to an end of his chant by and by and then asked us to give him some money, for which he would chant a long Sutra for our benefit. His request was by no means unusual. True Tibetans believe that one acquires great merit by the chanting of sacred books, and since the average man is too ignorant and too lazy to chant himself, he frequently hires a priest to perform his duty for him. This is one of the principal ways in which a priest makes his living.

The monks earn their livelihood in various ways, some of which are not at all compatible with their religious status, for they sometimes break out in bands and waylay and rob travelers. It happens also occasionally that a gang of the more turbulent monks will attack and plunder merchants and pillage villages.

The money and produce received by the monastery from various sources is not divisible among the inhabitants except in one or two instances, such, for example, as the *bu-la,* or fees received for performing funeral rites, and the alms which are given at harvest time to the "holy" men. Other revenue the individual monks receive are presents given by the rich in payment of the expensive ceremonies which follow some time after the death of a member of the family.

The monks have no definite income or salary, either from the monasteries or outside source. If their families are well-to-do, they may have allowances, and the cost of their education is borne by the family. In other cases, where the parents are landed proprietors, the inmate of the monastery will receive the produce of a field set aside, and called the *lama-i-shing* (lama's field). Such revenue is insufficient and must be supplemented by the monks' own earnings, a state of things which brings about much abuse of their powers. The means of augmenting allowances are various. If the monk be a full-fledged *ge-long,* he will be in request at marriages and other ceremonies; he will be called on in cases of sickness to recite prayers, and to be in attendance at births and on other occasions to cast horoscopes. For these services he receives payment in kind or money.

Many monks are money-lenders and carry on their usurious dealings, both in and outside the monastery, and charge high rates of interest.

After harvest, it is the custom for the monks to tour the districts about a monastery in small bands, chanting outside each house. The husbandmen present the singers with grain, and this is divided up in the monastery according to the degree, or grade, of the inmates.

Another means of obtaining additional goods is practised by lamas who waylay travelers in the village rest-houses and streets, demanding alms in return for their benediction; and some members of the fraternity hire themselves out to work in the fields for payment.

The monasteries own considerable property, their wealth being derived mainly from lands in the vicinity of the establishment. These lands are farmed by hereditary tenants, who pay no rent but deliver one third of all produce to the landlord—in this case, the monastic establishment. The delivery of this tribute is effected in various ways, sometimes direct by the husbandry, though more often by appointed collectors who, while engaged in gathering the produce, drive a thriving business, the profits of which they share with the overlords. These men travel round the villages and farms receiving the dues in wool, butter, and other goods, and sometimes coin. The collector then takes the opportunity to sell brick tea from China and such like articles, the poor tenants being compelled to purchase something. It happens also that where the ecclesiastics are the sole proprietors of the lands round about their establishments, practically taking in the territory of a whole government area, the *dzong-pon* or lay governor of the provincial dzong, or castle, is appointed as tax-gatherer; and as he, too, in such cases becomes a merchant, it can be readily understood that the tenantry suffer considerably, for the castellan has means at his disposal to enforce trade.

The revenues obtained by the monasteries is to be applied in three chief ways:

They are to be used for reparation of the fabric of the building and the acquirement of articles utilized in the temple, for the provision of certain provender, including beer, for the monks at festivals, and for procuring supplies of butter for the lamps kept burning before the holy images. But before account is rendered the higher officials secure choice pickings for themselves.

While the monks are exempt from all forms of taxation and impositions, the helpless husbandry have not finished with the overlords by mere rendering of the tribute. On them is the onus of providing transport-animals, cattle and ponies, to carry the borax, wool, and other goods in which the monastic authorities traffic, post-animals, and so on.

Monks are likely to get into a bad temper when a request for money is refused and so in this present case we gave our newly acquired friend a couple of trangkas, for which he bellowed another twenty minutes for our special benefit.

He was not the only one to pester us. The whole village seemed to swarm with mendicant minstrels. They swarmed into our courtyard and went through an amateur version of a devil-dance, wearing, however, only simple black masks. For orchestra they had only a huge drum and some brass cymbals, but these made a terrific noise. This even was drowned by the singing of the woman performers. A real devil-dance, of course, has only male actors, but in these village shows the majority of the players are women. Their performance seemed to last indefinitely, and we were forced to give them some coppers on the understanding that they break off and leave us in peace.

Later in the evening the monk left us; he was journeying by night, and we had the whole common room to ourselves. Lhaten suggested that I occupy the vacant dais, but I told him to do so, as I did not know when some other person might arrive.

I had been very glad to find ourselves alone, but I was soon brought to understand that Satan was even more glad, as it gave him an opportunity of making an attempt at blackmail. He saw how keen I was on getting to Lhasa and thought I would pay any price to avoid failure. Consequently he demanded a thousand rupees under threat of informing the local authorities who I was. My first instinct was to knock him down; but I knew that this would do no good, and so I was forced to make a compromise. I promised him two hundred rupees in the event of our getting to Lhasa, a sum less than I should have given him in any case had he worked satisfactorily. As the same time, I demanded from him a letter repeating his outrageous offer. Naïvely enough, he gave me this, whereupon I informed him that he was now in my power, and that if we were turned away or sent back from Lhasa as the result of any action of his, I could have him thrown into prison in India on the charge of blackmail. After matters had thus been satisfactorily settled, we composed ourselves for sleep.

The next morning we started off at our usual time, two hours before sunrise. We had first to skirt the curious Trangka hill and then strike out across the plain. This proved more uneven and rolling than usual and also very sandy, so sandy that the usual tracks which served as a guide to our road had been obliterated, and we were in fear that we would once more lose the way. I insisted, therefore, that we keep near the river-bank, as I felt that in this way we should not go so very far astray. This hindered progress a good deal, as the river winds in and out over the wide valley bed. Could we have only seen our direction we might have made many short cuts, but in the darkness vision was limited, and a comprehensive view of the valley formation was impossible.

The sunrise was particularly beautiful; a sandy soil, over which the air contains many particles of sand, always makes for beautiful sunrises and sunsets.

Once it was light we could go forward with greater freedom. In the morning my illness did not affect me so badly, and so we were able to put mile after mile behind us.

About eleven o'clock we came to the village of Namu, in the center of which was an important-looking monastery. Several of the monks were walking about the streets, and some of them stopped to look at us as we passed through. I heard later that this monastery has the reputation of being particularly reactionary. A small group of the monks came up to us, and one of their number began asking searching questions, for our Sikkimese costumes, which differ on certain points of detail from those worn in the central parts of Tibet, had probably awakened his suspicions.

After Satan's attempt at blackmail the preceding evening, I was very much afraid that he might give me away, in view of the threatening attitude which the monks assumed, but to do him justice, he was now firmly fixed in mind to get me to Lhasa. He was, moreover, a most consummate actor, and answered, or rather evaded, all questions most skilfully, so that we were allowed to pass on. It would seem, however, that our inquisitive friend was not completely satisfied, for Diogenes, who was lagging a little behind, was also stopped and asked not only about himself but about us. His simple mind had got the necessity of secrecy firmly fixed in it, and his naïve answers helped even better than all of Satan's volubility.

Our inquisitor was obviously a person of some standing in the temple, and was probably the *chö-trim-pa,* or provost, who sees that the monks conform in their actions to the Canon Law.

Every large monastery has a large number of office-holders. These offices and their titles, duties, and privileges differ considerably among the various orders, and many monasteries even inside one order depart a good deal from general custom, but among the Gelugpa, or reformed or yellow-hat monasteries, which now constitute the established church of Tibet, the usual monastic offices are more or less as follows:

At the head of the monastery is of course the abbot. He is either a reincarnation of divinity (*trü-ku*) and therefore selected as an infant, or is the specially appointed head (*kenpo*), whose selection generally lies in the hands of the authorities in Shigatse or Lhasa.

The organization of the temporal side of the monastery is in the hands of a treasurer or *chandzo,* and a high steward or *chinyer.* The welfare of the monks is looked after by a *lob-pön* or professor, who regulates the studies and may himself teach the senior students, and the above-mentioned *chö-trim-pa,* who maintains order and sees that the monastic regulations are obeyed. There are frequently two such officials, aided by several subordinate orderlies.

The main temple building and the great ceremonies

conducted therein form the jurisdiction of the *umdze*, or chief celebrant or dean, the *ku-nyer* or sacristan, and the tea-dispensers or *cha-ma,* etc.

These offices are usually held for a limited period, and are filled by election by and from the community of monks.

In addition there are a number of monks who are given special duties, such as the medical monks, the exorcist, the monastic painters, accountants, and tax-collectors, chamberlains and cooks, etc.

I had intended to halt in this village for our midday meal and rest, but we were sufficiently frightened by the presence of the monks to make us go on for another hour before stopping. Here we found an outlying farm-house, where we took our customary rest without interruption.

In the afternoon our road lay, for the most part, right along the river. The range of mountains which had run parallel to the Brahmaputra about four miles from the river-bed, having a broad plain in between, now began to close down on either side: on several occasions we could look straight down into the clear depths of the principal stream. Here I noticed an incredible number of fish, some of them of gigantic size, while on the banks were countless ducks and cranes. Their number was due to the Tibetan scruple against fishing and shooting. This scruple is based on religious dislike of destroying life. Inconsistently there is no prohibition of the killing of domestic animals, and the Tibetans are probably the greatest meat-eaters in the world.

Once or twice we caught sight of a boat making its

way down the river from Shigatse. The Tibetans are very primitive in the construction and navigation of their boats. Their craft are made of leather, square in shape, and are as clumsy as the ancient British coracle. On the lakes even these boats are unknown. In Tibet several temples and villages are to be found on islands in the midst of lakes, and, on account of the lack of boats, communication can only be had with the shore for a short time during the winter, when the water freezes and the people are able to walk to and fro on the ice.

Late in the afternoon we came across another long stretch of sand. The wind at this time was blowing very strongly, so strongly that we had great difficulty in walking, but I noticed that the sand was singularly little disturbed. This impressed upon me the fact, of which I had been but half-conscious before, that for the most part the wind sweeps along two or three feet above the ground, and that a gale can be blowing, and yet if one be lying down it is scarcely noticeable.

The sand also led me to another very curious observation. At one place quite a respectably sized stream ran down from a side valley, as if to join the Brahmaputra, but about three quarters of a mile away from the main stream it gradually lost strength, and about half a mile from its would-be confluence it disappeared altogether as if swallowed up by the sand! It was probably absorbed into the ground and ran as an underground current into the great river, but certainly the sight of the disappearing waters was most disconcerting.

Plowing through the sand was very weary work.

We had now gone for several miles without seeing any sign of habitation, and I was so exhausted that I seriously thought of camping out here in the open; but the others insisted on pushing forward, and finally we came to the bare, bleak village of Tangtru.

Just at this point the Brahmaputra, which hitherto had been split up into a number of small streams winding over a large bed, converged into a single narrow stream which ran with exceptional force and rapidity. With their backward navigation the Tibetans are not capable of dealing with such conditions, so that the river traffic which goes on along the Brahmaputra for many hundreds of miles stops here. Sixty miles further downstream, so I was told, it is resumed again, but because of the current boat communication between Shigatse and Lhasa is impossible. The village of Tangtru is the last stop of the boats on the upper section of the river, and we could see here a number of boats laid up by the side of the river. These leather boats become water-logged if they are allowed to stay too long in the water, and so the boatmen are always careful to haul them up on the bank as soon as they come to a resting-stage. Being made of very thin leather, they are surprisingly light, and I noticed one or two men who balanced their clumsy craft on their heads and carried them up to the courtyard of the rest-houses in which they were staying.

Considering Tangtru's importance as the base for navigation, I was surprised at its desolate appearance. The soil around here was too sandy for brick-making, so that the houses were constructed entirely of stone—

boulders, rough and unhewn, and stuck together indiscriminately with rude mud mortar.

Before long we were installed in a rest-house of the usual kind save that the walls were very damp, which made it more freezingly cold than ever as night came on. Provisions, it seems, were very difficult to get here. Chang, the barley beer, could not be supplied (this was the only village in Tibet where I ever found a scarcity of chang), and we could only with difficulty get fuel enough to boil our tea, so that as soon as we had eaten we crept away to the comparative warmth of our blankets.

The Tibetans seem to regard fire as useful only for cooking, which is strange enough considering that so much food is eaten raw! For purposes of warmth it is very sparingly used. Fuel is too scarce, and the Tibetan fuel, particularly, burns too fast to permit of its use for general heating; consequently the Tibetan when he feels the cold takes refuge in more clothes and at night, or in wintertime, carries on his back a whole wardrobe.

The next morning we were later than usual in starting, and it was nearly dawn before we got away. I was very much worried by the slowness of our progress but could not see what could be done to improve matters until we got extra transport animals, and unless we had some guide who knew the road, with us. We seemed to lose a lot of time straying about by our early morning journeys in the dark.

The whole of this morning's march lay along the cliffs which inclosed the Brahmaputra on each side. In some cases we had less than six inches of roadway carved from the rocky walls, and when we came to a particularly difficult bit, we had to unload our animals and carry their bundles across ourselves lest the poor beasts be pushed off the track and fall into the seething torrent hundreds of feet below. Everywhere was bleak bare rock; in many cases the rock had been carved with sacred inscriptions, and with bas-relief sculpture of various buddhas and bodhisattvas; some of these were crude, but many were beautifully done.

It was a very unusual thing to see bare rock in Tibet. The alternation of extreme heat and cold during the seasons and between day and night had broken up the surface of the rocky portions of the country so as to expose to sight only fine earth or sand. Even the mountains have generally a well-rounded look, but here the cañon or gorge in which we found ourselves must be of recent geological formation, for the great boulders showed no sign of weathering.

The valley of the great river of Tibet, the Brahmaputra, or Tsangpo, the name it is known by in that country, presents many interesting aspects to the explorer. The river flows for nearly thirteen hundred miles from west to east through the center of Southern Tibet, for the most part in a broad valley. Into this valley drain the smaller rivers, pouring their waters into the main river, which at flood season becomes a broad single stream, turbulent in places, but at ordinary times is made up of a number of narrow waterways running along distinct channels worn out in the main bed.

The depression or valley of the Brahmaputra for several miles beyond Tangtru has geological surprises for the observer. From the confluence of the river Rong down to a point where the main waterway branches off to Lhasa the formation of the valley is new and unexpected. It is a geological paradox which I can hardly attempt to explain fully here. In general the valley of the Brahmaputra is an old formation with down-like hills sloping gently to the wide river-bed, the rocks covered with soil, and a quantity of vegetation and herbage. But for some strange reason where the Rong joins the main stream there commences a totally new type of formation; the hills are rugged, with steep valleys and bare, unweathered rocks. This continues for about fifty miles, when again the old type of valley reappears. One can only surmise that at some comparatively recent date the river carved itself out a new and narrower course in the middle of the older and broader bed. Navigation is impossible along this reach for the crude hide boats of the Tibetans.

In addition to being narrow, the track was also very uneven, and we had to clamber up and down the face of the cliff. Later in the afternoon the road straightened and broadened out again, and we were able to increase our pace.

On account of my illness I had got in the habit of falling behind the others, and this practice very nearly led me into serious difficulties. A peasant came walking from the opposite direction and passed me without comment, but on looking back I saw that he had met with three horsemen, one of whom was obviously an official, who stopped the man and began to ask questions.

This is no unusual thing in Tibet. The Tibetan official loves to vaunt his authority and when riding along the road, if in no hurry, frequently stops pedestrians and demands where they are going and why. In many cases the poor peasants, fearing persecution, give the official a monetary present.

I was not very much worried as to the poor peasant's fate, but it occurred to me that the horsemen who were following us would shortly overtake me and put me through a similar catechism. My party was now nearly half a mile ahead, and so I determined to catch up with them so as to let any questioning be answered by Satan.

I had been feeling utterly fatigued and hardly able to crawl, but with this fear in my heart it was remarkable how soon I recovered and managed, in spite of my thirty-five-pound load, to "hit up" a pace that would have done credit to a marathon athlete. My bundle bobbed around on my back and one or two things fell out, our supply of salt among them, but this I did not mind, and I managed to flop along so fast that I caught up with my party shortly before the riders overtook me. They must have been surprised at the display of speed which I had given them, and did indeed pull up to ask a question, but I was obviously so out of breath that I could not speak, and Satan answered for me. After a short inquiry the official party rode on, and we were left in peace again.

CHAPTER VIII

THROUGH THE RONG GORGE

AN hour later we arrived at a thriving little village called Kulunga, where we halted for our midday meal and rest.

In great contrast to Tangtru, I found this village extremely lively, prosperous, and progressive. The *nemo* of our rest-house was very much interested to learn that we were Sikkimese and wanted to know whether living so near to India we had adopted any Indian customs. I was anxious to find out what the good lady considered typically Indian and was surprised to find her well informed, for she had never been outside her native village and had, of course, never seen an Indian in her life. She informed us that what distinguished Indians was that they ate no beef (or rather, as she put it, they ate no yak), that they insisted on eating in privacy, turning their backs on the rest of the world at meal-times, and, finally, that they observed caste rules.

Lhaten assured our friend that though the Sikkimese were unfortunate enough to live near the barbarians, we had not allowed our good Tibetan blood to be corrupted by heathen practices.

In point of fact, the Tibetans are not nearly so democratic as their scorn of the Indian caste system might lead one to suppose. Technically speaking there is, of course, no caste in Tibet, but there is a sharp distinction preserved between patrician and plebeian families. Tibet has some thirty or forty "great" families, which in other countries would be called a nobility. Below these there are some hundred and fifty or two hundred families which constitute a squirearchy, or upper middle class. Below these there is the broad mass of the population, consisting of peasant farmers and petty merchants. Lowest of all in the social scale come the outcastes, who are taboo because of their occupation; this applies such "impossible trades" as a butcher, a tanner, or even the makers of bows and arrows.

Entrance into the official world is in nearly all cases reserved to members of the "upper classes," and there is very great prejudice against intermarriage of the classes. The priesthood is open to all, except in some parts to members of outcaste families, and a bright young priest has a fair chance of advancement, though there is a strong tendency for priests drawn from the aristocratic families to occupy even the higher ecclesiastical positions.

Generally speaking, the cleavage of the classes is even greater in Tibet than anywhere in Europe, and this in spite of Tibet's contact with China, in some ways the most democratic of countries.

While I was resting after our lunch, Lhaten went "scrounging" around the village in order to purchase more salt and more barley. In this way he met a small party of men belonging to this village who were going to the town of Yase, several miles away, on the road to Lhasa, in order to buy supplies for their village. They were going up light and coming back heavy, so that Lhaten arranged with them for us to join their party and to be allowed to ride two of their ponies. In this way we not only got fresh and very useful guides, which would enable us to continue our early morning journeys without fear of losing the way, but also for the next two or three days Lhaten and I would be able to ride as well as Satan. Lhaten quickly came back to tell me of the new arrangement. I was overjoyed, for on account of the weakening effects of the dysentery I was beginning to fear that I should be physically unable to reach the Forbidden City, even if no other obstacles lay in our way. I insisted, however, that Lhaten and Satan ride the two fresh ponies, while I mounted our own worn-out nag, as I thought he would not be able to keep up with the others, and this gave me a good excuse for not being always in the close company of our new companions.

In much more joyful spirits, therefore, we started on a new phase of the journey. It had been such a long time since I had been in the saddle that I began before long to feel stiff and sore, but even this was far preferable to the agony of having to walk with a heavy load in my then critical physical condition.

Shortly after leaving the village, we left the banks

of the Brahmaputra and began to ascend a broad side valley in the center of which ran a tributary, the famous Rong River. Beyond this point it was impossible to follow the banks of the main stream. The flanking mountains continue to narrow down on either side, and the Brahmaputra for the next sixty miles becomes a series of rapids running through a narrow gorge with precipitous cliffs, sometimes more than a thousand feet high.

Consequently, though Lhasa lies on the north side of the Brahmaputra, we had now to make a long detour to the southeast, following the Rong River up to its source, the Yamdro Lake. We could then strike to the north again and, crossing over a mountain range, return to the Brahmaputra near where the Kyi River, on which Lhasa stands, runs into it from the north. By following up this second tributary we should arrive at last at the Sacred City.

On the way up the Rong Valley that afternoon we passed in front of a small and miserable-looking monastery. Alongside the roadway were a number of prayer-walls. In these were placed a large number of prayer-wheels. Following the example of my companions I dismounted from my pony as we passed by the walls and turned each wheel, but I noticed one or two other passers-by were not as punctiliously religious as ourselves, though they were scrupulously careful to keep on the right side.

These particular prayer-walls were of interest to me because they contained inscriptions, invocations, which were not in Sanskrit as is usual (even "*Om mani padme hum"* is Sanskrit) but in Tibetan and were, moreover, written phonetically and not according to the classical spelling.

Unlike Chinese, to which Tibetan is very distantly related, Tibetan has a regular alphabet consisting of thirty letters and four vowel signs. Spelling was standardized in the eighth century, and it is probable that at that time words were pronounced as they are spelled. Phonetic decay, however, has rendered a great many letters silent, and in very many cases the majority of the letters composing a word are not pronounced. Most frequently it is the first and last letters which are victimized. Thus, for example, *dbugs* is pronounced U, *mkas-po* is *ke-po, dngul* is *ngü,* etc. More confusing still are the rules whereby *pyin-pa* is pronounced *chim-pa, krag* is *tra,* and *bris-pa* is *tri-pa.* To the uninitiated, therefore, the spelling of a word is no indication of how it is pronounced. And even educated Tibetans make many mistakes in spelling. The grossly uneducated will spell things phonetically; that is, when they can write at all, and that rarely happens.

Very late in the afternoon we came in sight of our halting-place for the night, the village of Ringpo, over which towered a dzong, or castle, of the usual Tibetan type, though placed in a very unusual position.

The formation of the land and the position of the castle, monastery, and village of Ringpo were so extraordinary that I memorized the general outline with a view to making a rough sketch if an opportunity should occur.

The Rong River runs in a steep, narrow gorge which seems to have been worn away by the waters out of the bed of the older glacial valley, the natural level of the land. At this place the river gorge has divided into two streams, leaving an island in the middle. The summit of this island is level with the surrounding glacial valley. On this crag the castle is perched, while at the foot of the gorge under the castle nestles the main village of Ringpo. The monastery is built half-way up in the steep outer flank of the slope above the village. On the glacial plain on either side of these gorges one finds isolated houses.

This queer formation of a gorge cutting through an earlier broad glacial valley appears elsewhere, certain reaches of the Brahmaputra suggesting a similar effect; but nowhere did I see it so accentuated as at this particular spot.

I always had a great fear of staying too near a dzong with its resident corps of inquisitive officials, one of whose principal duties is to keep an eye on all travelers and newcomers to the district; and had we been alone, I should have insisted on staying at the little village about a mile this side of the dzong. But our traveling companions, who obviously possessed cleaner consciences than we, insisted upon staying at a rest-house right under the dzong, and I dared not raise any objection.

Once more we found the rest-house common room overcrowded, so that all of us had to sleep in a corner of the rest-house itself; our companions—three young men they were who had not yet got beyond the curiosity of youth—showed a disposition to be talkative and tried to engage even me in conversation. But I knew my conversational limitation in Tibetan, and after answering a few questions I put an end to further inquiries by rolling myself up in my blanket and going to sleep.

For the last several nights, my sleep had been interrupted by dreams of food. More particularly did I crave for some form of sweets. Often when I went to sleep would I dream of some pudding or pastry or even plain sugar. I dreamed it lay just beyond my reach and in my sleep would physically strain to reach it, an action that generally caused me to wake up.

In general I am not particularly fond of sweets and never would have supposed that I would miss them, but the absolute absence of any form of sugar or sugar substitute showed me how integral a part of our diet such foods have become.

Tibet is probably one of the few places in the world where sweets are unknown. India, even Bhutan and Sikkim, China and Japan, have all sweetmeats of some description; and even where sugar as such is unknown the sweet potato or some fruit such as the mango offers an excellent substitute; but a Tibetan knows nothing of such things, and when he first tastes them dislikes them. This is all the more strange because sugar is heating and would aid in counteracting the cold, but for this purpose the Tibetan prefers to use butter and fat.

The lack of sweets, however, probably helps the people in preserving their teeth. Contrary to usual supposition I found a large number of peasants with white, well-preserved teeth, and yet the Tibetan is never known to brush his teeth in any way or at any time.

In spite of my experience of Tibetan early rising I was certainly astonished when prodded awake at 1:30 in the morning and told to begin the journey, but our companions were in a hurry to get on and intended to make a long march that day. Usually at that time of the morning there is very little wind, but on this occasion a regular wind was blowing, and I noticed then and later, that in the *rongs* or valleys of Tibet the wind is much stronger because more concentrated.

It was pitch-dark, and I could see no trace of the road, but our guides continued steadily on without once hesitating. It is extraordinary how well Tibetans can see in the dark, though a peculiar disease of the eyes, through which one is totally blind at dusk, is not unknown.

Our road was curiously uneven. Sometimes it ran along the older, upper valley and sometimes along the lower, newer valley, and a good deal of time it was lost in continually ascending and descending the forty or fifty feet of cliff which separated the two.

We passed the important town of Rachampa in the dark and continued steadily on our way until at dawn we reached a point where the Rong River divides in two. Following a tributary to the right was a road which led to Gyangtse, only two days' march away. Three months previously I had been living in comparative comfort in that city, and I could not help but reflect upon the great contrast it presented to my present situation. If it had not been for my parole I should have been able to start my secret journey from Gyangtse and would have avoided all our terrible sufferings in the passes. I must confess that I felt a terrible temptation to abandon the Lhasa journey and to follow the road to Gyangtse, where I should be able to secure medical assistance and once more be in a position to command proper food and clothing; but I remembered that we were now less than a week from Lhasa, and this determined me to muster all of my energies for the final stages of the adventure, upon the success of which so much depended, and so I followed the others along the road to the left.

The wind continued to beat against us, and at times we had great difficulty in making progress. I was surprised to find in this narrow, gale-swept valley a number of thriving villages. The Rong Valley is, in fact, very famous historically, and its very bleakness seems to produce a sturdy set of men; many of the soldiers in the new Tibetan army are recruited from this district.

Shortly before noon we halted at the small village of Trumsa, where we had our usual rest and lunch-breakfast, our first meal, although we had been traveling about ten hours. In the courtyard of the rest-house I noticed a number of chickens, and my mouth watered at the sight of them, as my stomach revolted at the eternal putrid yak- and sheep-flesh.

Chicken is supposed to be an unspeakably filthy food in Tibet, and custom forbids its use. Eggs for some reason are also placed on the taboo list, and many strict lamas who consume huge quantities of mutton refuse to eat eggs on the ground that it has deprived a future chicken of life.

In conformity with Tibetan prejudice I had hitherto kept myself both from chickens and eggs, but while in this village it occurred to me that if there were chickens here they were scarcely kept for ornament, but that in spite of all prejudice and pretense they were occasionally eaten, when no one was around, for, as the Indian proverb has it, "Where there is no eye there is no caste."

In my desperate desire for a change in food, I decided that if the local Tibetans were so wicked as to eat chicken there was no reason why we should not also do so, and through Lhaten I arranged for the purchase of two fowls. I found that we could get them for a trangka (threepence) apiece but that the *nepo* (landlord) insisted that we catch them ourselves, as he would have nothing to do with such indiscretions.

Lhaten, the syce, and Diogenes now began a merry chase, but the fowls had never had their wings clipped and showed a remarkable ability to fly when they found themselves near capture. The chase continued fully half an hour, to our enormous amusement. I noticed that the reluctant *nepo* laughed the loudest of all, but in the end our game was bagged and we moved off once more. For a comparison of prices it may be added that the fodder for our animals at this stage cost two trangkas, and the handful of yak-dung for boiling our tea cost one trangka.

In the afternoon, as I expected, the gale grew worse, and as the wind was sweeping down from some glaciers in the upper valley, it was bitterly cold, the coldest day in fact, that I had experienced in Tibet. This brought it very clearly into my mind that the Brahmaputra Valley is the warmest part of Tibet, and the farther we got away from it the colder the atmosphere became.

In these circumstances it is easy to understand the surprise which I felt when, about four o'clock in the afternoon, on passing a village situated in the lower valley, near the water's edge, I saw a number of persons lying stark naked near the roadside. I thought they must be raving lunatics, or else corpses, to be thus exposed to the cold. But as we came nearer I discovered that they were ordinary Tibet peasants lying in shallow pools of steaming water. The village in question, I learned, is famous for its natural hot springs. Great curative powers are ascribed to the waters, and the Tibetans sometimes overcome their disinclination to wash and will then soak themselves in the steaming water for hours.

The crudity of the arrangements is curious. Instead of having a room, or even a courtyard, built around the springs, they are left here completely exposed, and it seems incredible that the people are not taken by pneumonia on getting out of the hot water and exposing themselves unguarded to the icy-cold winds. This crudity is all the more curious because on one point the peasants have shown a certain amount of art. They have scooped out the various shallow pools into which the hot water from the spring runs, and by diverting a small stream of cold water they form pools of varying temperature, from some that are just tepid to others in which the water nearly boils.

The hot-water springs of Tibet generally are impregnated with various salts; in particular, chlorides and sulphates of potash and magnesium; some contain iron; others are simply plain water without any noticeable impregnation.

But in addition to the great importance that is attached to the healing properties of the hot springs, the Tibetan has an ulterior motive for bathing in the sulphurous waters. He is a verminous creature, and his Buddhistic beliefs preclude the hunting and slaughter of the insects which infest his body and clothing. The springs, then, provide him with a simple means of ridding himself of vermin without trespassing too far on his religious scruples.

We had not remained immune. The native rest-houses are overrun with these pests, and I had already found that a number had attached themselves to me. At first the sense of their presence was extraordinarily uncomfortable, but by this time I had become so accustomed to them as to forget their existence. Nevertheless, I should have been glad to get rid of the present host by means of a bath in the hot sulphur-water, but I dared not attempt to do so, lest some of my disguise be washed away at the same time.

Such springs are very common in Tibet. Rarer in the central provinces, they occur chiefly in the regions at the higher altitudes in Tibet, in the salt lakes area, and more concentrated in the Yeru Tsangpo district. These springs are sometimes geysers rushing up high in the air. Others bubble up gently into natural pools and basins in rock and firm ground. On the higher plateau, at about sixteen thousand feet above sea-level, the cold descends to a mark thirty degrees below zero, sometimes to forty degrees, and the ground is frozen for eight months of the year. Here the waters of the gushing fountains sometimes freeze in the air, and high stalagmites are formed. The temperature of the springs varies, and it is sometimes easily possible to cook food in the water. A reading has been taken showing 183 degrees at a place where on account of the extreme elevation the boiling-point of water stands at 183.75 degrees Fahrenheit. The range, however, is very wide, but I often saw Tibetans lying naked in the warm pools when, exposed to the air, even wrapped up in several garments one over the other, the cold winds cut through one incredibly sharply and the penalty of carelessness was frost-bite.

One thing surprised me. Considering the large number of hot springs, it was interesting to note that Tibet is lacking in volcanic mountains and in fact contains no volcano past or present of any importance.

After leaving the hot spring village we found the valley had a quite different formation. In place of the broad or upper and the narrow or lower valley, the hills closed down on either side, and of the valley there was left only a narrow gorge, eaten out by the river, with high perpendicular walls, rising two or three hundred feet above our heads. We had, therefore, to keep to a narrow ledge within this gorge only a foot or two from the edge of the river, the waters of which were here covered with a thick layer of ice, over which, at some places, where the stream widened out, we had to cross.

It was long and very wearying work, and it was not until after sunset that we came to a place where the gorge opened out a little and here found the village of Rampa, where we were to rest for the night. We had been eighteen hours on the road.

The syce, in accordance with his orders, had plucked and cleaned the chickens while on the march, so that, once arrived in our rest-house, we were able to stick them in a pot and boil them without attracting too much attention. What a blessed relief it was to have good cooked food again after ages of dieting on raw, putrid flesh! And yet how strange it was to feel that we had to eat it secretly!

That evening I had a further proof of Lhaten's loyalty. His own dress was slightly warmer than mine, and, having observed how bitterly I was feeling the cold, he insisted on changing clothes with me, as he declared that he had less need for warm clothes than I. I had started with three Tibetan dresses, and in accordance with Tibetan custom I was now wearing all three at the same time, one over the other, except that I reversed the usual practice and wore my worst dress—this was now Lhaten's dress—on the outside, for the more poor, miserable, and oppressed I looked the less danger there was of detection.

Staying in the same rest-house we found a Lhasa lady who was on her way to Shigatse to visit some relations. Among the poorer travelers women share and sleep in the same general common room as the men, but, being of a better family, this lady was given a special, though smaller, room adjoining for her private use. But she obviously preferred company to solitude, for she came into our room after dinner and stayed for about an hour, joining in the common chatter.

She was a great gossip and had much to say regarding the various notabilities of Lhasa. Needless to say most of her information was rather of a scandalous nature, and probably only about one fourth of it was true; but at the same time the conversation proved very useful to me, as it told which of the Lhasa officials were easy-going and modern in their ideas and which were old-fashioned and rigorous. I was interested to note that though she had tall tales to tell about many of the abbots of the Lhasa monasteries, some of whom were also *truku,* or incarnations, even her ribald tongue had nothing to utter against the private life of the Dalai-lama.

The good dame's accent was nearly as interesting as her conversation. It belonged to the pure Lhasa breed and was in great contrast to the speech of every one whom we had so far met, for we were still, and ever since entering Tibet had been, in the province of Tsang (the capital of which is Shigatse), which possesses a dialect of its own.

Dialects are very common in Tibet; nearly every village has verbal variations peculiar to itself. This was, of course, one of the chief reasons that I got through undetected, for I could always put accentual errors down to some outlying dialect. These variations of Tibetan speech can be grouped under three or four main headings.

In the first place, the two main types of the Tibetan

population, the nomads and the town-dwellers, have each tended to develop linguistically along lines of their own, though for the most parts the two types are able to understand each other. Among the settled communities of Central Tibet, the Tsang dialect as spoken in Shigatse and the U dialect as spoken in Lhasa hold the field. There are probably as many people who speak the one as the other, though at present the greater political preponderance of Lhasa tends to make the U dialect the official language of the upper classes all over the country.

Outside of the central provinces, the principal Tibetan dialects, some of them very far removed one from the other, are Ladaki, spoken in the far west of Tibet, and Kampa, spoken in the great Kam province, which lies between Tibet proper, and China. Finally the Bhutanese, the Sikkimese, and the Sharpa, or the Tibetan inhabitants of Nepal, have each a specially developed Tibetan dialect of their own. The Mongolians and the Chinese who have taken the trouble to learn Tibetan (and many Mongolians, particularly, speak Tibetan very well) seem, in nearly all cases, to have acquired a Kam accent.

Even more far-reaching than the difference between the dialects as regards geographical position is the distinction between the ordinary and the honorific languages.

Most Oriental languages have been influenced by this principle. In speaking to an equal or a superior one uses certain elegant and high-flown phrases, while in speaking to a social inferior one speaks more curtly and shortly. But in Tibetan this distinction has been carried to absurd lengths. There is not only an ordinary and an honorific language, but also a high honorific language used in addressing high dignitaries such as the Trashi-lama of Shigatse or the Dalai-lama of Lhasa.

The differences between the three styles of address apply to nearly every word in the language. Thus, e.g., the ordinary word for to say or tell is *lap-pa,* the honorific word is *sung-nga,* and the high honorific word is *ka-nang-nga;* the ordinary word for foot is *kang-pa,* the honorific word is *shap;* the ordinary word for eye is *mi,* the honorific word is *chen* (spelled *spyan*), and so on indefinitely. It is impossible to infer from the ordinary word what the honorific term will be or vice versa; consequently when one wishes to learn Tibetan one *must* learn two and in many cases three words for every single object, because to use an honorific word to an inferior or an ordinary word to a superior is considered the grossest insult.

Our lady visitor kept us awake for some time with her stories but at length withdrew to her room. She had with her no female attendants but had three male servants, and I noticed that all of them occupied the same room as their mistress.

Not daring to join too much in the conversation I had long since curled myself up in my rugs and, as soon as we were left alone, fell fast asleep, worn out by the fatigues of the day.

By half-past two we were up and off again. For a long time our way lay along the same gorge formation that we had experienced all the previous day, but instead of the road's lying at the foot of the gorge alongside the river it now ran up on the side of the cliffs, about thirty or forty feet above the edge of the stream. The nature of the path was such that we had to walk.

During the first part of the journey, when it was still pitch-dark, I could do without my goggles and managed to follow the trail without stumbling, but at the first hint of light I put them on, as our traveling-companions were right in front of me. I was now, more than ever, in inky blackness and tripped against the man ahead of me and shot over into the ravine. The cliff had seemed perfectly perpendicular, but fortunately I discovered that there was just enough of an incline to break the full force of my fall, though I came down with a terrific thump upon the ice-crust of the river. The ice, unable to stand the strain, cracked and broke, and I was precipitated into the freezing water below. Thus, in place of the warm bath which I had coveted the night before, I was forced to take an involuntary cold plunge.

It is at moments such as these that one forgets matters of disguise, and I must admit that in my surprise at finding myself in the water I uttered a few strong English oaths. I had lived for a year at a university settlement in the East End supposedly in order to help the poor. The benefit which the poor got from me was more than dubious, but I managed to enlarge and improve certain aspects of my vocabulary. Fortunately my present efforts ended in a gurgle as my head sank under the water, and our Tibetan companions above were too startled and too far above me to catch in any way distinctly what I said, so that no great damage was done. The river was shallow, only some three or four feet deep, and Lhaten and the syce managed to fish me out before I could come to any serious harm. I found, on being hauled up, that my servants had been more frightened than I; both Lhaten and Satan wasted ten good minutes in abusing me for my carelessness, and I found that in spite of my superior advantages of education, their supply of appropriate words was much greater than my own. Before long we were able to continue our journey, though I was badly shaken by the fall and had somewhat injured my right hip. For this reason I was very glad to find that a little later the road widened out, and we were once more able to ride.

Shortly after dawn, and after passing another village, the valley once more entered into an entirely new type of formation. The gorge disappeared, and the valley became broad, flat, and even, the river running through the middle of this valley without having carved out a cañon or ravine.

I was interested to see how one valley could show three such entirely different geological features. At the mouth, near the Brahmaputra, the river seemed very old and weary; near the source the river seemed young and new. Personally, I am sure that the secret of this lies in the fact that until comparatively recent times the great Yamdro Lake extended to where we now were, and that it has gradually receded to its present boundaries and thereby lengthened the upper part of the river by many miles. We occasionally met parties coming from the other direction. I was much amused to notice that quite a number of the people we met, particularly the young men and the boys, wore masks. This, of course, had nothing to do with disguise but was merely a means of protecting their faces from the biting cold and cutting winds. These masks were made of leather, yak-leather, and had weird features painted on them, making their wearers look like mountain elves.

Yase, the destination of our friends, was not many miles away, but we halted about ten o'clock at a little village on the road, as one of the men had a married sister who was living there, and here we had our usual "brunch," or breakfast-lunch, and rest.

I was interested to find that marriages took place between families living so far apart, for here was a woman who had married a group of brothers living three days away from her native home; but, contrary to my expectations, I found that in Tibet such matches were by no means uncommon.

This is partly accounted for by the Tibetan dislike of marrying near relations. There are very distinct laws in Tibet covering consanguinity, though these laws are not strictly observed. Nevertheless, despite seeming laxity of morals, both before and after marriage, and the freedom exercised by woman and man in matters of sexual relationships, marriage is not, as a rule, contracted with kinsmen less than three or four degrees removed. The law of Tibet forbids alliances within seven degrees of consanguinity, but this is disregarded as to the letter of the law. In the lower ranks marriage is not unknown between close relatives where neither party claims a common parent, and I believe cases do exist of marriage between nephew and aunt, and son and stepmother, though, needless to say, such cases are rare.

I had one bit of luck in this village. Lhaten went through the baggage trying to find a needle wherewith to mend a tear in my clothes caused by my fall earlier in the day and found in the bottom of one bundle a handful of rolled oats which had fallen out of the tins we had used in the passes. I hailed the discovery with great joy, for my stomach revolted against the eternal barley-flour of Tibet. As we were halting with a private family and not at a rest-house, there were no other travelers to observe what we were doing, and our companions were busy gossiping with our hosts; so I managed to cook the oats while no one was looking. A cupful of milk was procured on grounds of illness, and I sat down to my feast. Alas, also there was no sugar, and so I had to revert to the barbaric custom of the Scots and eat my oats with salt, but, even so, after this secret orgy I felt a nobler and a better man.

Shortly before noon we set out on our journey again. As we went along I noticed a large number of springs, this time, however, of cold water, by the side of the road. These ran down to the river, which was now appreciably smaller. The river itself, being no longer hidden in a gorge, was exposed to the devastating rays of the sun, which had melted a good deal of the ice covering, so that we could see the water flowing in the middle; but so strong was the wind in the opposite direction that its blasts on the river made it seem as if the water was flowing backward and uphill; in fact, so strong was the illusion that the syce and Lhaten thought it to be real and bowed down in worship of a supposed miracle.

Before long our thoughts were turned in other directions, for we met a Lhasa nobleman and his suite traveling in the opposite direction to us. He had, it seemed, recently been appointed lay governor of a district in the extreme west of Tibet and was then on his way to take up his new post. All of the servants were mounted, and a little way behind came another twenty mules carrying the new governor's baggage. It was, indeed, a most splendid procession.

The harness was ornamented with tufts of red wool, and around the necks of many of the animals were strings of bells mounted on a leather strap, so that there was a vast amount of jingling as the procession passed. Most of the servitors were armed with modern and very efficient-looking rifles. and the leaders had also long whips with which they drove our own and all other parties out of the way.

The servitors of lower grade were clothed in dresses of red wool, though the wool was of the finest texture. On their heads they had huge flat red caps, like giant inverted plates covered with red braid. The governor himself and the higher members of his staff wore dresses of silk, beautifully brocaded, and for the most part yellow. Tibet, of course, is far too cold to support the silkworm, so that all silk has to be imported from China.

Although all along the way this official would be

housed in the best rest-houses, the services supplied would be equally primitive, so that the large retinue of servants was really necessary. Half of his servants are placed before and half behind him, riding single or sometimes double file. Two of the most important servants, however, ride some considerable distance ahead. These are the *machen,* or cook, and the *nyerpa,* or chief butler. They must get to the destined rest-house before the others, so as to have both food and room ready for the governor when he arrives.

The procession of a nobleman in Tibet is indeed an imposing spectacle, but most of the splendor is only gained by the severe oppression of the peasants along the route of march. The Tibetan peasant suffers under the system of indirect taxation known as the *ula.* According to the *ula* law, every family, in proportion to its wealth, must supply free of charge to every government official armed with a permit a certain number of riding- and transport-animals for the use of himself and his servants while traveling along the road. Not only do the peasants have to lend their animals to the officials free of charge, but they must also supply all the food for the animals without compensation. They must accompany the animals in order to feed and attend to them, and finally they must silently bear the loss of their animals should any of them die on the road, as very frequently happens on account of the outrageous usage which the ponies and mules receive at the hands of the officials' servants. Needless to say, this *ula* system is none too beloved by the populace.

As soon as the governor and his party came in sight,

all of us dismounted from our ponies and withdrew to the side of the road. Satan and the elder of our companions, being supposedly of higher ranks, contented themselves with removing their hats as the procession rode past, but I and the other members of the party were forced to give the more formal Tibetan salutation. This consists of opening the mouth and sticking out the tongue. Surely a most curious way of showing respect. The fists were also clenched and the thumbs were elevated as a sign of surrender, while Diogenes and I were even more humble and with our open palms pressed our right ears forward.

The governor, of course, made no answer to our salute; and, in fact, two of his servants, out of pure devilment, lashed out at us with their whips and gave me a stinging blow on the shoulder. I was quite satisfied, however, to get off as lightly as this, for I had feared that our party might be stopped and interrogated.

About two hours later we came to the village of Yase, where we had to halt for a short time and surrender our borrowed ponies, as our traveling-companions had now come to the end of their journey.

CHAPTER IX

ON THE LAST LAP—BUT SUSPECTED

IT was still very early in the day, and I had intended after a few minutes halt to push on to Pede Dzong, several miles further on; but on arriving at the village I received a most serious shock which necessitated a complete change of plans.

My long absence from Darjeeling had begun to excite comment, and when no news came from Sikkim as to my whereabouts suspicions began to be aroused. Finally the news that I had been seen near Lachen made it certain that I had entered Tibet and was probably trying to make my way to Lhasa.

Certain agents of the Tibetan Government immediately sent news to the Lhasa authorities of the rumors that had got abroad, and on February 7, the day I left Shigatse the Lhasa cabinet had been informed that I was probably already in the country and was without doubt making for Lhasa. The fact that no news regarding me had come from the outlying posts made them certain that I was trying to get there in disguise, and consequently the next day orders had been sent out ordering all the local officials to keep a sharp lookout for me, to have me stopped, imprisoned, and turned back immediately. Another day or two having elapsed without news of my capture, the Government had issued further orders that all travelers coming in the direction of Lhasa were to be stopped and examined so as to be sure that no one slipped through their fingers.

As the result of these orders sharp watches had been held at all the main roads, but as we had been journeying from Shigatse by a side road along which official communication is much slower we had hitherto heard nothing of these exciting events. But we had now come to the point where our side road joined the great highway leading from Gyangtse to Lhasa, so that here the wildest rumors regarding the "foreign devil" had become public property. Consequently we found the villagers much excited about the matter, and we were questioned as to whether we had seen anything of the intruder—questions, of course, which we answered in the negative.

It was very fortunate that we had been traveling with and arrived at Yase in the company of people who were well known in the village, so that not the slightest suspicion seemed to fall on any member of my party. Our Tibetan companions were to halt here, so that we were no longer to travel under their protection, and I became obsessed with fears as to what might happen to us during the next few days. We were still seventy-five miles from Lhasa, and as the whole of that distance would lie along the great highroad over which the strictest watch would be kept, I hardly knew what to do. So far we had escaped detection largely because no one was on the lookout particularly for us, and though I felt much more at home in my disguise and had greatly benefited by having been thrown into the closest contact with my fellow-travelers, I could not believe that I should escape detection if a close personal examination were to be made.

I had, however, either to give up the whole adventure or else to press on in spite of these new dangers, and, of course, I chose the latter alternative, though I determined to make no more dangerous experiments such as the eating of chickens or the surreptitious cooking of oatmeal.

Only one change was made in our arrangements. Between Yase and Lhasa we should have to pass through two towns which were the capital of districts and where there were governors and military officials in residence. These were Pede Dzong and Chushul. Ordinarily I should have spent the night in both places, but I knew that as a result of instructions from Lhasa much stricter watch would be kept in these towns than in the smaller villages, and so I decided to halt only at intermediate points. In accordance with this plan I concluded it unwise to go further this day and decided to spend the night in Yase.

It was still very early, and so, rather than spend the whole time in the rest-house, I went out for a long walk in order to add further details to the map of the country which I was making.

I took Lhaten with me, and also my materials for disguise, as I wished to repair any defects which time might have made, and it was easier and safer to do this out in the open than in the village. As soon as we were out of sight Lhaten touched me up, renewing my disguise as well as could be, after which I threw the pigments away, for I was afraid that our baggage might be searched at some time or other, when the discovery of such articles would give our secret away entirely.

We then continued our walk, as I wanted to catch a glimpse of the famous Samding monastery, which was not very far away. Just ahead of us we caught sight of an arm of the Yamdro Lake, the largest lake in Tibet, and one of the largest lakes in the world; but as we approached it I noticed that the river rapidly dwindled, then took a turn to the right, and vanished! This very much surprised me, as the Rong River is supposed to have its source in the Yamdro Lake—to be, in fact, the only outlet for the huge lake, which is fed, according to report, by several considerable streams. And yet the river has certainly no direct connection with the lake. Remembering the phenomenon of the hidden tributary of the Brahmaputra and the mysterious springs we had noticed that morning, I am inclined to think that a certain amount of water from the lake finds its way to the river by some underground source. In any case it cannot be much, for the Rong River is never very large, though geologically it seems to have been much more important in the past.

Just at this point, about the short stretch of land between the source of the river and the outer arm of the lake, I noticed an enormous amount of wild life, chiefly hares, cranes, wild duck, and the beautiful Brahman duck, which is quite common in parts of India and has

Superstition: prayer-flags and the horns of the Ovis Ammor (blue sheep of Tibet), a species of wild sheep deemed sacred, are placed on the roof of house to protect against evil spirits.

Tent dwelling of the wild Tibetan yak-herders

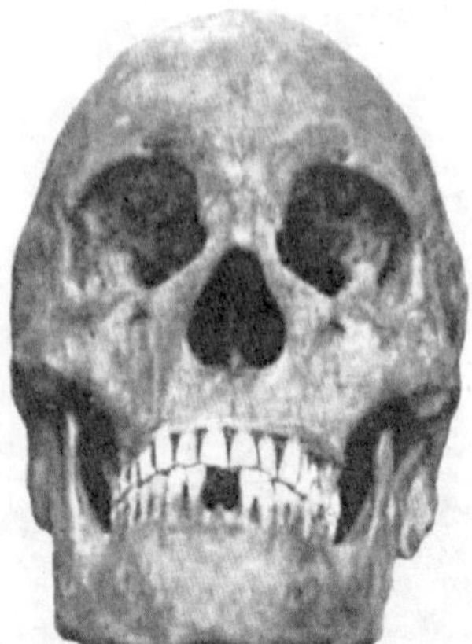

Skull (front)

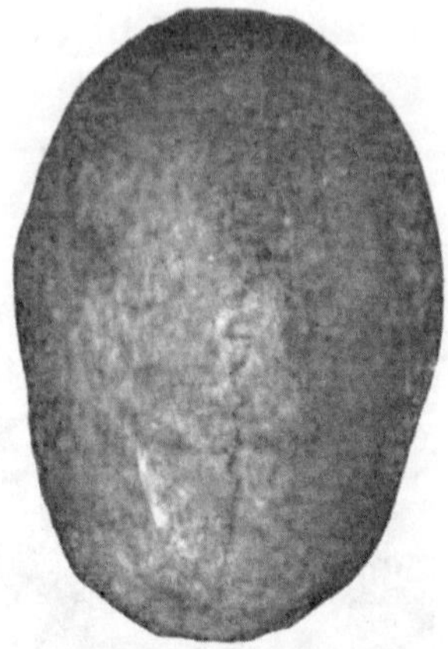

Skull (top)

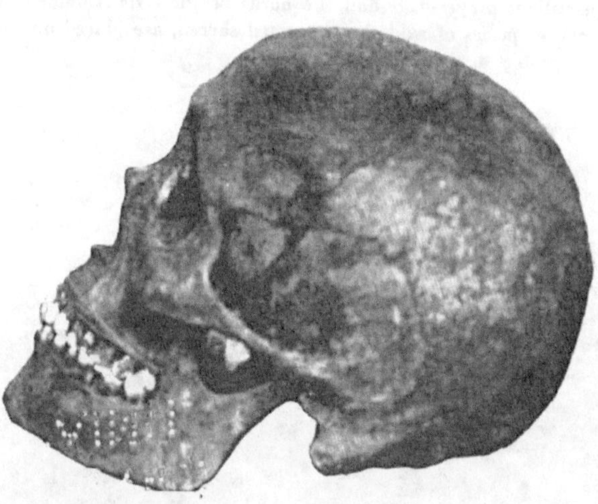

Skull (side)

the reputation of being uneatable. Once again the tameness of the animals and fowl was remarkable, and we were almost among them before they took to flight.

But we were soon to see that though they had little to fear from man they had numerous other enemies with which to contend, for lurking in the background were a number of foxes and wolves. On one occasion we saw a hare chased and finally caught by a wolf.

None of the foxes or wolves were either black or gray. They had all the sandy-brown appearance that fitted in so well with the landscape that, in fact, it made them invisible until they began to move.

With the usual conception of Tibet before one, that of arid wastes and absence of vegetation, the abundance of animal life, both wild and domestic, seems extraordinary. In a general visualization of Tibet, the very fertile tracts, particularly in the east and southeast, and also the pastoral regions are but dimly realized, when, as a matter of fact, the wide range and multitude of fauna in such parts are remarkable. Even in the higher plateaus and the little-known northern tracts at an average altitude of approximately sixteen thousand feet above sea-level animal life is exceptionally plentiful. The chief animals of Tibet one has come to assume as being yak and sheep, dogs and ponies, some goats, antelope and wild asses, whereas, while these are found roaming about in large numbers everywhere, in the valleys and over the upland pasturages wolves, black and yellow bears, lynxes, and in some parts tigers and leopards abound, and also smaller beasts such as hares, marmots, and the lagomys (a tailless rabbit), rats and other rodents, martins, weasels and badgers, otters and porcupines; wild fowl is plentiful—ducks, geese, partridges, sheldrakes, and sand-grouse.

Arrived at the shore of the lake we found the water covered with a thick sheet of ice. We here met the Gyangtse-Lhasa road, for the road runs on the sides of the lake for a considerable distance; but as there was no village along this stretch for some miles I was not afraid to halt for a few moments, or even to turn to the right and follow the road for some distance, until we came in view of the Samding monastery, which eventually we sighted at the extreme end of the lake, only a mile or two away, placed on top of a little hill which rose about three hundred feet above the level of the lake.

Samding (lit., the temple of soaring meditation) is one of the most famous shrines anywhere in Tibet. It is in many ways unique in that about half of the inhabitants are monks and the other half are nuns, while the head of the monastery with all its branches is a woman, a reincarnating embodiment of Dorje-pamo the pig-faced goddess, one of the most popular of the Tibetan deities.

Her monastery belongs to one of the red-hat or unreformed orders, which are frowned upon by the prevailing yellow-hat hierarchy, but an exception has been made in her case, and she is treated with royal honors by the Lhasa Government, sharing with the Trashi- and the Dalai-lamas the privilege of riding in a sedan-chair when she travels. She is also exempt from the rule that all nuns must shave off their hair and is permitted to wear her hair long, but on the other hand she is never permitted to assume a recumbent position. In the daytime she can sleep sitting up in a chair, but the whole night she must spend in meditation in the rigorous position demanded for this practice.

She is reputed to be possessed of various magic powers, one of which reminds us of the ancient Greek legend of Circe. The story goes that in 1717 Tibet was invaded by a body of Tartar soldiers who were Mohammedans. On approaching this monastery "their chief sent word to the Dorje-pamo to appear before him that he might see if she really had, as reported, a pig's head. A mild answer was returned him, but incensed at her refusing to obey his summons he tore down the walls and broke into the sanctuary. He found it deserted, not a human being in it, only 80 pigs and as many sows . . . under the lead of a big sow. . . . When the Tartars had given up all idea of sacking Samding suddenly the pigs disappeared to become venerable looking lamas and nuns, with the saintly looking Dorje-pamo at their head. Filled with astonishment and veneration for the sacred character of the Lady Abbess the chief made immense presents to her lamasery."[1]

I did not dare draw too near the monastery with its quaint inhabitants, for the Indians have a story that as a result of the visit of Sarat Chandra Das, many years ago, the water of the tiny Dumo Lake changed its color and became poisonous, and ever since then the inhabitants have been particularly keen in trying to keep for-

[1] Sarat Chandra Das, "Journey to Central Tibet," p. 189.

eigners away. As Samding did not lie on the way to Lhasa I did not see any reason for needlessly poking my head into danger, and so, after we had seen what we wanted, Lhaten and I turned back, retracing our way to the village of Yase.

Poor Lhaten had been much frightened by the news we had heard in the village and during our walk tried to dissuade me from going on with the venture. He suggested that if I go on I at least do so openly, so that the worst that could befall would be imprisonment and expulsion from the country; for, if I were caught in my disguise, he thought that I should certainly be killed. I told him that we had now gone too far to turn back, and I meant to carry on till the end, no matter how great the risk; and, though the faithful man grumbled, he promised to stand by me to the end.

Once back in the village we found the syce and Satan busy with accounts. They were trying to reckon how much they owed our traveling-companions for the loan of the horses. The Tibetans are extraordinarily bad at arithmetic and find it impossible to solve even the simplest problem of arithmetic in their heads.

Pen-and-paper calculations are also almost unknown among them, so that they are forced to count either on their fingers, with little stones, or with beads. This last is the most common way, and nearly every Tibetan is possessed of a rosary which he sometimes uses for religious purposes, to tell off his prayers, and sometimes for secular purposes to add up his accounts. In the larger cities use is also made of the abacus, which is so frequently employed in China.

Even with these aids the Tibetans find calculation very hard work, and it took our friends nearly an hour, squatting in the courtyard and fingering their beads, before they arrived at the sum which I had done in my head in a very few minutes.

This slowness of wits the Tibetans share with the Mongolians; and in consequence both peoples were, in the old days of Chinese influence, frequently fleeced by the more nimble-witted Chinese merchants. And this is one of the reasons for the deep-seated hatred which both the Mongolians and the Tibetans have for their Celestial neighbors.

I had found the ruse of joining a Tibetan caravan so useful in escaping suspicion in Yase that I decided to join another one and sent Lhaten around the village to find out if there was any other party on its way to Lhasa. He found that there was none which was going all the way to the capital, but in the next rest-house there was a party of three men who were going as far as Chushul, about forty-five miles from Lhasa; and, for lack of any one better, we arranged to go on with these folk.

To my regret we were comparatively late in starting, and it was nearly four o'clock before we left the village. In this case our new friends had no extra horses to spare, and so we were once more forced to walk. But I was not altogether sorry for this, for although my illness made me very weak, pedestrianism fitted in much better with my rôle of coolie, and I felt that in walking there was much less chance of discovery. It was now a case of walking into the lions' den, at least I felt it so; and accordingly as an additional precaution, I arranged to carry the largest and bulkiest-looking of the burdens. Satan, of course, was riding, and I kept close to the tail of his pony.

While it was still dark we once more reached the edge of the lake, but this time, turning to the left, we kept on for many miles along the water's edge. When daylight broke we could see before us, a quarter of a mile away from the lake, the great castle of Pede Dzong, sometimes written Palti Dzong. I had hoped to pass this under the cover of night, but our delay had exposed us to the sight of one of the watchmen on the turrets. We had no intention of halting in the little village underneath the castle, but as we were hastening through it two petty officials ran down from the *dzong* and commanded us to stop. They were obviously of no great rank but were clothed in long woolen dresses of a dark blue-red color, with the curious broad flat hats we had observed the day before. They carried no firearms but had long whips with bamboo handles. We were interrogated by these officials as to where we had come from and whether we had seen a foreigner on the way. At this moment I thought, indeed, the game was up, but though they subjected Satan, as master, to the closest possible scrutiny, I, as the servant, was only very cursorily examined, less attention being paid to me even than to Lhaten. Our traveling-companions were already known on this route, so that they were not physically inspected, although they were also questioned as to the people they had seen on the road. In my case they were content to tear open my dress, and, finding my chest to be as brown and as dirty as the others, we were allowed to pass. My eyes, the feature of which I was most afraid, they strangely enough passed over unnoticed, but in any case the Tibetan mind could not imagine that a white man should be willing to trudge thirty miles a day carrying thirty-five pounds on his back while his servant rode a pony in great state ahead of him.

We were eventually told that we could go on without any further trouble, and I was very glad to do so. Our companions suggested that as we had been delayed we should stay and have our rest in Pede Dzong; but Satan, to my relief, negatived this suggestion, and we put our best foot forward on the road.

For mile after mile our course lay along the side of the great Yamdro Lake, and we could begin to realize something of its vastness.

Set in a plain and surrounded by rich pastures, Lake Yamdro is one of the largest expanses of water in Tibet. It has a circumference of about 109 miles, and its waters are deep; while stretching out into it is the famous peninsula which terminates in the island-like head of To-nang. The peninsula joins the western shores by two narrow strips of land, and the natives liken it to a scorpion holding the shore by its two claws. At a point where one arm reaches the mainland has been built the renowned Samding monastery which I had seen the preceding day, while on the hills running down the center are four other monasteries owing allegiance to the mother superior of the Samding nunnery. Yamdro Lake is 14,000 feet above sea-level, and its waters are perfectly fresh, which is remarkable considering the fact that, apart from its dubious connection with the Rong River, it has no outlet.

The district supports a fairly large population, for to the south are low prairies which serve as pasturages for the nomad Dro-pas' herds, while on another plain, just beyond the mountains to the east, there is a deal of pony-grazing. On the north is a barrier of high mountains on a narrow strip which intervenes between the Brahmaputra and the lake, the river being two thousand feet below the waters of the lake. The space between is but about eight miles wide, but the Kampa-la, as this range is called, effectually prevents any leakage from the Yamdro into the river.

Off the south shore is the small island of Yambu where a branch of the Samding monastery is built, and not far from here a smaller lake stretches up to the boundary of the Yamdro, being cut off by only a strip of rocks. This lake, called Rombuza Tso or the corpse-worm bottle lake, is the burial-place of monks and is for this reason given so strange a name.

Tibet is the land of lakes. One can scarcely make a day's march without meeting with one or more sheets of water, mostly shallow ponds, though frequently of great size, lying in hollows in the plains or in scooped-out basins on the hills. More often than not the lakes appear in groups, strung out one after another or in batches in a circumscribed area. None of these lakes is supplied by an important stream, but presumably all rely on glacier drainage or on the melting of the snows to replenish them. Here are to be found the highest

The oracle of Tibet. He prophesied the month and year the Great War would end two years before the armistice. The Tibetan Government will not act without his soothsaying.

The Tibetan oracle as he is normally, with attendants

Gera monastery near Lhasa; the second largest in Tibet

Shigatse; the monastery, home of the Trashi-lama, the supreme abbot of Tibet

placed waters of the world, inland seas at an altitude of fifteen thousand feet. Hora Tso, which is 118 square miles in area and has several islands, holds the record in height; it is 17,930 feet above sea-level. This is in Northwest Tibet. The highest European lake is at Neuchâtel, Switzerland, at an altitude of 1,437 feet, the record in South America being 13,070 feet (Guatapuri Lakes, Colombia), and in North America 4,200 (Lake Waterton, in the Rocky Mountains, U. S. A.). The largest Tibetan lake is Kökö Nor, in the Nan-Shan mountain range of the northeast, which is 168 miles round, followed by Tsagyu Tso (or Chargut Tso), *Tso* being lake, though frequently the saline waters are called "Tsakka," i.e., salt-pit, which indicates to some extent the extreme salinity of most Tibetan lakes, especially in the northern territory.

A large number of these lakes are excessively saline, so that as the waters evaporate and recede from the shores, deposits of soda, potash, and borax are left as a fringe. The whole of the northern lakes appear to be heavily laden with salt, including the swamps and lakes of the Tang region, but in the Dro territory the waters are fresh and all contain supplies of fish. From native salt collectors and travelers it is reported that nearly all the lakes of the northwestern area are salt, and great quantities of salt are available in this district. Also pure chloride of potash is found in some places, being heaped up in piles. The cause is undoubtedly the wide-spread flooding of the rivers and the melting of the snows, which draws the salts from the ground and deposits them indiscriminately as the floods abate or the waters evaporate. The cold and heat take up the work, and eventually the wind scatters the salts or blows them into large mounds. Some lakes hold a quantity of impure nitrate of potash, which is collected and used for making gunpowder.

Near the lakes are found the hot springs which the Tibetans appreciate so much. Most of these contain a quantity of salts.

Everywhere one sees signs which suggest a tendency of the lakes to recede. And the traditions around the Manasarowar Lakes, near the Kumoan Himalayas, seem to bear out this view, for the tales treat of waters five hundred miles across, whereas in no place do they now exceed twenty miles in breadth. On the islands with which many of the larger lakes are dotted are built monasteries and shrines, which the peasants visit chiefly in winter when they can cross on the ice, for the Tibetan native is not a capable boatman and in summer has other things to occupy his time. Where the waters appear near mountain peaks of any importance, the peaks are given a masculine name, or male affix, while the lakes are always feminine—a curious conceit which is either rooted in traditions or has given rise to the strange stories which abound, in which mountain and lake have an animate existence.

As we went along the banks of the lake we noticed a great number of ground-mice. There were thousands of them, and I wondered what they could find to eat; as there were very few villages along this stretch they could not feed from stolen barley; in fact, the only thing visible on which they could subsist was a little moss.

It was, and has since remained, a mystery to me why these little ground-mice have chosen just this place to settle. Along the Brahmaputra Valley I had seen nothing of them, and in fact the only other place in Tibet where I found them was on the bleak Pari plain. There was one difference between the Pari mice and the Yamdro variety. Around Pari the mice were of a light-brown or grayish color, while around Yamdro their coat had in its brown a marked touch of red. But both varieties had one thing in common: they had no tail. They were very fat and stumpy-looking and in general appearance much more like guinea-pigs than mice. They had a curious way of squatting on their hind legs and surveying all about them until we came sufficiently near to frighten them, when they scurried into their holes. The ground was full of these holes; every two or three yards we came upon a fresh one. Satan, busy reciting his prayers for the day, did not notice them and allowed his pony to stumble in one of them, which resulted in a nasty fall. He had been going so slowly, however, that the fall was gentle, and he was not seriously injured; but on picking himself up he began cursing me with enormous gusto, as if I had been responsible for the mishap.

We had no time to argue. It was necessary for all of us to push forward, in spite of fatigue, at our best possible speed; for we had in front of us another difficult pass to cross that evening, and it was doubtful whether we could make it before nightfall, as it is supposed to be a full day's march from Pede Dzong. We shuffled along as best we could.

The poor pony was utterly exhausted, and Satan had great difficulty in urging him beyond a walk. What beating could not do, however, was effected by jealousy. For some extraordinary reason the aged donkey we had bought in Shigatse, and who had served us remarkably well, had won our pony's undying hatred. Both observed a strict neutrality with the mules but, by bites and kicks, tried to render life obnoxious to each other, and on this occasion, when the pony tried to fall behind, we had only to spur the donkey on in front to make the pony gather together all his energy to keep ahead. He obviously did not mind allowing a mule to take the leadership, but to resign his post to a mere donkey was too great a blow to his pride.

We kept steadily on all the morning without reaching any other village, and I was suffering from the pangs of hunger rendered all the more acute because we could see no resting-place along the coast ahead of us. A little after noon, however, we suddenly came upon a tiny one-roomed house, hidden in a depression. This house served as a midday rest-house for travelers along the highway and has been given the name of Tsakang. Here we stayed only half an hour and, having eaten as heartily as we could, started again on our journey.

Nearly the whole of the afternoon we plodded along the shore of the lake. We saw quite a deal of traffic. Two or three times we met caravans of mules carrying bales of wool down to Pari to be stored there until the spring, when the passes would be open. The wool then could then be taken down to Kalimpong. Nearly the whole of the wool trade of Tibet is in the hands of a small group of traders, most of them inhabitants of the Chumbi Valley; and a very good thing they make out of it. Even Tibet, in spite of its backward condition, is confronted with the very modern problem of monopoly and trusts. In the last few years several attempts have been made to break this wool combine, but in all cases they have failed. Frequently the would-be competitors have died mysterious and sudden deaths. Poisoning has been made into an accomplished art in Tibet and is very frequently employed in settling private feuds. Aconite is the poison most frequently employed, but others are not infrequent, and I believe that there are three or four poisons employed by the Tibetans which are completely unknown to the European toxicology. In addition to its secret use, aconite is also used openly in preparing poisoned arrows, with which the Tibetans were accustomed to fight. At the present day guns of modern make are rapidly displacing the aconite-tipped arrows except in the outlying districts, but the use of this and other drugs for secret poisoning seems to show no sign of abating.

All the way we could see that the lake was covered with a thick coat of ice, though with occasional seams indicating some flaw. Several times during the day we saw men walking across the frozen lake from the mainland to the peninsula or island in the middle, for hidden behind the hills on the great neck of land were several villages. In most cases these crossings were accomplished without difficulty or incident, but on one occasion, late in the afternoon, we were the spectators of a tragedy. Two men who were walking nearly in the center came to a point where there was a bad flaw in the ice. We could see they had to jump across a seam. The ice on the other side was obviously weak, for it cracked under them and they were precipitated into the freezing water below. They attempted to crawl out, but at first they could not find a block of ice capable of supporting their weight, and soon they were so numbed by the cold that they fell back helpless and sank beneath the water. We could see their heads appear once or twice, and then they sank again—and disappeared forever.

I was astonished at the phlegm with which my companions looked on at a catastrophe happening before our eyes. We passed one of the caravans just at this time, and its members paused for a few moments to look at the tragedy taking place a few hundred yards away, but they continued their amiable chatter, and no one made any move to save the unfortunates. Help was, I suppose, impossible, the victims were too far away; but I remembered the cold plunge to which I had been subjected on the preceding day, and I could not but shiver at their fate.

Once or twice we saw where formerly there had been villages of moderate size which had now become deserted. This is a sight which is very common in Tibet, for Tibet presents the appearance of a dying country, though in the last few years, since 1912, there have been signs of revival. In this particular instance the downfall of these villages was due, so my companions told me, to the abolition of fishing. Although fish is considered a dirty food, the Tibetan peasants not infrequently eat it, and the Yamdro Lake is well known for the size and excellence of its fish; but the present Dalai-lama, who is more than usually strict in his observance of religious injunctions, issued strict orders that the catching of fish should be stopped, and although in the more out-of-the-way places this order is not very strictly observed, in the villages nearer the highway the order had a very deleterious effect, and the poor villagers, finding their chief means of livelihood gone, were forced to go elsewhere.

In Tibet far greater attention seems to be paid to animal welfare than to the welfare of human beings.

About four o'clock in the afternoon we came to a parting of the ways. To the right a road continued along the shores of the lake, leading to the villages and the pasture-lands on the other side. To the left a trail started up to the side of the mountain leading to the Kampa Pass. We had to follow the latter and soon began a steep ascent. The Yamdro Lake lies fourteen thousand feet above sea-level, and the mountain range dividing it from the Brahmaputra Valley, which lies just on the other side, is about a thousand feet higher. The upward climb was not, therefore, very long, but we and our animals were all so fatigued—I particularly, on account of the nervous excitement of the morning—that the ascent seemed endless. Half-way up one of the mules suddenly sat down, and it required all of our efforts to get her on her feet again.

The latter part of the climb was considerably less steep, and shortly before sunset we arrived at the top of the pass and could once more see the Brahmaputra Valley stretched out before us. The scenery was magnificent, being in fact the finest view which I had ever seen in the country; but as I was acting the part of a Tibetan peasant it was impossible to stop too long to admire natural beauty.

As usual, just at the top of the pass we found two chortens or shrines. We added our stones to the little pile in front of each and also tied a rag apiece to the brush sticking out above the stone-heaps. We then recited a charm (*mantram*) in honor of the gods, rested for a few moments, and then began our long descent. The descent was much longer than the ascent, for whereas the pass lies only a thousand feet above the level of the lake, it is three thousand feet above the level of the Brahmaputra Valley, which lies much lower. The descent was in places extraordinarily steep and rendered somewhat dangerous by the darkness, which was now rapidly falling. In one place we came upon the body of a mule that had fallen from the upper portion of the road almost immediately above us. The corpse lay in the little stream which ran down from here to the village at the bottom of the valley. We later found the stream was the water-supply for this village, but the Tibetans are not at all fastidious in these matters, though they have a healthy dislike of drinking cold water, water being only drunk in the form of chang or tea, the preparation of which renders it more or less safe.

It is curious to find how in many cases popular superstitions have as their basis a certain amount of truth.

The Tibetans regard tea as a preventive of typhoid and other forms of fever. The truth is, of course, that in order to prepare the tea they have to boil the water, thereby killing the germs.

It took us about two hours and a half to descend the pass, and we came at last to the Brahmaputra Valley itself. Here we found the village of Kampabartse, and here we rested for the night. Our rest-house, I was glad to find, was not in but on the outskirts of the village. It was in conformity with the general type, the common room being but a walled-in stall in one corner of the courtyard, but I noticed several points of difference between the inhabitants of this village and those of the villages in which we had hitherto stayed. This had reference to the language, one or two minor customs, and also the dress of the people, more particularly the women. The hair-dress of the women was one of the most important changes. This transformation was due, we found, to the fact that we were now in the province of U and had left Tsang behind us, the technical dividing-point being the pass. We were now, therefore, not only in Tibet but in the very heart of Tibet, in the province of which Lhasa itself is the principal city.

It was thrilling to feel that we had come so far in spite of the innumerable obstacles which had stood in our paths, but I knew that the nearer we got to the capital the stricter the watch would become.

That evening we were to encounter one peculiar difficulty. We had changed a good deal of our Indian money into Tibetan currency, but the hire of the ponies to Yase had taken a good deal of our stock, and on arriving at Kampabartse we found our little store of Tibetan coins was completely exhausted. We had, of course, some of our old friends, ten-rupee Indian notes, and Satan tried to get our landlady to change these, but we found the old dame had never seen one and was very suspicious of them. In Pede Dzong, which is a much larger community, we should have had little or no difficulty in changing them, but in thus staying at the smaller villages to avoid the officials we had got ourselves into additional hot water.

The old *nemo* proved as adamant as any boarding-house landlady in Bloomsbury and, discovering our financial difficulties, refused to let us have any fuel or chang until we had paid cash; and what we proffered as cash she refused to accept.

In these circumstances we hardly knew what to do. Satan said that the only thing to do was to sell something. But what in the world had we to sell? Lhaten suggested one of the tin pots in which we were accustomed to boil our tea; for cooking utensils are among the things the traveler in Tibet must take along with him. We had two, and one must be sacrificed. Just at this moment I remembered that in addition to our ten-rupee paper notes I had a few silver coins in my bundle, and I quickly got these out; and calling the *nemo* back, we proffered them to her. She still seemed hesitant but after clinking the silver coins together she decided to accept them, and so after all we secured fire and something to drink.

I had been very much afraid that our possession of

only Indian coins might lead to suspicion as to our identity, and so we were careful to tell the good lady that we had been on a trading tour in Kalimpong, where we had been paid for our goods in Indian money and had not yet exchanged it for Tibetan, as the rate of exchange was more favorable in Lhasa—a point which was in fact true. But I was grateful to note that she was not at all upset about the matter and said that only a few weeks previously some travelers had attempted to pass off some one-rupee notes on a rest-house in the same village.

Fortunately while all this colloquy was going on we were alone, for no one was staying at the rest-house except our party, and our three companions had gone off to see an acquaintance in another part of the village.

After our meal, as I wanted to put the *nemo* in a good humor, I suggested to Lhaten that he call her in and give her a cup of chang. This is frequently done in Tibet, and the old lady was not slow in accepting our invitation and in fact stayed on interminably and regaled us with her gossip.

I was nodding in one corner and paying little attention to the conversation when suddenly I heard the woman mention that a foreigner was trying to get to Lhasa, and as we were coming from Kalimpong she asked us if we had seen anything of him. Needless to say we possessed no information regarding any such person. Lhaten added that though we had heard the rumor concerning him, he thought the whole thing was probably false.

The good lady said she would like to see the "foreign devil" and give him a good piece of her mind, but she was sure that so great was the vigilance of the officials and so powerful was the spiritual force of the Dalai-lama that the intruder would certainly be detected and sent back to his own village.

I was interested in this latter statement as showing the implicit faith which the Tibetans have in the divinity and power of their suzerain. In spite of the many vicissitudes which have marked the reign of this and previous holders of the office, most Tibetans really believe that the Dalai-lama is omnipotent, and nearly all have faith in his omniscience.

The fact that the present ruler was twice forced to flee the country at the peril of his life is glossed over or forgotten, or sometimes explained away, and our hostess was firmly convinced that by means of his spiritual powers the Dalai-lama could have told at any moment where I was and what I was doing. The only class of Tibetans who are skeptical on these matters are the monks, particularly the Lhasa monks, and those in immediate contact with the court.

The old lady left us at last. Our companions returned soon afterward, and before long all of us were sound asleep.

Very early the next morning we were off again and painfully made our way in the dark, for there was no moon, and it was only the extraordinary road knowledge of our companions that allowed us to make progress. For several miles our route lay along the south side of the great river; the murmuring of its stream a few hundred yards away was frequently in our ears.

In the gloom we passed through several sleeping villages, one or two of which had some fine old trees about them. The watch-dogs outside the houses barked at us, but we went on without stopping. A flank of hills began to close down on the river, forcing us nearer the banks, and here we found the roadway sandy. We were up to our knees in sand, but still we plowed on in silence.

CHAPTER X

THE LAST FIFTY MILES

JUST before dawn we came to a very important landmark, the famous Chaksam Ferry, placed where the outreaching hill forms a cliff overhanging the river. Here is to be found a regular service of boats which carries passengers from one side of the river to the other.

This is the only ferry along this portion of the Brahmaputra, and for some reason I had been terribly afraid of this spot, as here it was possible to see each traveler so closely that I felt sure that an official would be posted here to examine us. I was, therefore, particularly annoyed to find that the ferrymen were not yet awake and refused to cross until it was fully light. I shivered in the cold for many minutes, and then, not wishing to remain too near the ferry hut, continued for a few minutes along the cliff to catch a nearer glimpse of the monastery a few hundred yards further down.

This monastery is a place of some repute, though it has only some hundred inhabitants. Its fame is largely due to the fact that it is the starting-point and base of the great iron suspension-bridge which formerly spanned the Brahmaputra River at this point.

The great bridge is still standing, and very pictur esque it looked in the early dawn, but it is no longer serviceable, as in recent years the river has greatly widened its banks, so that the further or northern end of the bridge now forms a small island standing in the middle of the stream. The Tibetans did not have energy enough to extend the chain-bridge to the present bank and so have fallen back upon the ferry system for getting from one side to the other.

Such is the decay of Tibetan vigor for the old bridge was well made and has stood the test of centuries. It was built by the King Tantong, who was born about 1385 and is now a saint in the Tibetan religion, his image being worshiped in the adjoining monastery. This bridge was not his only engineering achievement, for he is said to have built 108 temples and shrines and seven other chain-bridges over the Brahmaputra. It is said that some of his other bridges higher up the river are still in use.

It was now quite light, and it was high time to hasten back to the ferry. On our way back we were overtaken by a group of nuns from a nearby convent, who also intended crossing the river. They were gaily chatting and occasionally burst out into shrieks of laughter. Apparently their religious professions did not interfere with their enjoyment of life. The heads of all these nuns were shaven, but I noticed that some of them wore curious thick wigs of coarse wool, colored a dusky red.

I was glad to find the ferrymen were at last getting ready. There were three or four of the Tibetan yak-hide coracles lying beside the bank. The nuns and the three or four other foot passengers got into these, and though they sank deep in the water and because of their unwieldy shape, turned round and round in the center of the stream, causing the women-folk to squeal excitedly, they reached the other side safely.

We had several animals with our party and so would not cross in these *kowa* or coracles. For travelers such as ourselves there was provided a large, rectangular flat-bottomed wooden boat, the only one of its kind I believe anywhere in Tibet.

We had a great deal of trouble in getting the animals into the ferry, and the awkward-shaped boat was very slow and cumbrous in its movements; but at last with a bump we reached the other side, a broad sandy plain. Contrary to my fears, no attempt was made to search or examine us. This may have been partly due to the fact that the ferry is privately owned, being in fact the property of the monastery which we had seen, a considerable portion of the revenue of which comes from the toll exacted from each passenger. For our whole party, however, consisting of five persons, a pony, two mules, and a donkey—our companions, of course, paid their own fee—we paid only three trangkas (ninepence) ferry charges, so that in this case monopoly does not seem to have brought about excessive charges.

Our road now lay for several miles along the north bank of the Brahmaputra. Our companions were anxious to get on to Chushul, their home, and, without waiting for us, trotted on ahead. Satan, who, of course, was also mounted, accompanied them, and we agreed to meet at Chushul.

At this point the Brahmaputra Valley is a little under twelve thousand feet above sea-level, very low for Central Tibet, so that it forms one of the warmest and most fertile parts of the country; consequently we could see villages lying only a very few miles apart and passed through two or three on the way to Chushul.

In one of these there was an inviting-looking courtyard, which stood upon our left. Paris, the mule, also saw it and suddenly bolted into it, and it was only with the greatest difficulty that we could get her out. In fact, she kicked up such a rumpus that the whole courtyard was in an uproar before we could get under way. The poor mule was only trying to give us a signal that she had come to the end of her resources, but it was a signal which we could not understand, and which, alas, in any case we could not have heeded. The good farmer into whose courtyard we had broken was not at all inclined to take matters philosophically; he cursed us most roundly and even pursued us down the road to throw stones at us and to give us a full account of our ancestry on both sides.

This little incident wonderfully refreshed us, and we continued on our way in a much better frame of mind. The plain soon narrowed down to a road that was just sufficient to let us pass along in single file, and then we rounded a tapering cliff and found ourselves in the important town of Chushul.

Our companions had stationed a boy outside to wait for us and to show us where their house was, so that before long we were able to halt and take our midday rest.

Chushul occupies an important strategic position. At this point the Kyichu or river of felicity flows into the Brahmaputra. Lhasa lies about forty-five miles up the Kyichu, so that we were here to depart from the great river again.

In 1910, when the Chinese invaded Tibet and the Dalai-lama was forced to flee to India, the Chinese sent a detachment to capture his Holiness and bring him back. A Tibetan rear-guard commanded by Namgang, the present Tsarong Shapé, commander-in-chief of the Tibetan army, took a stand at this place and by a magnificent battle managed to keep the Chinese back for several days, giving the Dalai-lama time to reach the frontier in safety. This battle was destined to be the turning-point in Namgang's career and thereby a decisive point in Tibet's destiny.

On the top of the near-by hill are the ruins of an old dzong or fort, but this has long since been destroyed; and though Chushul is the center of an administrative district and has its two governors, these officials are now housed in a large dwelling inside the village, adequate and imposing, but obviously having nothing of the castle or fortress in its construction.

This was very interesting to me, as indicating a gradual change in Tibet's social organization. Just as in Europe the walled city has disappeared and with it the use of castles as the headquarters of the governing powers, so at the present time in Tibet, many hundreds of years later, a similar tendency is evident, and probably there as elsewhere the dzong or castle will give way to the palace. In some ways it is a pity, for the castles form one of Tibet's chief glories.

Among the various buildings belonging to the Government at Chushul I noticed one which had an enormous hole in one wall. This was pointed out to me, and it was explained that not long previously an elephant was sent by the maharaja of Nepal to the Dalai-lama. On his way up to Lhasa he had been housed in this building and during the night had leaned against the wall, with the result that the whole side had given way. Frightened by the damage which he himself had made, the elephant had bolted and caused tremendous turmoil and excitement before he was captured.

While we were resting after our lunch, our hosts regaled us with tales of the dishonesty of Chushul people as a whole, the wicked tricks which were played upon travelers to deprive them of their money and valuables. I could well believe these tales, as the Chushul thieves have a reputation throughout the country. but I was surprised at the naïveté with which local inhabitants confessed such things. But in other ways it is interesting to observe how the Tibetan people have a shrewd suspicion of their own weaknesses.

We were singularly lucky in staying with acquaintances in Chushul. In this way not only were we saved from the wiles of thieves but, as I found out later, we escaped a searching examination on the part of the officials.

Chushul is so much regarded as the gateway of Lhasa that especial orders had been issued to the rest-house keepers here to report the arrival of any unknown travelers so that they could be searched by the officials, and it was believed impossible that any one could escape from the Chushul net; but our traveling-companions, who were, of course, well known in the place, vouched for us to the officials, and we got through without difficulty.

Even so, I was very anxious to get away from this village as soon as possible, and shortly after noon we started out again. Very much to my regret we had now to go on alone, as our friends were staying behind, and we found no other party to which we could attach ourselves.

We were now in the Kyi or Kyichu Valley. For about ten miles it preserved a wide-open formation and looked nearly as broad as the valley of the main Brahmaputra River. For the first few miles it was very thickly inhabited.

Between two of the villages we saw a very interesting marriage procession.

The marriage ceremonies of Tibetans of all ranks and classes are more or less alike, and as there is no caste system, though the aristocrats and officials are a proud, domineering race, it sometimes occurs that rich men claim wives from among the women of the poorer people, though it is very rare that male commoners marry into the families of the higher grades. Most frequently when an aristocratic girl fails to contract a good match she ends her days in one of the numerous nunneries.

Matches are first arranged by go-betweens, after

which the would-be bridegroom makes a formal offer of marriage to the bride's parents. Consent, which is ever delayed while a form of traditional bargaining goes on, is finally conveyed to the bridegroom's parents, who then make a present of a large quantity of wine to the house of the bride, when a general entertainment is provided, at which all of the families and their servants attend to dispose of the wine. *Kata,* the Tibetan ceremonial scarfs, are also presented to all and sundry by the bridegroom's parents.

This is a preliminary to the conveyance of the dowry, or purchase-money, called *rin,* which is paid over to the bride's father at a repetition of the previous ceremony.

The bridegroom does not go to fetch his bride but deputes about seven or eight male friends to induce her to leave her home. They stay with her parents for three days, when, laden with clothing and, if fairly well-to-do, a pony, a yak, a milch cow, and perhaps some oxen, also jewelry and plate and other articles for domestic use, she prepares to join her future consort. It is strange to note that the custom of wedding presents prevails in Tibet, and the bride is loaded with all sorts of gifts, according to her rank, by friends and relatives. A party of the bridegroom's friends come to escort her to her new home, where, when she arrives, she is seated on a cushion on a raised dais, where she remains with the bridegroom until a local lama performs a short service and prayers are said. The two chief parties have little to do or say, but the bridegroom's parents make a declaration that henceforth the bride will be owned by the bridegroom and his brothers solely, a part of the service which will scarcely appeal to the modern Western woman. Feasting follows, with presents to the bridegroom, and this continues for three days, when normal life is resumed after the wife has exchanged her bridal wardrobe for dress presented her by the husband. Sometime later there is a renewal of festivities, but these ceremonies are not nearly so elaborate in the case of the common people, though generally the main customs are observed.

While, however, there is one bridegroom, all his brothers become husbands of the bride and are proportionately responsible for her welfare. Marriage takes place at a relatively early age—between fifteen and twenty-five years of age—and very often the bride is older than her man.

I was very much amazed to find a marriage taking place at this unusual time, shortly before Tibetan New Year, and can only suppose that some urgent private reasons must have dictated it.

Later in the afternoon the soil became much more sandy and the little villages ceased. It also became very difficult to walk, and it was only with the greatest difficulty that I could continue to place one foot in front of the other. I felt so numbed by illness, weakness, and fatigue that I could think of nothing but one step at a time. Just at this point Paris, the mule, suddenly collapsed. She sat down and refused to move.

I was now at my wit's end. Satan got off his pony, and we added some of the mule's load to the packs the pony was carrying; but even so, much was left over, and we ourselves could not carry an ounce more. We sat down by the roadside in despair trying to think what we should do. While we were still arguing the point we were overtaken by four or five peasants who were carrying curious spears. They saw our sorry plight at a glance and told us that the village of Jang-me was only three or four miles ahead, and that they would, for a small fee, carry Paris's discarded packs on to that village, where we could stay for the night and try to make further arrangements.

We were very glad to accept their offer and once more pushed on. Once her load was off her, we managed to get Paris on her feet again, and we even persuaded her to accompany us to the village.

Soon afterward the valley narrowed down to a rocky gorge with many twists and turnings, and we were seldom able to see more than a few yards away.

About an hour later, while we were still in the gorge, a peculiar incident occurred which I feel it necessary to relate, as it so nearly led to my undoing. I had pressed on a quarter of a mile ahead of the others and was suddenly compelled to urinate. No one was in sight at the time, and I so far relaxed my disguise as to perform this duty in European fashion, i.e., standing up, instead of following Tibetan custom and squatting down.

Just at this moment a Tibetan official accompanied by two retainers, coming riding around the corner and surprised at my attitude, immediately stopped and asked me who and what I was. I was surprised to notice how so small a thing as standing or stooping should awaken so much suspicion, and in my confusion could only stammer out that I was ill and was but a poor peasant coming with his master on pilgrimages to Lhasa.

Fortunately for me, at this moment Satan and Lhaten put in an appearance. Lhaten took in the situation at once and came to my assistance in a very effective way. He rushed up, struck me with his whip, reproved me for dallying on the way, and ordered me to go on immediately. I was thus allowed to go on while the other two stopped to talk with the official. Evidently their tale must have been very effective, for in a few moments they came on and waved to me that all was well.

I was interested to find, many months later, on my return to Europe that Sir Francis Burton had a very similar experience on his secret journey to Mecca many years previously, though in his case the affair ended more tragically.

Not long after this the gorge opened out to form a basin, and here we found the twin village of Jangtö and Jangme, or upper and lower Jang, some thirty miles away from Lhasa. We went to a rest-house recommended to us by our spear-carrying porters, and soon had our animals unloaded and sat down for our much-needed rest. But after our evening meal we had to put our heads together and arrange for our transport for the next day; a most fateful and important day, for it should bring us to our goal, the city of Lhasa.

But we were at our wit's end, not knowing what to do as regards our transport.

We went out to inspect the two mules, and what we saw was certainly unpromising. Paris was obviously drooping from exhaustion, and the other poor mule, though seeming somewhat better, was distressingly afflicted with saddle-sores. In fact it was really worse than this. The shoe-blacking and the other things which the syce had rubbed on the early sores to cure them must have been septic, for the whole back of the miserable creature was now swollen with a great abscess.

No one could look at the creature without a feeling of pity, but I was surprised to find that Satan became really ill and was so affected that he began to pray very volubly to the gods. This feeling of mercy toward animals was all the more surprising considering how heartless he had been toward the sufferings of his fellow-travelers and the merciless way in which he had beaten Diogenes.

This, however, was only another case, strange but frequent, where a man has more feeling for dumb animals than for his fellow-man. This seems to be particularly true of Tibet, where the killing of a man seems in many instances less serious than the killing of an animal.

Sorry as I felt for the animals, I felt even sorrier for ourselves because of the desperate situation in which we were placed by their collapse. Here we were only thirty-odd miles from Lhasa, and it appeared almost impossible to get on. To go on without our transport was out of the question; our animals had given in, and I did not have sufficient money to buy any more. At this time I had only three hundred rupees left, and once these were gone I should be utterly helpless, penniless in the midst of a strange and savage land. I could not therefore afford to buy any other animals, but I told Lhaten to go around and try to hire some animals for the last day's journey. He tried in several places but in vain. Had we been provided with *ula* or government passes the peasants would have been forced to provide their animals, but without this pressure they refused to part with any of them in spite of tempting offers.

At last, however, he met an old farmer living on the outskirts of the village who seemed open to a proposition. He refused to rent his ponies for money, but upon hearing that we had two mules to dispose of he agreed to take the mules off our hands, thinking that a little rest would put them on their feet again, and in return for the mules he agreed to give us outright one pony and to lend us two other ponies as far as Lhasa.

The old farmer thought he was making a very good bargain, because in Tibet a mule is worth nearly twice as much as a pony, and here he was getting two mules for one pony, and a poor, miserable, forlorn-looking pony at that.

I, however, was quite satisfied at the turn of affairs, for it allowed us to move on the next day, and I learned later that Paris died not long afterward, so that this unpromising bargain turned out to be the only successful horse-deal with which I was ever connected.

Before long we were all asleep but so exhausted by the day's vicissitudes that it was nearly four o'clock before we started off on the last day's journey.

It was still dark, but we had no fear of losing the road, as we had with us the two sons of the old farmer who were coming with us to Lhasa to bring back the two ponies which had been lent to us.

For two or three miles our path lay along the sandy banks of the river, but after this the river valley narrowed down considerably, and we were forced to clamber up and along the sides of the rocky hills which flanked the left bank of the river. The road was terribly rough and stony, and many huge boulders lay in the way, but it was obvious that the roadway was artificial and in parts had been carved out of the hillside by human hands. This was the first time I had seen a deliberate attempt to construct a road. Everywhere else there were simply tracks made by the passage of thousands of mules and ponies, which had passed over the plains and over the passes at the most convenient spots. I was surprised that so much trouble had been taken to build a road along the cliff, as it seemed to me that it would have cost less time and trouble to divert the Kyi River, which wandered to and fro over the river-bed in such a way as to leave space for a road at the foot of the cliff.

I was told, however, that the apparently mild, peaceful-looking river was subject to great floods changing it to a raging torrent which not only filled the valley but also dashed in waves up the side of the cliff. Even more important was the fact that several places in the sandy banks at the foot of the cliffs were quicksands which eagerly devoured everything which rested on them.

It was difficult to believe this until we came to a place where we could see a little donkey which had slid down the sides of the hill and was already half sunk in the moist sands, which were gradually drawing him in. The peasants were trying to drag him out with their leather ropes, but as we passed them it seemed a fairly hopeless task.

For several miles our way lay along the awful rocky road, but at length we were able to descend to the bed of the valley again, and we were able to force our ponies on to a trot. About noon we reached the village of Netrang, where we stopped for our usual breakfast-lunch and rest.

During our brief stay here I found time to visit the somewhat neglected shrine of the great Indian priest Atisa, who came to Tibet and instituted several important reforms. These reforms later brought about the rise of the yellow-hat sect, which is now the established church of Tibet. Atisa died here in 1052, and the shrine erected on his remains, even though neglected, is still considered one of the most famous and holy places of the country.

Early in the afternoon I started out again on the road, for we still had many miles to cover that day. I departed as usual before the others, thinking they would catch up in a few minutes, but something delayed them, and I had to go on for several miles alone. I felt rather frightened at this, as I met several people on the road, and in case of examination I wanted some one by me who could do most of the talking.

Fortunately I seemed to awaken no suspicion in

any one and was only given an occasional hail; nearly all of the people, I noticed, were going toward Lhasa and very few coming away, for the next day was the beginning of an important festival season, so that Lhasa was attracting a large number of visitors.

I was riding very slowly, giving my servants an opportunity to catch up, so that I was frequently passed by small mounted parties on their way to the capital. I noticed that no man of apparent opulence rode alone or unescorted. In every case there was at least one servant riding before and one behind.

I overtook and passed, however, a number of travelers on foot. Most of these were obviously pilgrims of great poverty or if they possessed means they were wise enough to hide it. One such pilgrim attracted my especial attention, as he was measuring his distance along the ground. He would stand up straight, his hands stretched above him, and then, prostrating himself on the ground, would mark the place to which his finger-tips extended. He would then step to this point and go through the same process.

When I came near him he stopped and begged me to give him some money, saying he was a pilgrim who, to make up for certain past misdeeds, was making pilgrimage in this slow and laborious fashion to Lhasa. He added that he had started his journey from Shigatse and had been just a year on the road. He had been supported all this time by the donation of pious travelers who had passed him.

I tossed him a small coin and then passed on. Such acts of devotion are not uncommon in Tibet, though this was the first such devotee that I had seen. More usually such prostration-walking is confined to the circumambulation of a temple or city. His method of travel gave me a humorous reminder of the leeches of Sikkim, though in other respects I thought these blood-sucking creatures had more in common with the rapacious monks of Tibet than with this simple, naïve peasant.

The valley had widened out considerably, but immediately ahead of me was a steep-rising hill which ran at right angles to the flanking mountains right down to the water's edge. I ascended the shoulder of this hill, thinking I would catch a distant glimpse of the Forbidden City from the top, but on passing through the shoulder I saw only the great valley ahead of me, a valley that gradually widened and then became two valleys, one running to the left and the other to the right.

Of the city of Lhasa there was no sign, but immediately ahead, several miles away, there ran a range of mountains, and from where I was I could see, on the lower slope of these mountains, a huge and very impressive group of buildings rising tier by tier in ever-increasing splendor. This I knew must be the great Drepung monastery, the largest monastery in Tibet, and, in fact, the largest anywhere in the world. In theory it is supposed to have only seventy-seven hundred monks as residents, but in practice this number is far exceeded, and at present the population of the huge monastery is more than ten thousand.

Inside of the city of Lhasa there are of course

numerous temples and monasteries, none of them of great numerical importance. But in the neighborhood of Lhasa, apart from numerous minor ecclesiastical establishments, there are three great monasteries, each with its hordes of fighting monks, its colleges, its own hierarchy, and each possessed of enormous landed estates scattered all over the country. These three monasteries have a great deal to do with the government of the country, and even the Dalai-lama and his cabinet dare not face their wrath.

Of these the largest and most powerful and at the same time the most reactionary and turbulent is Drepung, the monastery which now lay directly ahead. It was, I knew, only four or five miles from Lhasa. The second in size was Sera with nominally fifty-five hundred monks (in practice many more), which, I was told, lay two or three miles north of the city. The last of the trio was Ganden (Gal-ldan) or paradise monastery, with nominally only thirty-three hundred monks, which lay about twenty-five miles from the city—a day's journey away. Though the smallest from the historical point of view, Ganden is the most important, as it was founded by Tsong-Kapa, the organizer of the ruling yellow-hat order of Tibetan Buddhism.

I descended to the foot of this spur, and there I found a huge bas-relief carving of the seated Buddha, of gigantic proportions, and of considerable artistic worth. Here I decided to wait until my servants could arrive, as ahead of me the plain seemed full of life, and numerous mounted parties were passing to and fro.

My little party arrived eventually half an hour later. The delay, it seemed, was due to the little donkey bought in Shigatse. So far she had kept up with the other animals with seemingly no difficulty, but she had now begun to lag behind, showing every sign of complete exhaustion, and so we stopped for a few minutes to give her a rest and an extra feed and then pushed on again.

We now had to make a long detour to the left, as the river had widened out considerably, and much of the plain in front of us was marshy and covered with stagnant back-waters.

Mile after mile we covered always in the direction of Drepung and still no sign of Lhasa. Earlier in the day my servants had been very chatty, but now a feeling of desperate fatigue had come upon us all, and we rode on in silence.

At length we came to an old village surrounded by majestic and ancient willow-trees, and here we ran into a swarm of beggars, who followed our party for more than a mile gesticulating and clamoring for alms; for were we not pilgrims coming to Lhasa, and was it not therefore our duty to acquire merit through charity? The few karmanga thrown them did not appease them, and eventually Lhaten had to drive them back by threatening them with his whip.

The traffic had now increased enormously. From the numerous villages scattered over the plain there came small mounted parties hastening along the great highway to get into Lhasa in time for the great festivities which started that evening. Many of these were prosperous ecclesiastics who showed most obviously that the gods favored and the people feared them. Many of these parties looked askance at our quaint little caravan dragging itself wearily along the road. Several times we were asked whence we came, and on one occasion when Satan told him that we came from near the Sikkim frontier he was then asked if he had seen anything of the foreigner who was said to be trying to get to Lhasa. A brief denial brought the matter to an end; but it showed the rumors about my presence had been widespread and had caused considerable excitement.

A mile or two beyond the village we came to a point where the river bifurcated. The main Kyi River turned sharply to the right, while its large tributary, the Ti River, ran in from the left. We had now to cross over this tributary by means of a very large and imposing bridge more than a hundred yards long, with masonry piers and substantial stone embankments.

For some time past I had been so torpid with fatigue that I had failed to notice the surrounding landscape, but suddenly Lhaten called out to me to look to the right. Doing so I felt a great and sudden thrill. In the distance, eight or nine miles away, I could see the Potala, the great palace of the Dalai-lama, the god-priest of the Tibetan people, and I knew that on the other side of the hill on which the palace was perched lay Lhasa, the abode of the gods.

The goal was at length in sight, and I knew at last that the long weary journey, the exposure, the privation, the illness, the constant fear and danger of detection had not been entirely in vain.

CHAPTER XI

THE GOAL ACHIEVED—WE ARRIVE IN LHASA

WE halted for some minutes to gaze at our objective, as we still had several miles to cover. The road was teeming with people, for the most part peasants bringing in grain, butter, and yak-dung to the city. Ponies, mules, and donkeys were in abundance, many of them with jingling bells around their necks. Many of them were progressing slowly, but so fatigued was our little caravan that most of them overtook and passed us.

At last we came to the foot of the hills which I had seen several hours earlier and then turned to the right to follow the Kyi Valley up to Lhasa, which always remained in view but which still seemed incredibly far away.

I was incredibly exhausted, but now that the goal was in sight I hoped that we could complete our journey without further incident. But just when we had passed under the ruins of the old Dongkar Castle and had the great Drepung monastery towering above us, a few hundred yards up the slope of the mountain the little donkey suddenly and mysteriously collapsed.

Lhaten and I jumped off our ponies and helped the syce lift her on her feet and readjust her load, and we then made desperate attempts to get her on the move again. It was in vain, but the little incident caused something of a crowd to collect, and among the crowd I could see many of the Drepung monks, some of whom jeered and others shouted out advice to us.

Drepung is well known as the chief center of the anti-foreign agitation, and many of its monks are fierce brawlers who back their opinions with their actions, so that I became very much embarrassed at the attention we were receiving. Satan, who became even more nervous, left us entirely in the lurch and rode on ahead, not wishing to seem associated with us in case of exciting developments.

In the end we took off the donkey's loads and added them to the ponies on which we were riding, but I left the syce and Diogenes behind with orders to try and bring the donkey on later, as I thought that in Lhasa we might possibly be able to sell her for something.

While the mob were still interested in the syce's struggles with the donkey, Lhaten and I slipped on our ponies and, accompanied by our two Jangme guides, continued on our way.

Half a mile further on we found Satan hiding behind a little adobe hut. Seeing that we were alone and unmolested, he consented to come out and rejoin the party. It was neither the time nor the place to say anything, but I was thoroughly disgusted with the rascal's cowardice in leaving us in the lurch.

We had left the imposing mass of Drepung behind

us, and had now only three miles or so further to go. The road was now dotted with small groups of Drepung monks making their way back to their monastery after spending the day in the city.

Our goal now loomed up very clearly before us silhouetted against the evening sky. The city itself was still invisible, and what we saw was two hills surmounted by buildings. The smaller and more pointed hill on the right was called the Chakpo-ri, or the iron mountain, and the quaint, square, tower-like building on its summit was the lama college of medicine. The hill on the left, larger but more rounded, was surmounted by the Potala Palace. As yet we could only glimpse the gilded spires of the roof of this building, as the major portion of the palace was built on the slope of the other side of the hill. The main city, I knew, lay about a mile beyond the two hills, but I wanted if possible to halt that evening at the little village of Potala-shol, which lies just at the foot of the palacc on the other side of the hill.

In order to get there we had to pass through the narrow opening between the two hills. So narrow, indeed, was the opening that a huge *chorten* or shrine had been placed over it, and we had to pass along the tiny roadway running *through* the shrine.

So narrow was the roadway that we had to dismount and pass through single file; but, once through, what a sight lay before our eyes. Before us ran a long and magnificent avenue leading to the city of Lhasa itself, the chief buildings of which could be seen looming in the distance. Immediately on our left we were face to

Medical college, Lhasa, on hill

Frozen ground and lack of wood or vegetation for fire drive the Tibetans to cut up their dead in the hills and leave the remains to the vultures

His Holiness the Dalai-lama

face with the gigantic structure of the Potala Palace, which covered the whole face of the hill.

Though we had seen the rear of the palace many miles back, this sudden appearance of the main building was most impressive, and I halted almost dumfounded by its splendor. It is a building wrought partly in stone and partly in sun-dried and whitewashed brick, nine hundred feet in length and more than seventy feet higher than the golden cross of St. Paul's Cathedral; it possesses a simplicity and yet a stateliness of style that cannot but impress even the most sophisticated. The upper center of the building was red, the remainder white.

In the plain at the foot of the hill were numerous outhouses belonging to the palace, used as stables, storehouses, and the residences of minor court officials, and adjoining these, though outside an encircling wall, were several private buildings—residences and shops.

A number of the residences also served as rest-houses for travelers; to these we directed our attention. But here we met with a fresh difficulty. Every one of these was already crowded; not only were the common rooms literally crammed with people, but large numbers had also bivouacked in the open courtyards.

Largely by accident we had arrived at Lhasa at the most holy and important time of the year. That evening, February 15, was the last day of the Tibetan year, and the next day, February 16, was the Tibetan New Year and the opening day of the New Year festivities, which were to last three weeks. So many imposing pageants and ceremonies are held during this time that it is small wonder that thousands of devout pilgrims crowd into the capital to gaze in awe and wonder, and in addition the city was overrun by monks from the three great monasteries of Drepung, Sera, and Ganden, and other ecclesiastical centers, many of whom were to take an active part in the religious celebrations which attend the beginning of the year.

It is estimated that in spite of its holiness and importance the population of Lhasa at ordinary times is only about twenty thousand (this does not include, of course, the monks of the three outlying monasteries), but at New Year time the population becomes more than five times as great and certainly exceeds a hundred thousand.

In spite of this fact I had thought it would be possible to squeeze in at some odd corner, but I was now to realize that it was impossible to secure a place at any price where we could lay our heads for the night. Every rest-house in the village was tried in vain, and the rest-house keepers became abusive when we attempted to push our claim for space.

The last rest-house we tried furnished us additional excitement in the form of the largest dog I have ever seen. He was unlike most Tibetan dogs, and looked like an overgrown St. Bernard. When Lhaten began to expostulate with the *nemo* of the house and to demand that we be allowed at least to sleep in the courtyard, the *nemo's* only reply was to let loose the great dog, who at once snarled and jumped to the attack.

The Tibetans are afraid of dogs, and every one in sight scattered immediately; in spite of our utter exhaustion my little party managed to make its way out of the courtyard in really record time.

As it was now quite obvious that there was no place for us anywhere in the Potala-shol, we determined to go and try our luck in the city of Lhasa itself, a mile or so further on.

The syce and Diogenes who had been left behind with the donkey had not yet caught up with us, and we waited several minutes for them to arrive; but in the end we decided to push on without them, as it was rapidly growing dark, and it was imperative that we get some shelter for the whole party as soon as possible; and so we set off down the long avenue leading to the city.

Although, of course, unpaved, the avenue was remarkably pleasant, not only on account of the breadth and evenness of the road but also on account of the park-like pleasure-gardens which lay on either side of it. These pleasure-gardens were private property, partly belonging to the Dalai-lama and partly owned by other aristocratic families, and were separated from the road by high, well-constructed adobe walls; but they were filled with trees, willows mostly, and though it was winter and the trees bleak and black, after the many miles of bare, lifeless, plantless plains, these trees, which reared their heads high over the walls, lent to the great avenue a remarkable sense of beauty and grace.

We met many people on the avenue who were obviously filled with the holiday spirit. Among the crowd was a group of young officials, who, relieved from their ordinary pomp, were obviously out for a gay time and made many ribald jests at the expense of the various little groups of pilgrims making their way to the city.

One of them, keener-eyed than the rest, nudged his companion and pointed me out, and I heard him remark that I looked remarkably like a foreigner; but his friend, seeing my poor shabby clothes, my woebegone appearance and general air of humility (due, I am ashamed to say, to a lively sense of fright), laughed at him and remarked that I was obviously only a misbegotten servant of a lousy Sikkimese. A rather pretty peasant girl hove in sight just at this time, and as the attention of the young sparks was attracted elsewhere I once more passed on in safety.

A little later the road turned to the right, and we soon came to a canal, which was formerly the main stream of the Kyi River but which is now only a stagnant backwater. But this stream was crossed by a famous bridge, the Yutok-sampa, or turquoise bridge, a curious structure which has walls and a roof, making it look like a long corridor. Here there was supposed to be a guard to examine all travelers seeking entrance to the city, but to my delight we passed over unnoticed. The city proper began some two or three hundred yards further on and was entered through a low Chinese archway.

It was now too dark to see much of the city as we passed through. We had, moreover, only one object in view, a shelter of some sort for the night. We were destined, however, to meet the same disheartening reception that we had found at Potala-shol.

Our two guides claimed to know all the rest-houses

in the city, and, following them, we went from courtyard to courtyard. Many of these courtyards housed as many as fifteen or twenty families, and every family was approached in our desperate search for a room, or a share in a room. In each case we were given the same answer: every space was already overcrowded. Over an hour was spent in wandering from place to place, and I began to fear that we should have to spend our first night in Lhasa sleeping out in the open streets. To make matters worse, these streets were now crowded with drunken brawlers in honor of the occasion.

Men were shouting long songs in honor of Arak, and several laid hands on some of the local ladies, who seemed none too unwilling, and more than once a fight broke out between various groups of revelers.

I was in great fear of detection, after our experience a little earlier, and I knew that, if detected, I should be seriously injured if not actually murdered by the irresponsible mob; so I determined to make one more desperate effort to get safely off the streets.

We were now in the very heart of the city, standing in the great central market-place, and I noticed to the left of us a large and rather imposing three-story building. We were told by the guides that this building was the property of the Government and was divided up into a number of small dwellings (we should call them apartments or flats) and used by some of the important Lhasa officials.

Such people were not, I knew, in the habit of taking in travelers, but I sent Satan and Lhaten inside to tell some one that we were a small party of devout Sikkimese pilgrims just arrived and without lodgings and to implore him to allow us to make use of some small room for the night.

They were gone about twenty minutes, while I was left alone to look after the animals and to try to keep as much as possible in the darkness.

Eventually my two servants returned, announcing success. We were to be granted lodgings for the night, though we should have to move on the next day. Wearily I drove our animals into the great courtyard of the house. As was to be expected, we found stable space on the ground floor; and, once the ponies had been attended to, we prepared to ascend the two flights of stairs leading to the apartments of our host. But I had now reached the end of my tether. Nervous excitement had kept me up thus far, but by this time I was so weak from illness and fatigue that I could not climb the quaint ladder-like staircase and had to be carried up by my servants.

We came eventually to our host's apartment, and in its tiny little out-room I was dumped down. This little room was obviously used chiefly as a passage, a scullery, and a store-room for argol—the yak-dung fuel—but I was more than delighted to be able to occupy even this.

So weary was I that I immediately fell asleep, but a little later I was awakened by Lhaten with food, and the best food I had had for many a day. I inquired of him whether anything more had been seen of the syce or Diogenes, whom we had left behind many hours earlier, and found that Satan had been out looking for them but in vain. They were lost in the crowd. We were a little worried by this but I thought that with daylight the next day we could possibly find them.

In the meantime I was concerned with a much more important matter. Our host had not deigned even to come out and look at us but had remained in his inner room, but the small pet dog he possessed, attracted by the smell of food, came out to inspect us and immediately began to cause trouble. The sense of smell must have told him that I was different from the others, for he began barking very vigorously at me, and at me alone. We tried desperately to silence him but without avail. His yapping began to attract attention, and I feared that in this way I should be discovered. It seemed very curious that I should be in Tibet all this time, undergoing frequent examinations, and never be discovered, and that here on our first night in Lhasa I should be suspected.

At this exciting crisis I quickly made up my mind, somewhat against the call of reason, to reveal myself. In the first place, I thought it was better to reveal myself voluntarily than to be found out by others; and, secondly, I had always had it in the back of my mind to reveal myself when I got to Lhasa. This was partly out of a silly boyish feeling of braggadocio—to show the Lhasa Government that I had been able to get there in spite of their efforts to keep me out. I was also afraid, if I came back to India and told any one that I had gone to Lhasa and come back from it in disguise, that my tale would not be believed, so that by revealing myself I should have definite proof that I had been successful in my undertaking.

If I were to reveal myself, I knew that it must be to the upper and more responsible officials that I should do so. Fear of the British Government would probably keep them from violent action, so that at least my life would be safe; for I knew that if I were discovered by the irresponsible mob I should have very short shrift of it.

As unusual circumstances had brought me to the very home of officialdom, I decided to use our host as the channel of communication to announce my presence to the Dalai-lama. Consequently, while the little dog was still barking, and to the consternation of Satan and Lhaten, who thought I was out of my mind, I doffed as much of my disguise as was possible at a minute's notice, and, making my way into the inner rooms, I eventually found myself in the presence of my host; and to him I immediately announced my identity.

I have never seen so surprised and astonished a person. He gazed at me for several minutes in blank and speechless bewilderment, but when he recovered himself sufficiently to speak he managed to give me an even greater surprise, for I discovered that the man who had been kind enough to give us lodgings after we had been refused admission at at least fifty other places was no other than Sonam, the official who had charge of the new communication system between Tibet and India and the intervening points. It was through him that the news had come that I had entered Tibet and was probably in disguise, and it was through him that the orders had gone out that a special search should be made for me in order that I might be stopped and turned back.

What wild freaks the Goddess Chance plays upon us at times! It seemed hardly credible, this dramatic meeting, and yet here we were, facing each other.

At first I thought I had walked straight into the lion's mouth and had revealed myself to the person who would be most hostile to me, but I soon discovered that things were more favorable. Sonam was a Lepcha, born in Sikkim, had seen a good many Englishmen, and had been very much impressed by the white man's prestige; and he had been partially educated in Kalimpong. The Lhasa Government had brought him to Lhasa on account of his knowledge of the foreign devils, and because he would hence be able to help the Lhasa officials in their attempts to improve their means of communication.

After the shock and surprise of the first meeting had passed away, Sonam and I sat down to a long and serious talk as to what was to become of me during the next few days. He himself was very friendly and promised to do everything to help me out, but he warned me that I was likely to have a very troublous and dangerous time ahead, as I had arrived in Lhasa just at New Year time when the fanaticism of the general populace was at its greatest height.

After some discussion we decided that the best plan for the immediate future was to inform the Dalai-lama privately of my arrival the next day, and then to wait for further developments.

Nothing could be done until morning, but Sonam

was determined to make my first evening in Lhasa a pleasant one. I was much surprised to see the great trouble he took to make me comfortable.

He insisted upon making me change my quarters and occupy his own private room, while he moved out to the room next door, occupied by other members of his family. I was thus, for the first time in many weeks, furnished with comfortable and private sleeping-quarters.

Although I had already eaten the simple food Lhaten had prepared, Sonam gave numerous sharp orders to his servants, and a little midnight supper was prepared. The food was not at all in Tibetan style; some dishes were Indian and some Chinese. This meant that the food was *cooked,* and much more palatable than any I had had for a long time, and I sat down to the banquet with a relish, grossly overeating, considering how ill I was.

Chang and arak, the native beer and brandy, followed as a matter of course. Considering the perils which were to overhang me during the next few days, I thought it wise to emphasize my priestly rank and refuse these, but Sonam overcame these scruples, saying that even the high priests of Lhasa forgot their duties at New Year time and joined in the liquid rejoicing. Having thus started on the way to perdition, how easy it was to follow in it!

During his stay in Kalimpong Sonam had acquired a taste for cigarettes, a taste which he had found it impossible to overcome in spite of the terrible anathema against tobacco on the part of the government. The sale or use of cigarettes was particularly prohibited by the Dalai-lama, but, as with all prohibitory laws, there was the usual bootlegging. Sonam had managed to smuggle in a supply, which he kept carefully hidden and locked away; for in Tibet drinking is only a vice, while smoking is a crime.

As I was not a Tibetan, however, Sonam relied upon my broadmindedness in the matter, and, getting out his secret store of cheap, wretched Indian cigarettes, he offered some to me. It was the supreme symbol of the confidence he placed in me. I had not smoked anything since entering Tibet. At first the craving for tobacco had been very terrible, but it had now subsided and I had now almost lost the desire for it, but as I knew so much of my future safety in Lhasa lay in keeping Sonam's friendship I did not dare offend him by refusing and so went the whole gamut of wickedness by lighting up with him. Wicked cigarettes they were, filled with raw, acrid, coarse tobacco; but how soothing they were to the soul!

After our secret smoke was ended I went out to see how my servants were faring. This also gave me a chance to see something of Sonam's abode and of the way in which Tibetan officials live.

On one point Lhasa is curiously modern. Only the very wealthiest families can afford to have a whole house to themselves. The poorer families, even those with good official ranks, are forced to content themselves with what are called flats in England or apartments in America—a suite of five or six rooms inside one of the great Lhasa houses.

Sonam, having only recently come to Lhasa and having only a small family, was forced to content himself with only four rooms. This little flat was quite self-contained and had only one door connecting it with the outside world, a door leading from the out-room to the veranda which encircled the inclosed courtyard around which the house was built.

Of the four rooms, one was the little out-room, allotted to my servants, where fuel was stored, and except as a passage was very little used. Opening out of it on one side was the kitchen, where food was prepared, and where Sonam's servants also slept. It also served as a food larder. Opening out on the other side of the out-room was the large common room. This served as the family living-room, reception-room, dining-room, and bedroom; for here slept Sonam's family, which consisted of Sonam's brother, his wife, and a female cousin of his wife who was there on a visit.

On the other side of this common room was the inner private room, used by Sonam himself. This was the room which Sonam had given to me, while he went to the next room, the common room, where he joined the other members of his family.

It was extremely kind of him to treat me in this way, though it was obvious that prudence had something to do with the change of rooms, as we had decided it was better for me to keep my presence in Lhasa a great secret from the general public until it could be seen what attitude the Dalai-lama and his ministers would assume toward me; and as long as I stayed in the inner room I should run no risk of discovery, as it was entirely to one side, and ordinary visitors could come to and leave the common room without ever suspecting that any one was in the little room beyond.

In accordance with our plan, I gave my servants and Sonam gave his servants very strict instructions that nothing was to be said to any one as to my arrival. Sonam gave such a vivid description of what was likely to happen to the whole household in case the secret was betrayed that I felt pretty sure no tongue-wagging would take place, at least for the next few days.

After this, the excitement being at last over, I retired to my room for the night. There was still the terrible uncertainty of what the next few days would bring forth, as few of the other officials were as modernly minded as Sonam; but after crawling inside my blankets I was soon fast asleep, well content to let the morrow look after itself.

But early the next morning I was awake again. Lhaten came in with a cup of tea, and I then arranged for him to go out with Satan to the markets and buy provisions for the next few days; for even though I was housed in Sonam's flat, it was of course understood that in accordance with Tibetan custom my little party made its own housekeeping arrangements. It was further understood that my two servants while they were on the streets were to keep a sharp lookout for the syce and Diogenes, whom we had lost the previous evening. I was much afraid of what might happen to them, as I knew that neither one had any money on his person when we parted from them.

After they had gone I determined to see what I could of Lhasa. It was too dangerous to attempt to go through the streets, and in any case I felt too ill even to attempt a sight-seeing tour, but with Sonam's help I got up on top of the roof of the house and from there commanded a panoramic view of the whole city. It will be remembered that roofs in Tibet are perfectly flat, so that we were able to walk around in perfect safety, gazing at different parts of the city. The outer parapets of the roof rendered me invisible from the street, so that I had an ideal place from which to spy on all that was worth seeing, particularly as the house lay right in the heart of the city and was the highest building anywhere in the city proper.

To the west lay the Turquoise Bridge, and beyond it the pleasure-groves stretched up to the two hills dominated by the medical college and the Potala. Although a mile away, the Potala seemed to lose none of its magnificent splendor, and the rays of the early morning sun, falling on it, gave it an altogether fitting golden glow.

The Potala hill hid from view the Drepung monastery which lay beyond; but, about two or three miles to the north, at the foot of the same range of hills, a range which runs almost due east and west, lay Sera, the second of the three great monasteries. Drepung wields the largest political power, but the monks of Sera are particularly noted for the excellence of their liturgical knowledge. To have a Sera monk lead a religious service is a great honor, and in a country where religious services are believed to control the forces of the universe, such a reputation is invaluable. To anyone acquainted with great ecclesiastical organizations it will not be surprising to know that Sera and Drepung are deadly rivals and are constantly trying to encroach on each other's prerogatives. To the east the great Lhasa plain continued for about six miles before it was once more closed in by the mountains. Occasional manor-houses dotted the plain, and through it ran the great highway leading to Ganden, the last of the three great monasteries, and far beyond that to distant China and Mongolia. Entrance to Tibet from China, or on the part of the Chinese, is now prohibited, but the Mongolians are permitted to come on pilgrimage to Lhasa, and even then I could see two or three caravans of pious Mongols picking their way over the plain. Mongolian caravans are always recognizable, as they contain the great Mongolian two-humped camels, and in Tibet itself camels are not used.

To the south ran the Kyi River, the river of felicity —well named, for its waters make the Lhasa plain fertile. On the other side of the river the plain continued for another mile or two until it gave way to the southern range of east and west hills.

Immediately around me lay the city of Lhasa itself, some half a mile square. In the old days it was surrounded by a wall in true medieval fashion, but the wall has now been destroyed though small portions of it remain and can still be seen.

Lhasa consists of a cluster of houses of the usual Tibetan type, made of sun-dried brick and whitewashed, with flat roofs, and generally with a courtyard formation, most of them two stories high, though three-story buildings are not uncommon.

Here and there a building of more imposing style or proportions would thrust itself upon the eye. Needless to say, all such buildings were religious foundations. A little to the north was Ramoche, unusual because it was a temple and not a monastery—the oldest temple in Tibet—and famous as an historic mausoleum. In holiness it ranks second only to the Chokang, or cathedral, of which more will be said hereafter.

A little to the west of Ramoche was Tsomoling, and still further to the west, near the Turquoise Bridge, was Tengyeling. Tengyeling and Tsomoling are two of the four so-called royal monasteries of Lhasa. The third, Kunduling, lay beyond the medical college hill, while the fourth is situated on the southern side of the Kyi River.

These four monasteries have an interesting and unique position. They are enormously wealthy, having landed estates in all parts of Tibet, but they have remained very exclusive establishments. While Sera, Drepung and Ganden have grown steadily in numbers, these four lings have limited the number of their members, and none of them has more than five hundred monks, all of them picked men, whose daily routine is more than usually elaborate and strict. The abbot of each of these monasteries is a reincarnating embodiment of some Tibetan deity, and in times past these abbots had a virtual monopoly of the post of regent, or de facto king of the country during the minority of the Dalai-lama. As the present Dalai-lama was the first

Over the roofs of Lhasa, with Potala in background

One of the main streets of Lhasa: Potala in background, right; cathedral, center; medical school on hill, left

Lhasa: the Potala

The Potala, official court and palace of the Dalai-lama at Lhasa

in many generations to survive his coming of age, it can be seen that the abbots of these four privileged and aristocratic monasteries had a great deal to say in the government of the country. During the long reign of the present Dalai-lama, who is more than able to rule without the aid of a regent, these ancient establishments have lost much of their power.

The largest and most prosperous-looking monastery in the city was none of these four royal lings but the Muru Gompa, which lay a little to the northeast of where I was standing; but undoubtedly the chief attraction of Lhasa was none of the buildings previously mentioned but the great Chokang or cathedral which lay immediately before me, just to the south, on the other side of the market-place.

This Chokang or cathedral is the holy of holies for all Tibetans and Mongolians, the St. Peter's of Tibetan Buddhism, to which come thousands of pilgrims every year, and doubly interesting, moreover, because it is the center not only of Tibetan religion, but also of Tibetan government, for in one wing of this great building are the offices of the *lönchen* or prime minister, the Kashak or cabinet, and the Tsongdu or National Assembly.

In spite of its fame and importance, the Chokang is not nearly so marvelous in its size or its architectural beauty as the Potala, the palace of the sovereign. This is partly due to the fact that a number of smaller lesser buildings are built around the Chokang, so that one can scarcely see anything of the Chokang itself except the great entrance gate, which is on the west side, and its glittering spires or *gyepi,* which shoot high above all the surrounding buildings, rising as points from the rather picturesque Chinese-type roof. These spires or cones are made from brass and then heavily gilded, but it is said that the principal spire is made of pure gold.

This Chokang or cathedral with all its surrounding buildings, some of which are official structures, and others, particularly on the east end, private dwellings, constitutes a great square—the central square or block of buildings. Running around this block is the principal street of Lhasa, called the Parkor-ling or the Inner Circle. As the practice of circumambulating or walking around a sacred building is held in high regard in Tibet as a method of acquiring merit, it is the custom for every pilgrim who comes to Lhasa to make the circuit twice daily, once in the morning and once in the evening, always of course from left to right.

In addition to being the main thoroughfare of Lhasa, this Inner Circle is broad enough to permit a number of stalls to be placed in it, so that it also constitutes the great market-place of the capital. That part of the avenue which ran before the house in which I was staying was particularly open and broad and had therefore developed into the chief center of stall-marketing. For this reason the house itself was called Trom-si-Kang, or the market-seeing mansion.

Sonam told me that all the great pageants and processions invariably went around the Inner Circle, frequently starting from the place immediately below. I was overjoyed to hear this, as it meant that I could see everything of importance which took place without leaving the place where I was staying.

Sonam and I stayed for some time on the roof, he pointing out and explaining the principal points of interest, but at length he said that he must go down in order to get into communication with the Dalai-lama and inform him of my arrival. This being New Year's day for the Tibetans, the Dalai-lama was holding a great levee or audience at the Potala, attended by the principal officials, so that it was going to be difficult to get private access to him; but Sonam was going to arrange to have a little note handed to him giving him the necessary information.

I followed him downstairs, for I still felt very ill and weak, and wanted to rest as much as possible so as to secure a supply of strength with which to face any new eventuality.

Sonam went out to his office, while I returned to the little flat. Here I was delighted to find not only that Lhaten had returned but also that he had found the syce and Diogenes and had brought them home with him.

They had had a very uncomfortable time. The donkey had eventually died, and, leaving the carcass behind, they had come on to the city but were of course unable to find any trace of us and had been afraid to make too many inquiries lest it might awaken suspicion regarding my identity. Having no money, they had been forced to sleep out in the streets, but by begging they had secured a little food. They were wandering around the Inner Circle, the center of Lhasa life, when they were found by Lhaten.

Once back in my own room I managed to draw the cushions which formed my bed over so that they were by the window which looked out over the market-place below. In this way I was able to rest and at the same time observe many interesting aspects of Lhasa life. Incidentally nearly all the windows in the Trom-si-Kang were provided with glass panes which had been brought from India. This was rather unusual even for Lhasa, for in most cases cloth with rather wide meshes, or occasionally glazed paper, is nailed to the window-frame. In such cases there is usually a wooden shutter behind which could be closed at night and so keep out the cold.

The whole morning the market-place was full of revelers of both sexes and from every part of Tibet. These were singing, shouting, and dancing. The dancing interested me, particularly as it was unlike anything I had seen before. Three or four women would gather and form a circle. Each had in her hand a leather strap, strung with little bells, such as are hung on the necks of ponies in Tibet when a noble rides forth. The women would then begin to sing, and stamp their feet rhythmically, at the same time jangling the bells which they held in their hands. Gradually numbers of men—strangers—would gather around them, join in the song, and stamp their feet in the same rhythmic fashion. Verse after verse would be sung, and the stamping would go on for many minutes until the singers were out of breath or one of the women, weary and jostled from behind, would fall down. Then the party would break up, only, however, in most cases to form again a few yards further to the right, once breath and voice had been recovered. It was obvious that these parties were gradually making their way around the Inner Circle, performing the prescribed circumambulation of the cathedral square. It was quaint to see them performing the holy rite in this exceedingly jovial fashion.

Many of the revelers, grown men as well as children, amused themselves by firing off squibs or fire-crackers, some of them tiny things and some of gigantic proportions.

The shortness of the previous night's repose made me feel very sleepy; I was just dozing off when the whole house was shaken by a tremendous explosion, and I was on my feet in an instant. As this took place after Sonam had gone forth to announce my arrival, I thought at first that a bomb had been placed underneath my window, but on looking forth I saw that by accident the whole fireworks stall had exploded, stunning every one in the vicinity. Four persons were killed, and five more were seriously injured.

A large crowd gathered around the heap of victims. In this respect the world is the same all the world over. But no one seemed inclined to lend a helping hand, and every one was left to look after himself. This meant that the dead and seriously wounded were left lying on the ground for really an extraordinary time, until friends or relatives could learn of the mishap and come and drag the bodies of the victims away.

There was of course no hospital ambulance, for there is neither ambulance nor hospital in Lhasa, nor is there any kind of provision for first aid to the injured. When the victims were eventually taken away they were brought back to their own homes, and some monks—possibly but not necessarily from the medical college—were invited in to perform their ritual either for the recovery of the patient or, if he be dead, for the safe passage of his soul into a favorable reincarnation.

Even more surprising was the lack of policemen in Lhasa or of other officials to take their place. This is one of the chief reasons for the lawlessness of the city. Most of the city officials were out on holiday, but eventually a woebegone-looking person wearing official dress and armed with a whip arrived on the scene and ordered some scavengers to clear up the débris.

Fire-crackers are much enjoyed by the Tibetan peasants. They are probably brought to Tibet from China, but on account of the faulty method of manufacture, such accidents, I was told, are by no means infrequent, and the Dalai-lama is trying to abolish the sale and use of all such articles; but it is obvious that bootlegging in Tibet has been brought to a fine art, for I had seen the squibs sold in the open market-place. The story was, however, destined to have an interesting sequel.

Apart from illicit sale, fire-crackers are still officially recognized and used in one connection. Every night in Lhasa at half-past eight curfew is sounded, but not by means of a curfew bell. Instead, one of these giant squibs is let off at each one of the four corners of the Inner Circle, as a warning that every one thereafter should stay indoors.

The curfew law is principally meant as a protection for innocent and respectable persons. There is no attempt made to illuminate the dark winding streets of Lhasa, which are full of men who are beggars by day and highwaymen at night, and the Government finds it cheaper to order the people to stay indoors at night than to install illumination or to organize a proper police force.

The excitement from the explosion had hardly died down before Sonam returned. He told me that he had managed to have a note handed to the Dalai-lama in the midst of his audience announcing my arrival, but that at the time the Dalai-lama had merely read it and had said nothing to any one round him regarding the matter and had exhibited no symptoms of either surprise, anger, or excitement; but this was only to be expected from an experienced Oriental potentate.

Further developments were bound to come in due course, and there was now nothing for me to do except passively await them.

But it was certainly very trying to be forced to remain in idleness while one's whole destiny was being decided by the whim of other people. About two o'clock, however, two messengers arrived from Tsarong Shape, the commander-in-chief of the army and the senior secretary of state, with orders that I come and pay him a secret visit.

Tsarong is the personal friend and favorite minister of the Dalai-lama, and it seems that shortly after receiving Sonam's note the Dalai-lama had spoken briefly to Tsarong, telling him to see me secretly and find out what sort of a person I was; in accordance with these instructions Tsarong had now sent for me as soon as he returned to his private palace from the Potala.

As this was a first interview, I thought it better to attempt to win favor by putting on the lama or priest robes which I had been given by the temple in Darjeeling, and to which I was entitled; but I was careful to wrap my head up in one of the thick Tibetan shawls so that people could not see too much of my face as I passed through the streets.

Attended by all of my servants (such is etiquette in Tibet, where a gentleman will never think of paying a formal call without being attended by at least two or three servants), and following the messengers whom Tsarong had sent, I set out for his palace.

This was near Sonam's house, lying just beyond the great central block of buildings formed by the cathedral and its satellite edifices. This meant we had to go along the Inner Circle, the great market roadway which runs around this group of buildings. Along this road we passed in the prescribed left-to-right fashion, always keeping the central group of buildings on our right. At the two eastern corners of the Inner Circle I noticed two gigantic wooden poles, a sort of glorified May-pole, with a few prayer-tufts fluttering at the top. This eastern end of the central square was largely occupied by Kashmiri and Nepalese merchants. Many of these were closed in honor of the New Year, and those which were open had most of their wares displayed on little stalls placed outside the houses, rather than on counters inside of them. Eventually we came to the south side of the central square and arrived at Tsarong's palace, the entrance to which was, however, not on the Inner Circle but on a narrow side street.

Tsarong's palace follows the usual lines of Tibetan architecture. It was three stories high and built principally of stone, but the outer walls were of no great importance, having no windows on the ground floor and only small windows on the floors above. Obviously the life of the palace was centered around the courtyard or quadrangle, which we entered by a gateway which at night was closed by a huge wooden door, heavily barred. The courtyard was roughly paved but muddy and heaped with odds and ends, though much neater than most Tibetan courtyards. All around the base under the first balcony were the stalls for Tsarong's horses and mules, a goodly number, some still standing richly saddled. The house was built up around all sides of the courtyard, but the rather imposing mass of the main residential wing rose up immediately before us. Crossing over the courtyard, we entered this wing by a small and insignificant door lying to one side. In the gloom I could just distinguish the precipitous ladder which led up to the floor above. The ladder, with its round, slippery, iron-sheated rungs and polished willow handrail, was the only means of ascent.

Once arrived at the first floor above, I saw to one side a small preliminary waiting-room where ordinary visitors are kept until they can be interviewed by one of the secretaries, but as soon as I arrived one such official stepped out and led me to the chief formal reception-room, which overlooked the courtyard.

This was also the palace chapel; in Tibet it is always

wise to show one's religiosity to visitors. The whole of one side of the room was occupied by huge gilded images, with burning butter-lamps and offering-bowls in front of them. The other side of the room was filled by a built-in dais covered by thick woolen mattress-cushions which served as chairs. On both sides of the altar proper were pigeonholes for books—religious books of course, which were meant for adoration and not for reading. Violent colors covered every inch of wall-space, vivid greens and blues, scarlet and gold predominating; but the general effect, aided by the gloom, was not entirely disharmonious.

I was seated on the great dais, and tea was immediately brought in and offered to me, but there then followed considerable delay. My servants were kept in the passage outside, and I heard a good deal of whispering going on.

Eventually a lady stepped in accompanied by a secretary. The lady, I found, was Tsarong's wife, or, to be more exact, one of his two wives. She told me that Tsarong was ill. The ceremonies at the Potala in the morning had commenced before five o'clock, and in the cold of the morning he had contracted a severe chill and was suffering from high fever. He had now fallen asleep, and his servants were afraid to wake him.

I told the good lady I was quite prepared to wait, and that his Excellency was certainly not to be disturbed on my account. I was much interested to notice that the lady of the house had come in person. Among the Mohammedans to the east and north, and in India and China, the upper-class women are forced to lead a very retired life, are kept to a special wing of the house, and never come into contact with male visitors, even when the husband is present. Here in Lhasa, on the other hand, in good Occidental fashion, the lady of the house sat down and by conversation sought to lessen the tedium of my wait.

I was sorry that our talk proved so short, for it would have been interesting to get the point of view of a Lhasa woman of high rank, but a servant came in to announce that his Excellency was at last awake and would see me immediately.

I was then led up-stairs to the second floor, to a private room, very prettily decorated, where I found Tsarong lying on a dais. Unlike most Tibetan houses, this room contained a table and several chairs of Chinese design, and on one of these chairs I was seated.

One is always supposed to give rich presents when one visits a powerful official in Tibet. It is, of course, bribery, but the thing is carried on very openly. But I had no presents to give and presented only a ceremonial silk scarf, which one always does in Tibet when making any sort of a formal visit. Tsarong greeted me very kindly and excused himself for not getting up.

He was a squat little man, inclined to fleshiness, and there was nothing very imposing in his presence. Nevertheless he is the possessor of a very unusual personality and is the one really great man of Tibet. In my opinion he is destined to play in his own country the same rôle that Bismarck played in Germany and Ito in Japan, though, of course, he has to work with infinitely inferior material. Incidentally he is, in Tibet, the solitary instance of a self-made man. Although the Tibetans have no caste system, practically all the major offices of state, apart from the posts of incarnate abbot such as that held by the Dalai-lama, are occupied by members of the great aristocratic families. Tsarong belongs to none of these. In fact, his father ranked below an ordinary peasant, being a bow-and-arrow maker. This is an occupation much despised by the Tibetans, rendering a man practically an outcast. The name of Tsarong and the title of Shape are both acquired. As a boy he was known as Namgang. A spirited, reckless lad, his early escapades made Lhasa too hot to hold him, and at the age of fourteen he had to flee to Mongolia, where he became a roving adventurer. His chance in life came a few years later, when the Dalai-lama was forced to seek refuge in Mongolia in 1904, at the time that the Younghusband expedition marched into Tibet. The temper of his Holiness at that time was such that he found it difficult to obtain or keep any servants. Consequently he was glad to accept Namgang as a personal attendant. The loyalty and the intelligence of the new servant soon attracted attention, and the young fellow was advanced into favor. As a special mark of esteem he was raised from a position corresponding to that of a private soldier and given a commission. On the return of the Dalai-lama to Tibet, in 1908, Namgang was created a captain.

His greatest opportunity arrived with the Chinese invasion of Tibet in 1909-10. The Dalai-lama fled, this time to India, and the Chinese sent a pursuing army after him. Namgang, by his magnificent defense of

Chushul, kept the Chinese back long enough to allow the Dalai-lama to escape into British territory. Namgang then attempted to follow him, but his retreat was cut off. Eventually he managed to get through the Chinese lines by dressing himself as a courier of the Indian Government, carrying British mail from Yatung into Sikkim. In this way the young officer was able to rejoin his leader in Darjeeling. Incidentally, Tsarong took my arrival in Lhasa as a huge joke, for he reminded me that while I had got from India to Tibet in disguise, he had been able to accomplish the same feat in an opposite direction. In 1911 the outbreak of the revolution in China weakened the morale of the Chinese soldiers stationed in Tibet. Namgang took this opportunity to restore the Dalai-lama to power. He entered Tibet secretly, raised peasant revolts against the Chinese garrisons, and in the end forced them all to surrender. At the same time the old Tibetan officials, who had been in friendly relation with the Chinese, were either banished or killed. Among those who met the latter fate was a shape, or secretary of state, called Tsarong. He and his son were hacked to pieces in the streets of Lhasa by a party of fighting monks. The Dalai-lama returned to Lhasa in triumph. As a reward for his services Namgang was made a Shape and at the same time created commander-in-chief of the army and master of the mint. The old Tsarong having left no heirs, Namgang was presented with the Tsarong estate. Thereafter he assumed the title of Tsarong Shape. To make possession doubly sure, Namgang married both the daughter and the daughter-in-law of the old Tsarong Shape. The latter was the widow of the murdered son. Tsarong, therefore, is one of the few people in Tibet who openly practise polygamy.

Tsarong has retained the personal favor of the Dalai-lama and is now the most powerful man in the country. He is very modern in his ideas and wishes to see the same awakening in Tibet that has taken place in Japan. Acting under his advice, the Dalai-lama has instituted many reforms, which have had an enormously beneficial effect upon the country. Needless to say, these reforms have met with vigorous opposition on the part of the monks, and among the priestly party Tsarong inspires only fear and hatred. Numerous attempts have been made to assassinate him, and he is forced always to keep a strong guard about his person.

During this first interview, after we had conversed for some time on general matters, we turned to my own affairs. Tsarong, I knew, had been actively in favor of permitting our whole party to come to Lhasa from the first, and privately he was pleased that I had been able to carry through the secret enterprise. He told me, moreover, that the Dalai-lama was not entirely antipathetic. Nevertheless, as the Tibetan Government, acting under pressure from the monks, had refused me permission to come, and I had arrived in disguise, it was necessary for me to undergo certain formalities. He advised me to make official notification of my arrival to the city magistrates the next day. These officials would report the matter to the Kashak, or cabinet of ministers, consisting of a *lönchen,* or prime minister, and four shapes or secretaries of state. This body would consider what steps should be taken in regard to me. Tsarong, of course, is a member of this cabinet and promised to put in a good word for me when the matter should come before it officially.

Whatever the decision of the other members might be, he promised definitely, on his own responsibility, that I should receive personal protection. He suggested, moreover, that I should, in my report to the authorities, expressly omit the names of the rest-houses in which I had stayed and the people with whom I had traveled. Otherwise, the Government, or the clamor of the populace, might force him to take some active steps against them. From this I could see how powerless, in the face of fanaticism, even Tibet's greatest man could be. We parted with every sign of cordiality on both sides.

I had spent almost three hours with Tsarong, and it was nearly dusk when I came out of his palace.

We had now to return to our residence in the Trom-si-Kang, but we did not go back the way we had come. To do so would be to go in the wrong way, from right to left, keeping the cathedral on our left, and so we completed our circuit of the Inner Circle, going along the south side to the western end.

After a short time the road once more broadened out, leaving a wide open space. This was of great interest to me, as on the northern side of the space adjoining the main cathedral building was a curious sort of platform, rather elaborately decorated. This, I found, was the Lhasa pulpit, the only pulpit I ever saw in Tibet.

Preaching plays no part in Tibetan religion. The peasants are quite willing to pay money to the priests to perform ceremonies for them. This propitiates the gods and demons; why, therefore, should one be forced to listen to sermons? The monks, on the other hand, see no reason why religious secrets should be delivered to the masses, and so pulpits and preaching are alien to the religious system of Tibet—except for this one pulpit. This is used only by the Dalai-lama, who once a year, in the character of high priest of his people, delivers a short discourse to the Lhasa community, who are packed in the open space around.

This annual sermon is a very quaint custom, and I was very anxious to learn something of its origin, but I found no one who could tell me.

We now came to the western end of the central block of buildings. At the southwestern corner I could see the Kashak buildings, really a wing of the cathedral, but very important, as inside this building was the central government of the country, with the offices of the prime minister or *lönchen,* the four shapes or secretaries of state, and the Tsongdu or National Assembly.

A little beyond this, almost in the center of the western side of the central square, was the main entrance of the Chokang or cathedral—a huge and ornate gateway, hung with black curtains. This gateway was set slightly back, and in the open space in front I could see hundreds of persons prostrating themselves in adoration of the divinities who were housed within.

In the middle of the street, facing the cathedral, were two interesting stone tablets or monuments. One is comparatively modern, being built at the time of Chinese influence, and is called the smallpox monument, as on its sides are inscribed an edict dealing with the quarantine regulations for smallpox, the most common disease in Tibet. Curiously enough, this has been defaced by a number of cup-like depressions resembling the pock-marks of the disease with which it deals.

The other monument, surrounded by a high wall of stone, is a tall edict monolith, inscribed with the terms of a treaty of peace between China and Tibet executed in 783 between Repachen, king of Tibet, and the emperor of China. At this time Tibet was a warlike, independent country, ruled over not by monks but by a secular king; and the treaty marked the end of a war in which the Tibetans had been successful over the Chinese. One side of this monument was overshadowed by an ancient willow, which is considered by the Tibetans as thrice holy in that it sprang from a hair of the Buddha which was brought and planted there.

Continuing on our way, we eventually came to the northern side of the square, and, turning to the right, we passed along it till we came to a large shrine or *chorten,* supported on four pillars so that one could pass under and through it. Just beyond the *chorten* was the Trom-si-Kang, our own home, to which we were glad to return.

The day had been so full of thrills that I felt very tired and before long was asleep.

CHAPTER XII

LIFE IN THE FORBIDDEN CITY

THE next morning I found from Sonam that the city magistrates, who are joint mayors and judges of Lhasa, had their headquarters in the city hall or palace of justice, a building almost immediately opposite my window. Just in front of this building I noticed two stone rings fastened in the ground, several feet apart. I wondered what these could be used for. I was soon to find out. I saw a side door open. A woman was dragged out by several petty officials. She was stripped of every stitch of clothing and thrown on the ground. Her arms were tied to one stone ring and her feet to the other. Two men then appeared with whips and began to flog her, giving her 150 lashes in all. The lash cut into her flesh, causing huge weltering wounds. At first she screamed in her agony, but later she fainted away. Water was thrown over her to revive consciousness, and then the grisly work began again. I was anxious to find out what crime the woman had committed to merit this punishment and was informed that she was the vender of the fireworks and squibs which had caused so much damage the preceding day. When the sentence had been administered she was too weak to stand and had to be carried inside the building, where, I was told, she was flung down and left to recover by herself. I looked at the grim building and thought with a shudder of the ordeal I should have to undergo before the magistrates. Nevertheless, later in the day I sent Satan and Lhaten to them to announce my arrival in the city and to request that they forward the information to the ministers of state.

My servants returned and told me that the news seemed to have caused a good deal of excitement, which showed that my arrival had been kept very secret. The magistrates had further stated that the matter was so important that they could take no further action until they had consulted the higher authorities.

I knew that this would take another day or two and so settled down to inactivity for the rest of the day. For some time I amused myself by watching the crowd outside. New Year celebrations were in full swing and the revelers as numerous as on the preceding day, but there was not quite so much drunkenness and rowdiness.

In addition to the bell dancers, I noticed a number of children playing in the market-place; many of them, boys and girls both, were skipping, the skipping-ropes being either of wool or of leather. Many women were out with their babies. Most of them carried the babies on their back in Japanese fashion, and not on their hips, as do so many peoples, or in their arms.

The *chorten* or shrine which lay a few yards away seemed a special object of attraction for the women.

Many of them came with little prayer-cloths which they attached to the shrine, while others burned small quantities of brush in the adjoining sacrificial urn.

Burnt offerings of some sort play a part in all primitive religions. In Lhasa there was an even more striking instance of this: about two miles to the southwest of the city on the very summit of a precipitous hill was a gigantic urn in which very smoky incense is burned every day. It takes several hours to climb this hill, so that the wealthier devotees prefer to pay various coolies to carry the incense up for them, but the merit acquired by the act belongs to the donor and not to the poor coolie.

The afternoon of this day was marked by a very important event—the taking of a bath—the first bath I had been able to take since leaving Darjeeling; it was the first time I had been able to wash my hands since entering Tibet.

Even then to get this bath was something of a feat. Sonam had no bath-tub, nor was there anything like a tub anywhere in the whole house; but eventually it was discovered that one of the Nepalese a few doors away had a tin tub used for washing clothes, and eventually he was persuaded to lend it for the occasion.

It took some time to heat the necessary amount of hot water in the ordinary tea-pots and then pour it into the tub, but at last everything was ready—when to my horror I discovered that after all I did not want to take a bath. Cleanliness and dirtiness are largely a question of habit, and perhaps of climate. At first the steadily increasing layer of dirt had been a misery, but now with the Tibetans I had come to regard it as a secure protection.

I did not, however, dare go back on the idea after all the elaborate preparations that had been made, and so I scrubbed myself to a resemblance of cleanliness, though I knew that with my accumulation of filth I should have to get clean on the instalment plan.

Sonam and his family regarded my bath as a huge joke; and in one respect the joke really was on me, for thereafter I did suffer more acutely from two things, lice and cold.

The lice had been there all the time, ever since Kampa Dzong, but for some reason the dirt and grease had affected me so that I could not feel them; but now I became acutely conscious of their presence and set out to make war against them. But it was a battle of a million to one—and the million were successful.

The cold I had counted on, and I counteracted this by putting on more clothes. Even in Lhasa this is the one way of keeping warm. Lhasa, in common with the rest of Tibet, knows no other fuel than dried dung (the better classes here use yak-dung, the poorer classes horse- and mule-dung), and this burns up too quickly to use for anything except cooking, so that when the temperature drops the Tibetan merely dons an additional suit of clothes.

The water for the bath, and for all other purposes, came from a well in the courtyard; the conception of running water is entirely alien to Tibet. Every day the servants would go down to draw the necessary supply.

Lhasa, unlike most parts of Tibet, suffers from no

lack of water. The whole of the Lhasa plain is very marshy, and at no point does one have to go lower than four or five feet to strike water. For this reason the Tibetans believe that the sacred city is built over a great lake, which would rise and engulf the whole city were it not for the magic power of their god-king.

The shallowness of the well made the water very dangerous. Great manure- and refuse-heaps lay all around it, with the courtyard privy only a few feet away, so that any one interested in germs should have a life's work in studying the content of the water; but every one drank only tea—and prayed to the gods, and so survived.

The courtyard was also the community slop basin; everything left over, liquid or solid, was dumped into it.

The next day brought one further development. Early in the morning two officials sent by the city magistrates arrived to announce that a formal inquiry would be held in a few days' time and begged me to remain within doors and to keep the fact of my arrival secret until then. They were afraid that the Lhasa rabble, always excited to fever-pitch about New Year's time, might storm the place and tear me to pieces if they knew that I had come into the Sacred City in spite of all precautions intended to keep me out. They apologetically added that at all ordinary times the magistrates had control over the city and could guarantee my safety, but that at the present moment the place was so full of turbulent monks that they frequently found it impossible to keep order. The position was further complicated by the fact that for twenty-one days, beginning with the next afternoon, the city government would be handed over to two monks appointed by the Drepung monastery. This is an annual custom, and during this period even the Dalai-lama and his cabinet would have no control over the metropolis; any disorder would have to be curbed by the two temporary ecclesiastical mayors. These were known to be bitterly anti-foreign and would have little interest in protecting me from popular attack. I thanked the officials for telling me all this and promised not to go about openly but reserved to myself the right to wander about the streets after dusk or in disguise.

Cooped up as I was, the rest of the day promised to be very tedious, but things livened up very considerably when later on an official named Kyipup paid me a visit.

Kyipup's interest lay in the fact that he is one of the two Tibetans living who have been to England. Although Tibetans have such a fanatical objection to allowing any foreigner to enter their own land, there seems to be no feeling against a Tibetan who goes outside of his own country even when he returns. For this reason several Tibetans have wandered into Mongolia and China, chiefly bent on trade, and in recent years more and more people have found their way down to India, both in order to buy and sell in the Kalimpong market and also others bent on pilgrimage to the sacred places of Buddhism, which are to be found in India; for though Buddhism has long since died out in India, India was, of course, the land of its origin. Here the historic Buddha was born; here he retired from the world to lead the ascetic life; here he attained complete enlightenment and preached the first of a long series of discourses; and here at length he died. In Tibet the historic Buddha has been overshadowed by mythological divinities, but the Tibetan still regards it as an act of great piety to go to the places in India made holy by the presence of the human founder of his religion, so that even in Lhasa persons who have been to India and know something of conditions there are not uncommon.

But in the ordinary course of events nothing would have brought a Tibetan to Europe. When the Younghusband expedition was in Tibet in 1904, it was thought to be wise to get hold of two or three youngsters of aristocratic families and send them to England to be educated, at the Indian Government's expense. Some difficulty was found in securing such boys, as the better-class families were loath to intrust their offspring to the tender mercies of the foreign devils, but subsequently three scions of the lesser nobility were obtained with whom to try the experiment.

One of them, reputed to be the most promising, died before the success of the idea could be judged, but the other two, after spending several years in England, are now back in their native land.

One of them, Kyipup, who had come to see me, had been given a general education at Rugby, while the other, Mondron, was sent to a mining college in Cornwall, where he learned something of prospecting and mining engineering.

Both boys picked up English very quickly; in fact they soon forgot most of their Tibetan and had to write to their parents in English, so that the outraged families had to call in a native interpreter before they could get any idea of how their sons were faring. Kyipup was reported to be very good-hearted and honest but stupid, while Mondron made good progress in his studies but picked up a reputation for Oriental wiliness. Nevertheless, both boys adapted themselves to English life, and there was a good deal of interest as to how they would fare on their return to their native land.

On the whole, the experiment seems to have been a failure. The boys were considered denaturalized by their fellow-countrymen, and instead of being promoted to higher positions, they have lagged around the bottom of the official ladder. This is rather remarkable considering the recent efforts which the Dalai-lama, backed by Tsarong Shape, has made to reorganize his Government on a modern basis. Kyipup has been made an official in the new post-office, while Mondron was given an opportunity to use his talents and find gold. When he failed to bring forth huge quantities of the precious metal the upper officials decided that the fault must be not in the real absence of gold but in the young prospector and so promptly demoted him.

Kyipup is quite content to spend an easy-going and care-free existence in the post-office, so long as he can smoke vast quantities of cigarettes in secret; but Mondron, more ambitious, and realizing that the line of promotion lies in the church, has become a monk, though of course going on with his official work.

It may be that part of the unofficial disfavor with which they are regarded is due to a dramatic episode which took place shortly after their return. Fired with youthful enthusiasm they brought back with them a motor-cycle. The Dalai-lama, wishing to know more of the devil machine, ordered a demonstration to be made on the plain outside of Lhasa. The motor-cycle was duly started, but the tremendous noise that it made so startled the mules on which the Dalai-lama and his escort were riding that they ran away and very nearly caused the incarnate deity of Tibet to have a bad fall.

In an attempt to avoid high wrath for this misfortune the motor-cycle was immediately presented as a gift to his Holiness. Since then it has lain, unused, in a corner of the palace.

The difference in the character of the two boys was well illustrated by their attitude toward me. The naïve Kyipup came to pay me a visit and talk over old times in England. I found he remembered his English very well. Mondron, however, knowing that I was a *persona non grata* to the Government, carefully stayed away. He was already suspect with the fanatical monks by reason of his previous contact with the West and did not wish to get himself into further hot water by having it known that he had consorted with the foreign devil who had come to Lhasa in disguise.

The next day the two monks from the Drepung monastery who were to act as rulers of the city for the next three weeks made their official entry into the city about ten o'clock in the morning. In honor of their arrival the whole of the street round the central square, which I have called the Inner Circle, was strewn with sand so that the new lords of misrule would not have to walk on ground polluted by common feet.

Attended by a number of fighting monks from Drepung, who acted as a body-guard, they came in solemn procession and made a formal tour round the Inner Circle. The advance-guard called out from time to time, warning the populace to make way for the new rulers, while others, armed with long wooden staves, struck out at the mob as they passed by.

After the procession had gone round the central square it returned to the open space underneath my window, halting just before the Palace of Justice. The officials of the Palace of Justice, who at ordinary times have charge of the city, then came out of the building, and, with all their attendants, knelt down in the sand in token of deep humility.

The two new lords of misrule now proceeded, one at a time, to give a long harangue. This was delivered in a curious chanting tone while the speaker moved in a slow, curious, dancing gait. Both of the new rulers carried singular square black poles, wonderfully carved and decorated, attached to their hands by silk cords; one of them, I noticed, had an excellently trimmed mustache and beard.

The new rulers in the course of their harangue informed the officials that though they, the civilians, might remain ostensibly in power, yet for the next three weeks all ultimate power was to be in the hands of the monks, and that even the cabinet and the Dalai-lama were subject to their jurisdiction.

This, of course, was true. In times past punishments have actually been inflicted upon the Dalai-lama himself for some trifling misdemeanor by the two Drepung monks during their brief tenure of office.

These two ruling monks, let it be noted, are not the abbots or high priests of Drepung, nor any of its leading professors or scholars, but monks, of no particularly high ecclesiastical rank, who act as censors or deans of the monastic community.

Their appointment to the rulership of the city is due to the fact that during their period of office all the monks from the surrounding monasteries crowd into the city to join in the New Year festivities, and so the monks greatly outnumber the civilian population, and the ordinary civil officials find it impossible to keep order over the ecclesiastical bravos. At the end of the three weeks, when the monks leave Lhasa and return to their monasteries, the power of these two temporary rulers automatically lapses, but it is renewed again for a further period of ten days beginning on the twenty-second day of the second month of the Tibetan calendar, when the monks once more crowd into the city.

Although the visiting monks come from all the surrounding monasteries, the two lords of misrule are invariably representatives of Drepung. This is a privilege very jealously guarded by this great monastery.

It is said to be a privilege granted to Drepung by the fifth and greatest of the Dalai-lamas. It was this man who made the Dalai-lamas the temporal rulers of the whole country. He granted this right to Drepung in recognition of the great service which the monastery had paid in establishing his universal authority.

Since that time the annual custom has proved very vexatious to subsequent Dalai-lamas and has very substantially diminished their authority.

The present ruler, unusually keen and ambitious, has been very aggressive in asserting his rights and in curbing the authority of the usurpers. He has more than once hinted to the monks that a privilege which one Dalai-lama gave another Dalai-lama could take away. This statement was particularly pointed because, according to Tibetan belief, the present Dalai-lama is a reincarnation of his predecessors, including the fifth Dalai-lama.

The present ruler would undoubtedly like to carry out his threat and abolish the New Year regentship, but dares not do so on account of the great outcry which would follow; so he is wisely trying the better plan of gradually reducing the powers of the two lords of festivities to a shadow, leaving it as a part of the New Year pageantry; but he has still a long way to go.

After the harangue had ended the new rulers departed to their official residence and the procession broke up, but I noticed that from this time every priest in Lhasa assumed a much more arrogant tone and jostled any civilian whom he might meet out of the way. As a result of this new bravado a fight broke out in another flat in the same house in which I was living. Thirteen monks were having a banquet together and subsequently drifted into a theological argument. Evidently they must have differed on some detail, for they came to blows, and out of the original thirteen only eight survived. The other five were found dead in the morning. This case was the first to occupy the attention of the new mayors. During the remainder of my stay I heard of several other such instances.

The whole of the morning of the next day was taken up by another great procession in honor of the new officials.

This was really a historical pageant. Some of the members were on foot, while others were on horseback. All the participators were dressed in ornate silk costumes illustrating different important epochs in the country's past. Many were mere youngsters who wore masks representing various historical personages.

As usual the procession passed round and round the city several times, so that from my window I got an excellent view of the whole affair, but the most important event of the day, so far as I was concerned, was the second visit I was able to pay Tsarong Shape that afternoon. Officially of course he was not yet aware of my arrival, so that the whole affair had to be carried on very secretly. I found that he had now quite recovered from his recent indisposition and was in excellent spirits, though he warned me that I should have to look out for squalls in the near future, as some members of the Kashak were greatly angered at my arrival and had insisted upon an official though secret inquiry into the matter. In this connection he suggested one or two things I should stress when the inquiry came.

He once more promised that he would do all that he could for me behind the scenes and apologized for the fact that he was forced to act indirectly, but he said the monks were already extremely angry with him for the large number of European reforms that he had introduced, and were he to stand openly as my sponsor, it would be used as a means of stirring up wrath against him and against the modernist tendency of the government.

I could not wonder at the wrath of some of the reactionaries against Tsarong when I saw how very European he was in some of his ways. As commander-in-chief of the army he had seen the cumbersomeness of the native dress for the soldiers, and he had arranged for all his officers and men to be dressed in a style almost identical with that of the British army.

He himself was dressed then, as always, in uniform, preferring that to the dress of a shape to which he was of course entitled. He confessed, however, that though they looked incongruous with European uniform there were two articles of Tibetan dress he could not bring himself to discard. One was the huge turquoise earring which Tibetan gentlemen wear in their left ear. The other was the Tibetan topknot, or the fashion of twisting the hair of the head into a curious little knot on the top of the head, through which is thrust a little jeweled ornament indicating the rank of the wearer.

The wearing of this topknot is confined to the higher officials, from the fourth rank upward. Remembering Tsarong's rise from the lowest class, it was amusing to note that he could not refrain from the use of the badge of the old privileged nobility into whose ranks he had only recently climbed. But certainly if any one deserves this or any other token of rank it is Tsarong.

The little room in which I was received this time was fixed up in a European style, and the little dinner for which Tsarong insisted that I stay contained several semi-European dishes, the materials for which he imports at enormous expense from India. For drink we had two mixtures—one ginger-wine and brandy, the other crême de menthe and whisky; certainly the recipe for the latter must have originated in his own fertile head. Most surprising of all, he hauled out after dinner a huge English pipe, which he filled with strong shag and smoked. Considering the strong prejudice against tobacco, this was remarkable, but even Tsarong dare not smoke in public.

Another of Tsarong's secret hobbies is amateur photography. He has secured a photographic outfit and has taken some excellent snap-shots. The only people who object to being photographed are the monks, who as usual are fanatical upon the subject.

I noticed on the wall of the room a photograph of Tsarong and his two wives, taken by one of his underlings. I was interested to see how open he was about his bigamy; the two wives seemed to be on very friendly terms with each other, but I noticed that he was wise enough to have one wife living in one palace and the other in another.

Apart from his country estates in the Takpo Valley and elsewhere, Tsarong has three mansions in the neighborhood of Lhasa—two a mile or so outside the city—and one city palace, where I now was.

To my surprise, I found that he was building a new city palace only a few hundred yards away from his present establishment. I later found that the real reason for this was that he believes the present palace to be haunted by the old Tsarong and his son, who were murdered, and whose estates and women-folk he has inherited. Tsarong has had several children who died in infancy, and there is left to him only one sickly little boy. Medical science would account for this in another way, but even the modern and progressive Tsarong believes that these calamities are due to the ghosts of his predecessors who are thirsting for revenge, and he believes that in a new building the shades of the dead will be powerless.

We had a long and interesting talk that afternoon, and as no one else, not even servants, was in hearing, he spoke quite freely.

Tsarong claims to be, and no doubt is, a very devout Buddhist. He had prayers said for his recovery and even has a learned old *geshe,* or doctor of (Buddhist) divinity, come in to talk points of metaphysics with him; but he has no illusions as to the nature and value of the average Tibetan monk.

He asserts, and quite rightly, that there are far too many inhabitants of the monasteries. This surplus number weakens, he says, the economic structure of the country; and even from the religious point of view it is impossible for so many people to be really fitted for the monastic life. Consequently he is doing what he can to limit the number of entrants to the priesthood, and to place it on a more competitive basis.

Tsarong is anxious to open up Tibet to foreigners, believing that the country is now strong enough to maintain its independence in spite of their presence; but this I doubt. In any case, in spite of his influence, there seems to be little chance that he will have his way on this point.

Tsarong displayed a keen interest in European politics and to my surprise manifested a fairly accurate knowledge of the general trend of affairs. He stated that the Bolshevik revolution completely destroyed any sympathy which the Tibetan Government might have had for Russia. He quaintly added, "It would have been all right if the Russians had deposed their ruler; but to kill him was another matter." Considering how blood-stained Tsarong's own picturesque career was, I rather marveled at this opinion; but obviously the killing of a ruler and the killing of a subject were two different things.

Considering how European Tsarong is in so many ways, and the fact that he had spent many months in India, I was surprised to find that he speaks neither Hindustani nor English. At present he is trying to pick up a little English from Sonam's brother, who had studied in Kalimpong; but the lessons are still in the elementary stage, and we had to converse entirely in Tibetan.

After a long and pleasant sojourn with him, I returned to Sonam's abode late in the evening.

The next day the city had somewhat quieted down and I was called over to the Palace of Justice by the civil magistrates and asked to aid them in composing a letter to the Kashak, or cabinet, explaining how and why I came to Lhasa. I found the two officials up-stairs in a tiny room. They were clad in red silk robes, with purple facings that looked so exactly like my Oxford doctor's gown that I burst out laughing when I first saw them. They were seated on a dais at the end of the room. Over them was a golden canopy, and on a small lacquer table in front of them were placed jade cups with silver stands and covers filled with the usual buttered tea, which was constantly being replenished by small pages. Along each side of the room ran lower cushions, on which clerks were seated cross-legged. Generally, any person who is called before the magistrates is forced to kneel down on the bare floor before them, but a special exception was made in my case, and a senior clerk vacated his seat for me.

The senior magistrate expatiated upon the wickedness of my action in coming to Lhasa and said that many officials were extremely angry at my action and wished to see that I was given proper punishment, so that he advised me to be very tactful in my statement, which would be forwarded to the higher authorities, and urged that I make it include a special plea for mercy.

I then made a long statement in colloquial Tibetan which I thought would suit the purpose. This was then redrafted into literary or more properly epistolary Tibetan by the magistrates and dictated to one of the clerks.

The clerk took down his dictation on a black rectangular wooden board smeared with white chalk. He scribbled with a metal-pointed instrument which, clearing away the chalk, left the black surface exposed.

When the document had been duly copied on paper with Tibetan pen and ink, the board was again smeared with chalk and was ready for use again.

At first both magistrates, though courteous, had been very hostile in their attitude, but they were obviously pleased that I was acquainted with their language and knew something of the customs and beliefs of the land; and eventually by the intentional naïveté and simplicity of my answers I won something of their sympathy. But in keeping with my naïveté I managed to forget the names of all the rest-houses where I had stopped on the way, as I was anxious not to get innocent people into trouble.

After the official business was concluded, and while waiting for the clerk to make the final copy of my statement, I managed to have a long chat with the two magistrates on general matters. They asked me several questions about life in England, but unlike Tsarong they were appallingly ignorant of everything which took place outside of their own country. To them Tibet was the center of the world, the heart of civilization, and even their interest in European life was quite perfunctory: they asked questions in quite the same way that an average Englishman might inquire as to the cannibal tribes of the South Sea Islands. I found that apart from the highest court circles this attitude was common all over Lhasa.

For my part, I took the opportunity to secure from them a good deal of information concerning the native administration of justice. Law is at the present time a very vague thing in Tibet. The ancient customary code has broken down, and the magistrates now attempt to judge every case on its individual merits, irrespective of statutes and only slightly influenced by precedent. My new friends complained to me of their present difficulty in assigning proper punishments. Tibet has never had a prison system. Criminals are kept locked up only while they are awaiting trial. In former times it was customary to cut off a hand or a leg and to gouge out the eyes as a punishment for any serious offense. The present Dalai-lama considers these punishments to be inconsistent with Buddhism; consequently he abolished them a short time ago, so that legally the judges can now only inflict flogging or banishment for any crime, including murder. The Lhasa magistrates stated that these sentences were not sufficiently severe to deter other offenders, and expressed regret that the old system had been done away with.

Later I heard that the judges' regret at the abolition of the older punishments was possibly due to mixed motives. Practically all officials in Tibet are in the habit of taking bribes. In the old days a man was willing to pay a large sum to the magistrate in order to save his limbs or his eyes, but to-day the criminal is not so eager to expend an equally large sum merely in order to avoid a beating. Yet bribing persists, and a prisoner assigned so many lashes can have the sentence mitigated by paying to the magistrates the equivalent of sixpence for each stroke remitted. Even when a certain number of lashes has been prescribed the official whippers beat lightly or heavily according to whether or not the prisoner is able and willing to give them a present.

During the last few months the Tibetans have just begun to adopt compulsory labor as a punishment. In a notable case of this kind a clever young monk from Sera was found guilty of forging some of the new government paper money. In admiration of his skill he was sentenced to work for two years without pay as a craftsman in the new Lhasa arsenal.

The next development in my case took place two days later, when the cabinet, having read my petition, ordered me into their presence to discuss certain of its statements. I was told once more to muffle up my face and to come in ordinary Tibetan clothes so that no one should notice who I was as I passed through the streets.

The headquarters of the Kashak, or cabinet, it will be remembered, were in one wing of the great cathedral, though they have a separate entrance.

On this occasion I had little opportunity of seeing much of the cathedral proper. Subsequently, however, I had several opportunities of visiting it and may as well give a brief description of it here.

It should be remembered that this building is the very heart and soul of Tibetan Buddhism, the center of all attraction to the thousands of pilgrims who flock annually to Lhasa, the abode of the gods. To be quite correct, this cathedral is itself Lhasa, and the city is only the buildings which have sprung up around it. It is said to have been built in 652 A.D., but it has, of course, been restored and added to since then.

On passing through the great entrance-gates, one

finds oneself in the outer courtyard, the sides of which are occupied by covered and pillared verandas. The walls of this courtyard are covered with frescos long since rendered invisible from age. This courtyard contains only two things of interest: an outer chapel, where a number of important services are held—this is near the entrance to the inner courtyard—and, along the left wall, a throne for the Dalai-lama, where he and his attendants sit to witness certain ceremonies which are held in this courtyard.

Beyond the outer courtyard and separated from it by a long dark passageway, barred at either end by gates, lies the inner courtyard. The center of this courtyard is used as a flower-bed, and in the season the blossoms should be very beautiful, though of course it was now lifeless.

Immediately opposite, at the other end of the courtyard, was the chief shrine, but screened from view by a wall of open iron trellis-work. In front of this, on the two sides, are two statues of Maitreya, the blessed saint who now dwells in the Tusita paradise waiting for the time to come when he will descend to earth to be incarnated as the next Buddha, or savior of the world. The pillared walls of this courtyard were covered with hundreds of images of various buddhas and bodhisattvas.

Behind the walls ran a long dark passage all around the courtyard. Opening out from this passage were various chapels also containing important images.

In order to get to the great central shrine one has to go around by means of the passage. On the way one sees a statue of Shar-Tsong-Kapa, the great reformer of Tibetan Buddhism in the fourteenth century, the organizer of the all-powerful yellow-hat sect to which both the Dalai- and the Trashi-lamas belong.

Eventually one comes to the central shrine, the holy of holies, and stands before the chief image. This represents the historical Buddha when he was still a youth, when he was still a royal prince, and before he had renounced the world to become an ascetic. This image is supposed to have been made from life in India, then taken to China, and finally brought to Tibet. Its history is doubtful, but certainly it is the most holy image of Tibet, the object of the unbounded adoration of the Tibetan; and enormous wealth in the form of offerings is laid on its altar. The lamps which burn before it are of pure gold, and everything about the image is covered with enormous, though uncut, precious stones.

This great image of the central shrine represents Tibet's contact with the earlier, more primitive, Buddhism where the historic character of the founder plays an important part. The floor above is largely devoted to the worship of the fierce female demon, who acts as the dread guardian of Buddhism. Female deities are a late development in Buddhism, and this particular deity dates from an even later time (probably the seventh century A.D.,) when some of the gods and goddesses had come to be considered terrorizing and bloodthirsty creatures whose wrath must be appeased. The lady who was represented here, Peden (or Paldan) Lhamo, is the most terrible of the Furies. She has many forms, some mild, representing her as a gracious lady, the hearer of prayers, others which portray her as the goddess of black magic, of war, of disease, and of death.

In the upper room of the Chokang, or cathedral, there are images representing her in both aspects, but naturally one's eye is especially caught by the image of her in her more horrible phases. The color is black, representing mystery and death. She is riding on a fawn-colored mule, but she is clad in the skins of dead men and is eating brains from a human skull. Offerings of chang or beer, a substitute for blood, are made to her in other human skulls, while as the goddess of battle she is surrounded by all sorts of weapons.

All around the image and the room run hundreds of tame mice, who are sacred in that they are reincarnations of monks and nuns consecrated to her service. Mice are sacred to her in her character of the dispenser of disease, a curious forerunner of the modern theory that the rodents are germ-carriers.

Considering the terrible and bloodthirsty nature of the lady, it is rather curious and amusing to find that the Tibetans believed she was recently incarnated in the world as the late Queen Victoria!

It is only proper that a large chapel on the ground floor is dedicated to the more important of all Tibetan kings, Srong-Tsang-gampo, and his two wives. He is supposed to have lived in the seventh century A.D. Prior to his time Tibet was split up into a number of small warring savage tribes, utterly devoid of any culture, and possessing no means of reading or writing. Not only did he unite the country into one kingdom, but he made marauding attacks on his neighbors, China and Nepal, and forced the ruling families of both countries to supply him with a consort.

Both ladies brought with them something of the culture of their native lands, and through their influence Tibet began to assume a veneer of civilization. More important still, both queens were Buddhists. Not only did the king adopt their religion but he became an enthusiastic proselytizer. He founded the cathedral and opened up the country to Buddhist monks.

Srong-Tsang-gampo, the Constantine of Tibetan Buddhism, was later followed by Langdarma, who played the part of Julian the Apostate, and who attempted to root out the new religion; but he was murdered by a zealous monk, and thereafter the new religion continued to make steady progress—progress in fact so great that the secular line of kings was overthrown in favor of a hierarchy of monks. For a while, as we have seen, the chief power lay in the hands of the abbots of the Sakya monastery, hundreds of miles away, but eventually Lhasa became once more the capital under the rulership of the chief priest of the young but vigorous yellow-cap order. Nevertheless, not only is Srong-Tsang-gampo regarded as an incarnation of divinity (deification is the common lot of every great person in Tibet) but his spirit is supposed to be reincarnated in every succeeding Dalai-lama.

On this particular day, however, I was more interested in the southwestern wing of the cathedral, which is used as the headquarters of the Tibetan cabinet. Here I met the *lönchen,* or prime minister, his colleagues, Ngapo Shape and Parkang Dzasa. Tsarong was careful to be absent on this occasion, but in any case he rarely attends the cabinet meetings, as he usually spends most of the day on the parade-ground at Settam training his troops, or at Norbu Linga, the private residence of the Dalai-lama, in personal attendance on his Holiness. Another shape, or secretary of state, called Trimon Shape, was absent from Lhasa during the whole of my visit, being engaged on a political mission in Kam (or Kham), the great province in the east of Tibet. Parkang is the only ecclesiastical member of the cabinet, all the others being laymen. Technically, he is not a full shape, as can be seen by his title of Dzasa, but for several years past he has acted in that capacity.

The office and title of *lönchen* is very modern; its creation was due to special causes. Prior to 1904 the cabinet consisted only of four shapes (the literal translation of the name shape is lotus-foot). As a result of the Younghusband expedition, the Dalai-lama was forced to flee to Mongolia, and the government of Tibet reverted to the hands of the Tsongdu, or National Assembly, a Parliament consisting chiefly of representatives of the great Lhasa monasteries, and, consequently, thoroughly reactionary. This body considered that the military and diplomatic defeat of Tibet was largely due to the ineptitude of the then existing shapes. They were removed from office and banished, four new men being appointed to take their place.

In 1908, when the Dalai-lama returned to Lhasa

and to power, he felt that the ex-officers should be recompensed for the injury done them. One of them was already dead, but the other three were recalled to the capital. His Holiness did not dare depose the four existing shapes, and so he instituted the new office of super-shape, or *Lönchen* (literally, great minister), and had the three exiles installed as such. This was intended as a temporary measure, and the posts were automatically to cease with the death of the three men concerned; but for a time the cabinet consisted of seven men, three *lönchens* and four shapes. Two of the *lönchens* are dead, and the remaining one is an old and feeble man. On his decease the cabinet will once more consist only of four shapes, though there is some talk that the Dalai-lama will decide to continue the office of *lönchen* and appoint Tsarong to fill it.

The Kashak or Cabinet composed of the *lönchen* and shapes is a very important body. The Tibetans have never learned to differentiate the executive and judicial functions of government. Every governor is also the judge of his district, and the Kashak, in addition to being charged with the administration of the country, constitutes the High Court of Appeal. The executive powers of the Dalai-lama are all exercised through the Kashak. This body appoints and dismisses the governors of the fifty-three districts and all other principal officers. It issues laws and ordinances; but, in order to appease the turbulent monks, important points of legislative policy are placed before the National Assembly. The members of the Kashak are appointed by the Dalai-lama and are responsible only to him. Tsarong Shape, as commander-in-chief of the army and as master of the mint, has special functions assigned to him; but the other members of the cabinet are not individually charged with the supervision of a particular department or ministry. Their duties are to attend at the general meetings of the cabinet, before which all state matters are brought and decided.

The Kashak meets every day of the week except Saturday. Every Thursday it assembles in the presence of the Dalai-lama, either at the Potala or at his private palace, Norbu Linga, in which he prefers to reside on ordinary occasions. On that day the business which has transpired during the whole week is reviewed. The Dalai-lama takes a great deal of personal interest in these details, and frequently lays down certain lines of policy, which must be followed by the Kashak in deciding future cases. At the same time, he is careful never to insist on any point which he thinks may arouse public opposition. He has twice lost his throne and has no desire to do so again.

On the occasion of my visit I found the three ministers seated cross-legged in a shabby little room full of papers, little better than that occupied by the city magistrates. Ngapo and Parkang said very little, and the conversation which ensued was carried on almost entirely by the *lönchen* and myself. I felt that the other two were inclined to be hostile, but the *lönchen* maintained an even courtesy, though he was obviously upset by the trouble which my entry into Lhasa had caused the Government. He is a mild, timid man, with much more of the air of a religious recluse than of

Tibet's highest civil official. His policy is one of irresolution and compromise. His intentions are excellent, but he is easily frightened from carrying them out by the slightest show of forcible opposition. He has none of that devil-may-care attitude which makes Tsarong so charming.

He told me that the Kashak hardly knew what to do about me. He asserted that he and the other shapes had no anti-foreign prejudice, but as the National Assembly had been most vehement in rejecting the proposition that we be allowed to come on to Lhasa from Gyangtse, he was afraid that its members would become very angry when they heard of my arrival. Nevertheless, as I was here, the *lönchen* added, he had been persuaded—here I saw Tsarong's influence—to allow me to stay on for a further period, though he asked me to remain more or less in disguise, and without letting the populace know of my arrival, lest a riot take place.

The *lönchen* was anxious to know what made me so keen to come to Lhasa. It was impossible to get him to understand the pleasures of undertaking an adventurous and dangerous journey. Had I talked about anthropological research he would have thought me mad, and so I informed him that so keen was my thirst for knowledge of Buddhism that I risked everything to drink at Lhasa from the fountain of wisdom. The old gentleman then thought he would like to test my knowledge of Buddhist philosophy, and asked me to interpret a text, which may be translated as follows: "Salutation to the peerless teacher who has silenced all disputation by his explanation of casual origination, without beginning, and without ending, without permanence and without impermanence, without sameness and without difference, without coming and without going." This happens to be the first verse of Nāgārjuna's famous Madhyamika-Karika, written about the first century A.D. As luck would have it, I once spent six months for my sins in studying this work and its commentaries, and so I decided to take the opportunity of airing a few of the unintelligible polysyllables which I had learned in this connection, interspersing quotations from Sanskrit and Chinese, neither of which could the poor man understand. In fact, the old gentleman, though deeply pious, had very little knowledge of the technicalities of his faith, and had asked for the interpretation largely as a joke, but I kept him on the paradoxical grill until his brain seemed nearly addled.

The Tsongdu, or National Assembly, to which reference has been made, is a very important body, since in theory at least it has charge of the entire legislation of Tibet. There are, in name at least, two assemblies. One is the Greater Assembly. This consists of representatives of all the monasteries, of all officials, and of all members of noble families; but in point of fact the General Assembly never meets, except at very momentous times, and the conduct of affairs lies in the hands of the Lesser Assembly, the Tsongdu proper, a small and very exclusive body, consisting of some twenty-odd persons whose most important members are the representatives of the three great Lhasa monasteries, Sera, Drepung, and Ganden. There are also representatives of the four royal lings and of the highest nobility, but every member is essentially a Lhasa man.

This is in one way the weakness of the Tibetan Government. The higher officials, including the provincial governors, are all chosen from families which may have estates all over the country but are essentially Lhasa families, and the Parliament of Tibet is dominated by the local Lhasa monasteries. The peasants and even the gentry and monasteries of other parts of Tibet have no voice in the settling of affairs.

Nominally all matters of national importance must come before the National Assembly for its approval, as well as all matters, however trifling, relating to foreign policy, so that even the Dalai-lama, in spite of his divinity, is not absolute. At the same time it is the Dalai-lama who is the judge of what constitutes a matter of national importance, and in his constant reaching after personal power he and his cabinet now frequently decide matters which by right should secure the approval of the legislative body.

At the same time the Tsongdu is far from being a nonentity and even in the last few years has frequently vetoed plans upon which the Dalai-lama had set his heart.

Consisting, as it does, largely of monks, the Tsongdu is a very conservative and reactionary body whose steady policy it has been to check the Dalai-lama and Tsarong Shape in their efforts at reform and reorganization.

The Tsongdu meets in a large room forming part of the Kashak wing of the cathedral. The shapes, or

The monastery of Dreföng, near Lhasa, the largest in Tibet, housing about eight thousand of the turbulent, red (or fighting) monks

Dongtse monastery

ministers of state, are not allowed to be actually present and take part in the discussion, but they are present in a small adjoining room, curtained off, where they can hear everything that is said. Apart from the shapes, all meetings are held in camera.

After my meeting with the cabinet I returned to Sonam's dwelling, there to await further developments. Three days later I obtained my first glimpse of the Dalai-lama. He was far too much frightened to grant me a public audience lest it be made the basis of agitation against him, but his curiosity had been aroused, and he arranged for a secret interview, so secret in fact that even my servants and Sonam knew nothing about it. In the evening a messenger arrived and told me I was to accompany him to the Kashak, but after turning a corner I was led by him along another street which runs from the city of Lhasa to the great Potala Palace.

It was now dark, and it was therefore impossible for me to see much of where we were going, but after arriving at the village at the foot of the palace we entered a side door of the sacred inclosure at the bottom of the hill. Though from a distance the Potala looks like a single unified structure, it is really a cluster of many coödinated buildings and wings, used as residences for various officials, tombs, temples, and chapels, reception and ceremonial rooms; one wing is used as a training-school for officials.

We climbed up the hill to the base of the great Red Palace, the central block of which dominates all the others, and which contains the more important chapels and reception-rooms, and the private apartments used by the Dalai-lama when he resides in the Potala.

On entering the Red Palace and after going along a long passage I stumbled up an interminable number of Tibetan step-ladder staircases until I found myself in a small room very near the top. Here I was suddenly left by my attendant. At first I thought I was quite alone, but looking closer through the gloom I saw quietly waiting one other person—no other person that the Dalai-lama himself.

I had a long talk with the living god of Tibet, but though it concerned itself only with general matters I was forced to promise that I should keep the interview entirely secret. It was obvious that his Holiness was much frightened at the possible consequences of giving me an audience, and later when a crisis came he denied having seen me and forced me to do the same.

While, however, it is impossible to record what was said, I can at least say something of the impression he made upon me.

I found him to be a smallish man, lighter in build and with a face longer and more oval than most Tibetans. A childhood attack of smallpox had left slight traces upon his countenance, but these were almost invisible in the gloom. His head was shaven, as becomes a priest, but he had long, pointed mustaches, which he had learned in India to wax. He was a man who obviously was accustomed to be regarded as a god, and who, moreover, had a firm belief in his own divinity, and yet there was a great quietness, even modesty, about his manner. He has not the delicate, half-mystical appearance which characterizes the Trashi-lama of Shigatse. He is much more a man of the world, a careful observer of human nature, and a shrewd conjecturer of ulterior motives. His personal life is above suspicion. He is rigid in his celibacy and in his abstinence from wine and tobacco. His food is simple, and his dress on ordinary occasions is scarcely to be distinguished from that of an ordinary monk. He prefers to reside as much as possible in his villa at Norbu Linga, another mile beyond the city, instead of living in state, attended with pomp and ceremony, in the Potala, one of the most magnificent palaces in the world. Yet he is obviously concerned with this world's affairs. He is ambitious in a cool, calculating way, ever seeking to unify his power and to weaken opposition.

In his youth his violent temper frequently led him to commit some rash or foolish act, but the trials and tribulations of exile and deposition have taught him greater caution—one might almost say craftiness. He is afraid to commit himself to a policy without seeing what its effect will be. He would be the last person to claim occult powers for himself, and his intelligence is not gigantic. Fine points of metaphysics and theology he leaves to others, but he is possessed of a great deal of acumen and acuteness. Above all, he is blessed with the faculty of being able to choose wisely his human instruments. His most notable success along this line is Tsarong Shape, and the wisest thing he ever did was to place in Tsarong's hands much of the reorganization of the state.

As is generally known, the office of the Dalai-lama

is not hereditary, nor is this supreme ruler of Tibet elected by the will of the people. Rather is he chosen by a system which is unique in the governments of the world. In theory the Dalai-lama is an incarnation of the divinity Chenresi and is also an immediate reincarnation of himself. Within a short time, varying from a few months to two years, after the death of the pontiff the supreme council of monks announce to the people the discovery of the new Dalai-lama. The new Dalai-lama may be an infant of a few weeks or a child as old as two years, but in any case he must have been born subsequent to the death of the last Dalai-lama, whose soul is supposed to have transmigrated into the body of the infant. Sometimes before the death of the old pontiff the latter intimates to his councilors that he will probably be born in this or that part of the country or in this or that type of family. Such an intimation, of course, simplifies matters for the councilors when the time comes to make the choice. But where no such intimation is given, or where there is a division of opinion among the councilors, recourse is had to divination through the casting of lots. Not only the Dalai-lama is thus chosen to succeed himself as a new incarnate Buddha, but so are other high ecclesiastics, particularly the abbots of many important monasteries throughout Mongolia and Tibet. In the case of these less important lamas, however, the succession generally follows regularly, and each incarnation attains to a ripe old age. But the Dalai-lamas have been much less fortunate.

The first four supreme pontiffs were purely religious leaders and had no political significance; consequently they, too, had the average duration of life. It was the fifth incarnation who managed by the aid of the Tartars to make himself a temporal ruler of the country. Thereafter a great deal of political intrigue began to be bound up with the fortunes of the succeeding incarnations.

After the death of the fifth Dalai-lama there were a number of irregular successions, with various rival claimants for the divine office, each supported by various factions. Eventually the Chinese emperor was called in by one of the factions in order to establish their protégé on the throne and at the same time to protect them from foreign invaders. The Chinese did restore order but at the usual price, and in 1720 the Emperor Kanghi of China declared Tibet to be a vassal even though an autonomous state and appointed two *ambans* or political agents to reside in Lhasa. Though nominally only diplomatic agents, these Chinese officials exercised a great deal of power, and from that date until 1912 Tibet was forced to recognize the suzerainty of China.

Thereafter the succession to the throne was regular but extremely rapid. The administration of power lay in the hands of a regent, who was in turn largely controlled by the *ambans*. The regent was supposed to hold office during the minority of the Dalai-lama, but practically no Dalai-lama was allowed to survive his minority. The limit of life for the last four Dalai-lamas has been eleven, eighteen, eighteen, and eighteen respectively. In other words, the boy Dalai-lamas have all been puppets in the hands of the priestly oligarchy which ruled the country. These all-powerful priests, fearing that an adult Dalai-lama might not always be sufficiently plastic in their hands, saw to it that the supreme ruler was called to a new incarnation when he reached the age of majority.

The present Dalai-lama is the first one in more than a century to escape this fate. He is a man of acumen and of great strength of character as has previously been indicated. In no way has he manifested these characteristics more than in his supreme achievement; namely, escape from death up to his present age. The son of a peasant, his succession to the supreme rulership of Tibet was obviously dictated by political motives. At the time of his succession Tibet was much under the influence of China, and China did not wish the supreme rulership of Tibet to fall into the hands of one of the wealthy and powerful families of that country. Hence the choice of the peasant boy for this office.

This one-time peasant boy is now a man of fifty, one who has succeeded in wresting to himself, as Dalai-lama, the power that for so long has been usurped by the oligarchy of monks. Suspecting—and doubtless learning from hearsay—the fate of his predecessors, the present Dalai-lama, when he approached the age of majority, studiously avoided eating food that was not first tasted by his attendants and in other ways shrewdly avoided running into danger.

On reaching the age of eighteen he insisted upon claiming the power that was nominally his, and grudgingly this was granted to him. Emboldened by success and by the will to power, as well as the will to live, the present Dalai-lama embarked on his own responsibility upon a fearless if somewhat indiscreet foreign policy. His apparent over-friendliness for Russia and his overtures to that country succeeded in arousing the hostility of both Great Britain and China; that of the former in particular, of which the more or less direct consequence was the British expedition under Colonel Younghusband into Tibet in 1904. Upon the entrance of British troops into Tibet the Dalai-lama fled incontinently into Mongolia, from which country he later crossed over to China, and lived for a time in Peking. In 1908 he returned to Tibet but was destined to remain there only about eighteen months before "on the wheel of things" it became China's turn to act the part of invader of Tibet and the turn of Great Britain—i.e., British India—to act the part of host, offering refuge to the fugitive. From 1910 to 1912 his Holiness remained in India.

Since 1912, when, through the activity of Tsarong, the Chinese were ousted and the Dalai-lama returned to power in Lhasa, it has been the part of his Holiness to "set his house in order." It is a part for which, considering the many obstacles which have beset his path, he has shown unusual capacity. As the result of his activity, the present political situation in Tibet is one of unusual interest.

The country is sharply divided into two actively partizan groups. One is the court cabinet and is supported by a considerable portion of the lay nobility and of the peasantry. The other, represented by the so-called National Assembly, is largely composed of the nominees of the priests of the three large monasteries in the vicinity of Lhasa. Both these parties are largely autocratic, but the priestly party is by far the more reactionary. The court party consists largely of persons who have dwelt long enough abroad to absorb new ideas and is comparatively progressive. Incidentally the court party is pro-British, while the priestly party is strongly anti-British and pro-Chinese. At present there is no group which has any especial regard for Russia.

To-day the power of the court party is gradually on the increase, but it is interesting to speculate upon what will take place upon the death of the present Dalai-lama. Will Tsarong seize the reins of government and declare himself king, as it is sometimes whispered may be the case, or will he, perhaps more astutely, be instrumental in the choice of an infant Dalai-lama of a type that can be molded to his own point of view and way of thinking? Or will a very old prophecy be in reality fulfilled, namely, that the thirteenth Dalai-lama will be the last, that after his death Tibet will be opened up to the "white barbarians" of the West, and that the title of Dalai-lama will be but a memory of the past? Easy to put the question; but who can answer? My mind was dwelling on these things as I sat in amiable conversation with his Holiness.

At the end of an hour I took my leave and returned to Lhasa and my dwelling in the same stealthy way that I had come.

CHAPTER XIII

A PRISONER OF STATE

THE next morning the storm broke. I knew that after the news of my arrival had been communicated to so many persons it would be impossible for it to remain long a secret. Rumors about me had been spreading for the last several days and had eventually reached the ears of some of the more fanatical monks. Consequently in the morning I saw quite a crowd collected under my window. This continued to swell in size, and by the afternoon it had become turbulent. Two or three of the bolder spirits raised a howl and called on me to show myself, while others shrieked, "Death to the foreigner." Others then joined in, and a regular hymn of hate came up from below. Stones and sticks began to be thrown. Fortunately my flat was on the second floor and very inaccessible; but a few stones hit the window, and the glass panes were broken. But as the mob had no firearms with them, I knew they could do little damage unless they could get inside the house. All houses in Lhasa are built round a courtyard. The ground floor is given over to stables and store-rooms and has no door or window opening on the street except one great gate communicating between the courtyard and outside. Staircases leading to the first and second floors are all inside the courtyard. Consequently I had the great gate closed and barred and prepared to stand a siege. The crowd pounded on the gate and strove to get in, but the great beams held firm. In other lands there might have been danger of their setting fire to the place, but in Tibet all houses are made of stone or sun-dried bricks and are not inflammable. There was the possibility that the other inhabitants of the house might prove treacherous and by opening the gateway from within allow the crowd to enter; but though as a precaution I placed two of my servants on guard at the gate, I had no great fear, as it was known that a mob was likely to do damage all round, and I thought that every one else would have an interest in keeping the rabble out.

It was rather thrilling to have a crowd outside howling for one's blood, but though my servants were terribly frightened it seemed likely, from what I saw, to prove a safe amusement. At the same time, if by any chance the mob were to effect an entry, things would develop into something far more serious.

Consequently I knew that it would be safer for me outside than inside, and I decided, temporarily, to take refuge in another part of the city. None of the mob, I knew, had any idea what I looked like; consequently, I carefully renewed my disguise and, with my servants, slipped out by a small secret door in the back of the courtyard which led into another courtyard which in turn led into a small back street.

I was determined to take refuge in the residence of a petty official who was friendly to me, but in passing it occurred to me that it would be rather thrilling to see from the outside something of the mob around my house.

The crowd had its attention so fixed upon the spot where they thought I should be that they would never dream that their intended victim was standing among them. Consequently, on the way to my sanctuary I made my way to the front of the house and stood for a few moments on the outskirts of the throng. Not to be outdone by the others, I occasionally let out a yell myself, and to make things very realistic I picked up a small stone and threw it at my own window before passing on.

I heard later that troops had been held in readiness to rush to my assistance in case the mob had got into the house, but this proved unnecessary. When darkness crept on and the time for dinner arrived, the crowd gradually melted away, and I returned to my own abode by the same way I had left.

During the next few days small groups of people gathered in front of the house and occasionally made hostile demonstrations, but this never developed into anything serious, largely because it became known that I was under the protection of the Government.

Nevertheless, guards were posted at the door as a precaution against any unforeseen eventuality, and the Government implored me not to leave the house during the remainder of the period that the monks continued in the city, lest I should be recognized and attacked on the streets. After the monks had left and the city had settled down to normal, all danger would be at an end. Consequently from February 27 until March 13 I was practically a prisoner of state in the Forbidden City. But this period was far from unpleasant.

In the first place the period of enforced rest did me a great deal of good physically. The illness which came on me while I was still on my way to Lhasa had continued, and I had been far from well ever since entering the city. The excitement of the first few days had done nothing to improve matters, and I was more than glad to have this opportunity of quiet recuperation.

Inflammation of the lungs brought about several hemorrhages, but freedom from exposure and the efficiency of sheepskin blankets gradually brought about an improvement, though the improvement proved very gradual. For some reason coughing spells came much more frequently at night than in the daytime, and when I sat up, the coughing was less severe than when I lay down. On many occasions I could only get a few hours rest by sleeping propped up in a sitting position.

My dysentery proved even more troublesome. At first I thought of calling in some of the lamas from the famous medical college on the Chakpo Hill opposite the Potala, for I knew that in addition to their chants they were in the habit of giving certain herbs to their patients. In many cases their herbs are quite fantastic, and their drugs are based on the magic pharmacopœia of China; but for simpler troubles many of the herbs of the witch-doctors of primitive peoples are quite useful, and I thought that some of their drugs might do me some good, and at the same time I might in this way see how the lama doctors of Tibet go about their work. But I was strongly advised not to call them in, as it was more than possible that they would administer some poison in place of medicine, this being the simplest method of getting me out of the way.

The lama doctors of Tibet know nothing of modern western methods. The groundwork of their medical theory is based on the ancient Indian system incorporated in medieval Buddhism, but this system has been somewhat modified by ideas taken from the Chinese pharmacopœia.

Considering the fact that the Tibetans are in the habit of cutting up the bodies of the dead, it is surprising how backward the Tibetan medical system is regarding even anatomy. No advantage seems to have been taken of corpse dissection to improve on their knowledge of the shape and functions of the internal organs. Elaborate anatomical charts are indeed prepared, but in these the heart of a woman is supposed to beat in the middle of her chest and that of a man on the left. Red blood circulates on the right-hand side of the body and yellow bile on the left.

Surgery of a very primitive kind is practised but entirely without reference to antiseptics, and many persons in Tibet die from amputations which have brought blood-poisoning.

Crude and primitive as this Tibetan medical science is, it is very elaborate, and a man is supposed to study nearly ten years before he can master it, longer than the time required for a European medical degree; and many aspirants fail in their final medical examination. All told, there are less than one hundred qualified lama doctors anywhere in Tibet, and nearly all of these are resident in Lhasa. In the country districts an ordinary monk with a knowledge of ritual is considered sufficient to banish the disease-bringing demons. Pneumonia, venereal disease, and smallpox are the scourges which are most rampant in Tibet.

Some of the more simple and pious of my Lhasa friends became worried as the days went on and I showed no improvement, and wanted me to go in for the more ordinary Tibetan method of curing disease, the method used in the country, where no doctors are to be found. This would necessitate calling in some priests, but as no drugs were to be administered it was thought to be safe.

According to this plan some priests were to be called in to perform three rites on my behalf: one was the chanting of a famous metaphysical Buddhist work called the "Prajna Paramita Sutra" (Sher-chin), or the discourse on the transcendental wisdom; the second was the offering of food and drink to various demons, genii, and guardian deities to insure their good will; finally, in case these failed and I should grow worse, the monks should perform a ceremony called *chi-lu* wherein a little crude image of myself wrapped in some of my clothes would be offered to the gods of death with the idea that the gods could be deceived into taking this image instead of myself.

Two other similar cures are recommended; one was to eat some of the *rilbu* or holy pills which are prepared in somewhat different form all over Tibet. In nearly all cases they are round black balls about the size of a marble made of barley-flour and containing the relic of past saints, or even something from the body of living incarnations. Needless to say the Dalai-lama pills are considered particularly efficacious in curing disease, and I was assured of a supply.

The other means of conquering disease especially recommended was to purchase some animal destined for slaughter and set him free. It is believed that illness comes as a punishment for past misdeeds, and the saving of life is so meritorious that it will counteract all past evil and therefore do away with the cause of disease.

I was destined, moreover, to receive medical assistance from quite another source. Knowing that I was ill, Tsarong promised to send me some English medicines that he had had especially imported from India, but on arrival they turned out to be a dozen boxes of very moldy Beecham's Pills and three pounds of Epsom salts. Considering the crudity of Tibetan medicine it might be thought that a person initiated into the mysteries of European medicine would find a very warm welcome in Tibet, but the experience of the Europeanized doctors in Gyangtse and Yatung prove that this is not necessarily the case. It was thought by the Indian Government to be good propaganda policy to have a European doctor stationed at Gyangtse who could not only look after the health of the troops stationed there but also attend to various Tibetan patients—and by curing them win the good will of the people. Conservative prejudice, however, has meant that in most cases Tibetans who fall ill will first call in their priests; and only when they have given up all hope of recovery, and as a last resort, will a visit be paid to the English doctor. In many cases the disease has reached such an advanced stage by this time that it is impossible to effect a cure—and it is the European, of course, who gets the blame for the death of the patient, so that belief in the efficacy of European medicine is a matter of slow growth.

In my own case, what helped me more than any medicine was the fact that I could get proper food once more. Whereas, in the country districts it was possible to secure only barley-flour, tea, and putrid meat, which for purposes of disguise I had to eat raw, in Lhasa the menu is much more varied.

In the first place, the Lhasa plains are so much more fertile than any other part that many more crops will grow there. Peas, potatoes, and walnuts, for example, are cultivated, and from the extreme east of Tibet come apples and dried apricots.

The upper classes of Lhasa have been much affected by Chinese ideas, and many of their dishes are of Chinese origin.

The most common dish of the aristocrats in Tibet is a broth called *tukpa.* This contains a vermicelli or spaghetti, made of millet-flour, generally, and a mass of finely chopped boiled meat. This might be called the staple dish for a man will have seven or eight helpings

Sons of *lonchen* (or prime minister of Tibet); the younger, on left, is an official; the elder, on right, a monk.

Tibetan woman with traditional head-dress

Exterior of Gyangtse cathedral; monks at morning prayer

The cathedral of Lhasa

of this and will, in between these helpings, eat little bits from the various side dishes—curried meat, turnips, white radishes, etc., which are in front of him.

Another very popular Lhasa dish, consumed in great quantities by inhabitants of the capital, is *momo,* or meat dumplings. They are boiled pastry balls containing minced meat and onions and generally flavored with *sa,* a pungent wild vegetable nearly as hot as chile. There are a great many eating-shops which specialize in these *momo,* and they are usually crowded.

Even in Lhasa rice is not grown, and in any case the Tibetans have no use for it; but Lhasa contains many Bhutanese, Sikkimese, and Nepalese who can never get fully accustomed to Tibetan barley, and for their benefit rice is brought on mules from over the passes. This means that rice is procurable in Lhasa, but it is very expensive.

Most pleasing of all to me was the fact that one can get sweetmeats in Lhasa. The Chinese are very fond of various sweet even though tasteless cakes. They were even able to imbue the Tibetan nobles with a faint liking for these delicacies, and I was able to buy several boxes which had been specially imported from China. The cakes were all old and mildewed, but they were better than nothing.

Best of all, I was able to secure small quantities of sugar itself. The sugar was filthy and sold in tiny paper parcels containing only a teaspoonful of the precious material, and these packets cost a rupee (one shilling sixpence, or thirty-five cents) apiece, but so great was my yearning for something sweet after months of abstinence that I squandered a small fortune on these sugar packets.

To me the Chinese dishes, such as *tukpa* and *momo*, were scarcely more appetizing than native Tibetan food; but as raw materials were fairly abundant, and as there was no longer any necessity for secrecy or disguise, Lhaten was able to prepare for me a number of dishes for which my soul yearned.

I found that living expenses were much higher in Lhasa than anywhere else in Tibet, but, apart from sugar, rice, cakes, and other imported food, of course cheaper than in the outer world.

It may be interesting to some to see my average budget for food while I was in Lhasa; this does not include anything eaten by my servants:

Fuel	4	trangkas[1]
Chicken (whole)	4	"
Eggs (4)	2	"
Milk (yak's milk)	2	"
Potatoes	4	"
Meat	3	"
Rice (handful)	5	"
Sugar (3 packets)	15	"

A supply of this sort would last about two days, which shows that I did not stint myself after my long experience of half-starvation.

I was afraid that the long weeks of my imprison-

[1] It should be remembered that one trangka is approximately equal to threepence, or six cents.

ment were going to prove very tedious, but the time was made interesting in a number of different ways.

In the first place, during the New Year period there were a large number of pageants, ceremonies, and processions; and as many of these took place in the market-place underneath my windows I was able to get an excellent view of them.

More particularly did three of these affairs make a vivid impression upon my mind. The first of them took place on March 3, which was the fifteenth day of the first Tibetan month, and as the Tibetans have a lunar calendar the night of every fifteenth is always marked by the full moon.

The afternoon of this day was marked by feverish activity. Laborers were busy erecting great booths all around the Inner Circle. These booths were very imposing structures, many of them over fifty feet high. They were supported by huge wooden poles stuck into the ground, but the body consisted of canvas or cloth cut in various geometrical designs, each of special symbolic significance. The canvas was either painted or, more commonly, decorated with stained butter and was frequently inlaid with elaborate and beautifully carved butter images.

Before these great cloth structures wooden altar-tables were placed, and on these were put large numbers of brass lamps filled with butter, which were lighted once dusk had fallen.

About seven o'clock the Dalai-lama and all the great officials of state made a solemn procession lit by torches around the Inner Circle, followed by thousands of pilgrims. To the Tibetans it was a most solemn and sacred affair, and even to the outsider it was really very imposing, but a humorously incongruous touch was added by a large body of troops from the new army which Tsarong is training along strict European lines, who went before and after the Dalai-lama as a bodyguard.

The officials and the high priests were dressed in their medieval costumes, while the soldiers wore British uniforms and were armed with modern rifles. To make matters worse, at the most solemn and sacred moment in the whole procession the regimental band struck up "Should a Body Kiss a Body Comin' through the Rye?"

The lamps were kept alight, and large bodies of pilgrims continued to circumambulate the central square all through the night; but at the first sign of dawn the lamps were extinguished and the structures quickly dismantled, and by eight o'clock in the morning there was no trace of them. Considering the great laziness and slowness of the Tibetans on one hand, and the great size of the ceremonial booths on the other, it was really remarkable with what speed they were erected and pulled down.

This full moon ceremony had its origin in the great Kumbum monastery, which lies at the extreme northeast of Tibet, a part still controlled by China. This monastery was the early field of labor of the great Tibetan reformer Tsong Kapa, the founder of the yellow-hat sect, who brought this festival with him to Lhasa.

There must have been more than a hundred booths

in all. It is the duty of each monastery in the neighborhood and of each of the great aristocratic and official families to erect and attend to one. This duty entails a heavy expense, and there was a tendency a few years ago to neglect this obligation as far as possible, at any rate to demolish them early in the evening; but in spite of his great modernity in some respects the Dalai-lama is a great stickler for the strict observance of all religious ceremonial and has forced the people to erect the booths in the old elaborate manner.

The second important procession did not take place until the twelfth of March. This was even more military in tone. In fact, it was the ceremonial procession of the old national guard of Tibet. In the old days before the new army had been created, it was the duty of each of the great families and the important monasteries to provide and equip a number of soldiers who could be called upon for service in case of emergency or war.

In spite of the new army this old territorial army organization continues to exist. A quainter procession could scarcely be imagined. There were three main groups, one armed with bows and arrows, one with spears, and one with guns—but such guns. They were all muzzle-loaders, of old seventeenth- or at latest eighteenth-century design—top-heavy, lopsided but wonderfully inlaid and decorated. Any one of them would have found a place of honor in a historical museum. To add to the impressiveness of the occasion these ancient muskets were loaded with blank cartridges and fired, causing a deafening din. Nearly all the soldiers were in full armor of well-worked iron, reminding one somewhat of the old armor of Japan. They wore curious, round, basket-like shields, and had feathers in their helmets. Even the horses of the mounted soldiers were incased in armor. Three times this fantastic army went in procession around the Inner Circle, and then they marched away to the open plains to carry out their military exercises.

The next great pageant took place only the next day (March 13). This was more definitely religious, being a festival in honor of the Blessed Maitreya, the coming savior of the world. An image of the saint was carried around on the one vehicle with wheels of Tibet, a curious clumsy cart. Why in the world the Tibetans have never gone in for carts I could never imagine, as the open plains are admirably suited for wheeled traffic, but even the Dalai- and Trashi-lamas are content to go about in a palanquin, a privilege shared only by the abbess of Samding convent; and every one else must walk or ride on horse- or mule-back. Even the image-bearing carriage of Lhasa was pulled by men. Behind the cart marched in procession the glories of Lhasa, two real live elephants from Nepal, both of them presents to the Dalai-lama. Very fine but very useless presents they are, for neither the Dalai-lama nor any other Tibetan would dare ride on them, and even their keepers or mahouts have to be Nepalese, as no Tibetan would take on the job.

Behind the elephants came three great dummy animals, made out of cloth, very ingeniously designed and colored. They were of great size, and each contained several men. They represented the yak, the tiger, and the elephant.

Small boys played a very important part of this procession. I rather wondered at this until I was told the reason, which is certainly very curious. According to ancient Indian cosmology, the stature and the span of life of mankind are not changeless but undergo cycles of decrease and increase. At the zenith of human glory every man is a giant and the average duration of life is eighty thousand years, but gradually degeneration sets in. Stature and life-span decrease until all human beings are dwarfs and live for only ten years. After this comes a cycle of increase when man goes back to his original size and duration of life, but just at present, according to the Hindus and Buddhists, mankind is on the down grade. Every century man's life and size steadily, even though imperceptibly, decrease. The average life is already less than a hundred years and the average stature less than six feet, but this degeneration will continue for many centuries to come. When the nadir is reached, Maitreya, the compassionate savior, will arise. The boys in the procession, therefore, represent what all human beings will look like in the era of the future Buddha.

In addition to the processions, the tediousness of my imprisonment was also relieved by reading. By sending Lhaten out into the market I managed to procure a good supply of Tibetan books. These were of course of the usual sort, printed not with movable type but from carved-out wooden blocks upon very coarse paper. In many cases the print was insufferably bad, the whole page being but a black smudge. But this is quite understandable. Most of the peasant pilgrims who come to Lhasa like to buy a few religious books. To be possessed of holy writings is to acquire merit. It is quite unnecessary that they be read, and as they are not to be read why should they be well printed?

I told Lhaten to buy for me two groups of books, one being those which were most popular among the laity, and the other those which were most popular among the priests, and in due course he brought me back some fifty or sixty volumes. The books bought by the laity were largely trash, confessions of sins to the Buddhas of the past, recitation of charms for protection from evil, danger, and sickness, and an occasional biography of a Dalai-lama or other saint.

Among the books which were most popular with the ordinary monks were three works of considerable interest.

The first of these was the "Domang" (literally, many sutras), a selection of the most popular short discourses from the great "Kangyur" collection. This book is a gold-mine to the priest in Tibet, as he will be well paid for reciting or chanting various portions of it for the benefit of private patrons. The whole "Kangyur" is far too bulky to be portable, but the "Domang" can be carried wherever custom calls. The whole "Kangyur" contains much that is really beautiful and much that is really silly. Unfortunately the selections contained in the "Domang" are nearly all of the silly class, magic charms and incantations for winning the protection of gods and demons.

The second work was the collected poems of the great Tibetan saint Milarepa (spelled Milaraspa). He might be called the Tibetan St. Francis. A wandering ascetic vowed to poverty, and clad only in a cotton robe, he composed many religious songs and poems, some of which show high artistic merit. Among many magical and mythological puerilities there are very vivid descriptions of land and of people, though the whole tone of the poems is to declare the nothingness of all phenomenal existence.

The third book was "Lam-chen," or "Lamrinchempo," the stages on the Great Path (to Salvation). This is a very important work by Tsong-Kapa, the founder of the established church of Tibet, and professes to be a manual that will guide the disciple along the path that leads to ultimate emancipation; but it contains many discussions of the philosophic foundations of Buddhism and gives us an excellent insight into theoretical as opposed to practical Tibetan Buddhism—Buddhism as it is supposed to be rather than as it is.

Most of my time was spent in wandering through the dull, dry pages of Tibetan religious literature, but occasionally I was able to relax my mind by reading two newspapers published in English! These were subscribed to by Sonam as a means of keeping up the English he had learned in Kalimpong. Both papers were published in India, by and for Indians, and though printed in English were decidedly home rule and anti-British. One was the "Bengalee," moderate in tone, of considerable literary merit, and most persuasive in its arguments. The other was the "Amrita Bazar Patrika," a most violently seditious rag, full of scurrilous abuse. It is certainly a token of the liberalism of the Indian Government that it allows such a revolutionary paper to be published.

It was rather funny that it is these two papers which represent English literature in Lhasa. Even Sonam was rather ashamed of the "Amrita Bazar Patrika" and tried to hide it from me, though in the end I managed to get hold of it.

Formerly, I was told, the Dalai-lama himself subscribed to the "Statesman" and the "Englishman," two real English journals published in Calcutta; but as he was unable to read a word of them the subscription was stopped after a while.

The Dalai-lama is also possessed of two or three books in English about Tibet, and he has had portions of these translated for his benefit, but he takes very much to heart the criticisms which have been made regarding his people and their civilization. The Japanese priest Kawaguchi who managed to get to Lhasa in disguise won his intense dislike on account of a criticism of the character of Padma Sambhava, the wine-bibbing and sensual founder of Lamaism. I sometimes wonder what he will think of some of my own remarks about Tibet.

The Tibetan officials in Yatung and Gyangtse who are more in touch with the outside world sometimes forward to Lhasa foreign comments on Tibetan affairs, and a certain English official who was in Tibet made himself very unpopular with the Lhasa court on account of an article he wrote in a Calcutta newspaper of the filthiness of the town of Pari. Apart from the highest court and official circles, however, Lhasa remains in complete ignorance of the outside world and is completely unconcerned with what the outside world may think or say of it.

Perhaps the most interesting interludes in my prisoner's life were the frequent visits paid me by various Lhasa people. Through Sonam and Tsarong a number of persons were induced to come and see me so as to relieve the monotony.

Among my visitors were a number of priests of a more liberal turn of mind than the average, who, hearing of my interest in the study of their religion, came to talk with me. To one dear old man I became especially attached, and he came frequently and stayed for hours each time, consuming incredible quantities of buttered tea, discussing the fine points of Buddhist metaphysics.

Although completely ignorant of all Western learning—to him European religion, philosophy, and science were closed books—he was a man of great learning from the medieval Tibetan standpoint. His learning was exactly like that of the schoolmen of the Middle Ages. His geography was delightfully vague. To him the world was a cylinder and the sun and moon but tiny satellites which revolve round it; but for him such concrete material things were of little or no importance, for he was interested in the subtleties of Being and Non-being, the nature of substance, and the inherence of attributes. On these points his knowledge and his views were profound.

But with all his learning, he was as simple as a child, charming and naïve and possessed of an old-world courtesy. Sorrowing over the wickedness of the world, he was full of an unsophisticated piety that would have put half the saints of all religions to shame.

At first he talked of lesser things, of the Wheel of Life, to which sentient beings, blinded by lust and ignorance, are attached, going round and round the cycle of transmigration until the power of wisdom and purity sets them free.

But life and the wheel of life all belonged to the sphere of phenomena, and there would follow long talks on the nature and the ultimate reality of the phenomenal world; here would be expounded and criticized the views of the three main schools of Buddhist philosophy, the Sarvastivadins, who were realists, the Yogacarins, who were idealists, and the Madhyamikas, who were transcendentalists. To make the discussion a little more lively I professed to take the part of the idealists against the transcendental position of my teacher, and the old man would grow vehement in showing me the shallowness of my views and would come again every two or three days with fresh arguments and new illustrations.

Weighty texts were needed to clinch a discussion, and the delightful old philosopher gave to me, his newfound pupil, many precious manuscripts of the writings of ancient saints and scholars, Indian and Tibetan. These were indeed a priceless gift. I had come to Tibet largely in order to procure such things, and in this way I came into possession of many works that were other wise unobtainable.

Printed books I also secured now in large numbers. The more metaphysical and philosophical books are never kept in stock in the book-shops, but the old scholar managed to get several printed off for me. The wooden blocks for such books are kept in some of the larger monasteries; and when one wants a copy of a book one must bring one's own paper to the monastery, and for a small cost the monastery officials will have the paper stamped with the proper blocks, but as I was a prisoner the old man arranged everything for me.

This old priest was one of the most delightful men it was ever my privilege to meet anywhere in the world. His charm and the genuineness of the winning simplicity of his character was in most vivid contrast to the ignorance and boorishness of the average Tibetan monk, but I was to find that such characters as his are occasionally to be found even in the great Lhasa monasteries, more particularly among the small group of monks who have won the coveted *geshe* or doctor of divinity degree.

This degree is the goal of every monk in Tibet, but there are very few who acquire it, as in nearly all cases it requires twenty years of study and vast textual knowledge to pass the necessary examinations, and in spite of the thousands of monks I do not suppose there are more than a hundred real *geshes* in the whole of Tibet.

The *geshe* rank is the highest of five stages in the career of a Tibetan monk. When as a boy he enters the monastery he is merely a novice or an acolyte. After he has learned to read and write and has memorized a few pages of ritualistic texts he will gain the rank of *genye.*

This is the equivalent to the title *upasakha,* which in other Buddhist countries is given to pious laymen who never enter the monkhood but who are known by their devotion and charity to the order. But in Tibet the laity may not even have this dignity, which has become a preparatory stage in the priesthood.

Further study and a further examination brings the rank of *ge-tsü* (or *ge-tsul*), which in other countries is equivalent to the novitiate but in Tibet is a further stage in the hierarchy. Particularly in the provincial monasteries many monks never rise higher than this stage, and a monk of this rank is allowed to take part in most religious ceremonies.

Another set of examinations and suitable presents to the monastery officials leads to the rank of *gelong,* the fully fledged monk or priest, capable of performing all ceremonies, and eligible for practically all the offices, elective and nominative, in the monastery. This is as high as the vast majority of the monks ever go.

Finally come the few who devote themselves to a life of study and who, having passed a strict examination and having also successfully maintained a thesis in the public disputations, are given the title of *geshe.* There are also one or two other scholastic titles. Theoretically it is only a monk with the rank of *geshe* who can be appointed the *kempo* (*khanpo*) or abbot of a monastery—i.e., of a monastery which has an appointed abbot and not a reincarnating divinity at its head. The abbots of so many of the larger monasteries, however, are reincarnations, chosen by lot as children, that there are comparatively few very high posts open to a young ambitious and studious monk who has no family influence to back him in his social climb. There are, however, two very high ecclesiastical posts supposed to be filled on the merit basis alone. One is the *chikyap kempo* or abbot-general, the chief official in the ecclesiastical court of the Dalai-lama. This, however, is largely a political and diplomatic post designed to keep the Dalai-lama in touch with the great monasteries. A new appointment was made to this office while I was in Lhasa, the man chosen being a representative of the great aristocratic Pala family, which at one time underwent a great deal of persecution on account of its friendliness toward the British authorities.

The other merit post is that of *ti-rimpoche,* the abbot of Ganden monastery, the third of the great trio of monasteries. Ganden, being the furthest removed from the political intrigues of Lhasa, has the greatest reputation for learning, and the *ti-rimpoche* is supposed to be the greatest scholar in the country. Curiously enough he is usually appointed from among the chief scholars of the other monasteries.

Most of the *geshes* are really learned men, though unlike my beloved preceptor, their scholarship is usually more of the letter than of the spirit. They are loaded down with a verbal knowledge of the scriptural texts without the slightest idea of what they mean. But they are the only ones who have any real knowledge of the doctrines of Buddhism. I was surprised at the colossal ignorance of the average monk—ignorance concerning his own religion. This was the more surprising considering the examinations they are supposed to have undergone. Very few of them could give any clear exposition of what Buddhism really teaches. They could only repeat a large number of incantations.

A great many monks in the three great monasteries fail in all of their examinations and become what is known as fighting monks, *dok-dokpa* or temple guardians. They smear their faces with black grease and spend most of their time in brawling. It is their number and influence which have given these monasteries their current reputation for rowdiness.[1]

Kyipup, the boy educated in England, continued to visit me frequently, and both he and Sonam gave me much interesting information concerning the new Tibetan post-office.

From very early times Tibet has been possessed of a government courier service, with relays of ponies carrying messengers from the capital to the most distant provinces. These messengers were supposed to carry only government despatches, but in some cases they could be bribed to deliver private letters as well. During the great reforms of the last few years the Government has sought to transform this old courier service into a regular post-office service, whereby the carrying of private letters and even packets is legalized. Up to the present time only twelve post-offices have been opened, the principal places being Lhasa, Shigatse, Gyangtse, Pari, and various intermediary points. These

[1] I have decided not to bore my readers with any discussion of my researches into Tibetan Buddhism. This subject will be handled in a subsequent and more technical work. For a treatment of Buddhist philosophy in general, see my "Introduction to Mahayana Buddhism" and "Manual of Buddhist Philosophy."

places are in the center of Tibet, and the outer provinces are still covered only by the old courier system.

The mails are carried from place to place entirely by pony relays, but on the whole the service is swift. Gyangtse lies about 150 miles away from Lhasa, and letters come through in about two and a half days.

The Tibetans have printed a very interesting collection of stamps, and the postal system is supposed to work exactly on the European scale, but letters go through much more frequently as the result of a small present to the postman than because of bearing a stamp.

Tibet is not, of course, a member of the Postal Union, and there is no direct postal connection between Lhasa and the outside world, but there is a British post-office in the fort at Gyangtse, and there is a Tibetan post-office in the same city; and provided one has a friend in Gyangtse to transfer letters from one post-office to the other, it is possible to send to and receive letters from England and America while in Lhasa.

I was lucky enough to be able to make the necessary arrangements and so was able once or twice to secure longed-for bundles of letters from home which were waiting for me in Darjeeling; but, alas, among them were urgent notices that my current income tax was unpaid and information as to what was going to happen to me in case I did not pay up in ten days.

An even more striking instance of the new order of things in Tibet, rendered all the more striking because of the continuance of the old order alongside of it, is the telegraphic outfit which has been installed in the last two years. To be sure, the telegraph line only runs between Lhasa and Gyangtse, 150 miles; and very crude, very childish and amateurish it is, but a real telegraph system. It breaks down every two or three weeks, but it is soon repaired, and as many as five telegraphic messages are sent over it every week! By means of the British Indian telegraphic outpost at Gyangtse it is thus possible for one to be in almost immediate touch with the outside world while living in the most isolated and forbidden city of the world.

I was interested to learn that the telegraph had been decreed by an executive order of the cabinet, largely as the result of Tsarong's influence, and without the National Assembly's being consulted. Needless to say, this reactionary body was very indignant at the innovation, but it was even more interesting to know that this modern invention was to help in trying to keep me—a foreigner—out. It was over the telegraph that the news came that I was thought to be in Tibet in disguise, and it was over the telegraph that the orders had gone out to the local officials that search be made for me so that I could be turned back.

One of the most interesting of my visitors was a man called Champela. He has had a rather interesting experience. Although of pure Tibetan extraction, he spent his boyhood in Darjeeling and became thoroughly acquainted with the English language and customs. Because of his brightness he was given a good post in a bank. Then something went wrong, accounts could not be squared, and Champela, knowing that extradition laws do not apply in Tibet, fled to Lhasa, where he found government employment on account of his knowledge of foreign customs. He incidentally became official translator and interpreter to the Government when at length it became necessary for some one in Lhasa to know English.

Year after year he has remained in Lhasa, always desiring to return to Darjeeling; but the fear of prison kept him away. A year or two ago, through the magnanimous clemency of Sir Charles Bell, he received a pardon for the long-ago-committed and half-forgotten crime; but he is now an old man, terrified by the thought of the long journey back to India, and so his departure is postponed month after month and will probably be postponed year after year until he dies, still planning his return to the place of his boyhood.

The younger brother of Champela, called Karma Subum, had been my Tibetan teacher in Darjeeling. I had found him a man of unusual intelligence, one of the few Orientals capable of teaching his own language, and so in spite of past deeds I had looked forward to meeting Champela, and I was not disappointed. A mild, meek, humorous little man he was, who had led the most upright of lives since the crash of his youth; he was one of the most genuinely kindly men I have ever met. His numerous acts of courtesy made my stay in Lhasa doubly pleasant. At the same time he was one of the few men in Lhasa, apart from Tsarong, who take an intelligent interest in the public affairs of their own country, and he was full of reliable information. It was surprising to find how few Tibetans, even officials, had any idea as to the details of the country's administration, and in many cases when I had sought everywhere else for information I had to go to Champela to secure what I wanted.

Two or three of the things he said were worth recording. I was amused to learn from him of the large number of letters which the Dalai-lama receives from private persons in England and America. For the most part such persons assure his Holiness of their rigid adherence to his creed, their acceptance of his divinity, and their knowledge of the fact that he is a mahatma, one of the great hidden personalities who direct the course of evolution all over the world. The writer then adds that as he is different from the average materialistic Westerner he would be pleased if the Dalai-lama would permit him to come to Lhasa and study the ultimate mysteries in the home of the secret doctrine. In some cases the writer backs up his plea by stating that he met his Holiness during the latter's stay in Peking or Darjeeling.

It is the duty of Champela to translate all such letters into Tibetan, and they are duly read by the Dalai-lama; but no reply, not even an official acknowledgment, is ever vouchsafed. They are merely stored away and forgotten.

A similar fate used to attend official communications, letters sent by representatives of the Indian Government; the Younghusband expedition had as its proximate cause the fact that a letter from the viceroy was returned unopened. But the humiliation of Tibet as a result of that expedition taught the Dalai-lama a lesson. More particularly has the effort of his Government to maintain the independence won from China in

1912 taught him to seek support from India; and today all communications sent by the Indian Government, usually through the political officer in Sikkim, receive prompt attention, and a courteous even though sometimes evasive answer very promptly despatched.

I was glad to learn from Champela something more concerning the relationship between the Dalai- and the Trashi-lamas. Politically, the power of the Dalai-lama far overshadows that of his colleague in Shigatse, but religiously the potentates are supposed to rank as equals. I had always supposed that for this reason it was found more convenient for the two highest incarnations of divinity in Tibet never to meet, but it seems that interviews between the two do occasionally take place. Only two years previously the Trashi-lama had paid a state visit to Lhasa and had been entertained by the Dalai-lama.

Tibetan etiquette has it that though the two rulers are equal as touching their divinity yet they take precedence over one another in respect to their seniority as regards the flesh. As the present Dalai-lama is a few years older than the present Trashi-lama, the Lhasa ruler is able to lord it over his rival. This is probably one reason why the Trashi-lama was invited to Lhasa.

It is the duty of the Dalai-lamas to consecrate new Trashi-lamas, and of the Trashi-lamas to consecrate new Dalai-lamas, and supposedly all is love and good will between them. Actually, however, there is always bitter rivalry between the two courts, and in the present instance the Dalai-lama has a strong sense of animosity against the Trashi-lama on account of certain events of the last few years. It is well known that personally the Trashi-lama is a dreamer, a religious recluse who takes little interest in political affairs. But no doubt just for this reason he has been made a cat's-paw by other interested parties.

In 1904 when the Dalai-lama as a result of the Younghusband expedition fled to Mongolia the Chinese officials resident in Lhasa declared him deposed and declared the Trashi-lama the supreme ruler of the country. In spite of this fact the Dalai-lama managed by further direct negotiations with the Peking authorities to come back to Lhasa in triumph, and the Trashi-lama sank back to second place. But in 1910, when the Chinese officials discovered that the Dalai-lama was not subservient enough to suit them, a Chinese army invaded the country, as has been previously related; and when the Dalai-lama fled to India he was once more declared deposed and stripped of his divinity in favour of the Trashi-lama, who, though nominally the supreme ruler and possessed of all the privileges enjoyed by the Dalai-lama, was but a mere puppet.

The Tibetan rebellion of 1912 which brought independence from China meant also the return of the Dalai-lama, and the Trashi-lama only too willingly gave back the seals of office; but the Dalai-lama has never forgiven the usurpation of his power by his Shigatse rival and has ever since subjected him to various minor persecutions. These were borne for many years with great patience, but quite recently, since my return from Tibet, the news has come through that at last the Trashi-lama has sought refuge in flight, escaping either to Mongolia or to China, probably the latter.

This will very likely mean further trouble in the future. The Chinese have never resigned their claims to suzerainty over Tibet; they have resolutely refused to admit the claims of the Dalai-lama's Government and have only been waiting for a favorable opportunity for attempting once more to overrun the country. The Trashi-lama will be a valuable puppet in their hands. They can assert they invade Tibet only in order to restore the Shigatse potentate to his rightful position, and as the Trashi-lama has many devout adherents throughout the country, the Dalai-lama will have to look out for treachery from within as well as prepare against invasion from abroad. More particularly has the great modernist and Europeanizing tendency of the Dalai-lama's court as at present constituted and its friendship with the Indian Government won the ill will of many monks even inside the Lhasa monasteries—Drepung particularly has always been pro-Chinese—so that we can see that in spite of the present calm Tibet is full of the seeds of unrest.

Incidentally it may be added that it is almost certain that the Indian Government will continue its policy, pursued for several years past, of favoring the Dalai-lama at the expense of the Trashi-lama.

Two or three young *tsipon* or treasury officials also came to see me, and from them I learned that the Tibetan Government also has its financial embarrassments.

The trouble is that most of the government officials

become very wealthy while the Government remains very poor. Nominally the officials of every rank receive only a tiny salary, on the theory that as all the officials are chosen from the wealthy families they do not require large emolument but will be willing to donate their services to the state. But in point of fact the salary is the smallest portion of the income from any post. The acceptance of bribes, or "squeeze," is the openly recognized order of the day, and a great deal of money that should really go into the government coffers as taxes finds its way into the private pockets of the official. When even this proves insufficient, an official can generally secure a grant of land from the Government which brings in a tidy income.

The governors of the fifty-three provinces into which Tibet is divided levy a family tax and a land tax, the land tax being usually collected in kind, consisting of a varying percentage of the crop; but very little of the money raised in this way is ever available for the needs of the Central Government, for not only is much of the land owned by the monasteries free from taxation, but out of the tax money the Government is forced to grant a small annual subsidy to the monks of the great Lhasa monasteries.

A good deal of the ready cash for the current purposes of the Lhasa Government comes from three other sources; a tax on wool, a tax on salt, both levied according to quantity, and finally the profits from the mint. The Tibetans have found their mint a paying proposition, on account of the debased coinage which they issue and force the people to accept. In addition to the commoner copper coins, none of which are worth their face-value, a number of silver coins used to be issued, a trangka coin, a coin worth three and one third trangkas, and a coin worth six and two thirds trangkas, as well as a gold coin worth 133 1/3 trangkas; but with the march of civilization the Tibetans, or rather Tsarong Shape, who is master of the mint, has found that it is cheaper to print paper money than to issue silver coins; and so now Tibet has also a paper currency with notes for ten, fifteen, and twenty-five trangkas. No wonder that in place of the old single mint Tibet has now three mints and is establishing a fourth in the Chumbi Valley. One can only wonder how long this debasement of the currency can go before it results in a financial smash.

Tsarong no doubt sees this and is trying to strengthen the financial standing of the Government by a very bold move. This is no less than a law to force the lands owned by the monasteries and the privileged nobility to pay their fair share of taxes. The great aristocratic families have been accumulating their wealth for many centuries past, storing it up in their hidden treasuries. Tsarong is very keen to institute a levy on this idle capital and also to establish the equivalent of a sliding-scale income tax. How depressing it is to feel that even in far-off Tibet one is not free from the dominating financial slogans of the day!

Tsarong is naturally very eager to increase the taxes, as his new army, created since 1912, demands a great deal of money. A number of other reforms which he is proposing will also require a large amount of fresh capital.

The treasury and income of the Dalai-lama are, of course, kept quite apart from those of the state. In addition to privately owned lands and other sources of steady income, the Dalai-lama is annually in receipt of many valuable presents of great financial worth in the form of free-will offerings. His yearly income, therefore, is and has been for a long time greatly in excess of his expenditure. The Tibetans have no conception of investing their money. Their only way of saving it is by hiding it in the ground. Consequently, year after year large sums of money are added to the great pontifical treasury in the heart of the hill on which the Potala is built. By all accounts, the hidden coffers of the palace must constitute a veritable treasure-hoard. Each year the stock is added to, and there is a great prejudice against taking anything out. The only record of any diminution of this supply was in 1910 when the Dalai-lama fled to India, taking with him enough money to last for many years of exile. But since his return the money has been more than returned.

There was a great deal of excitement in Lhasa, during the early part of my stay there, over a fire which broke out in the Potala. By a curious coincidence I had been asking about fires in Lhasa only a short time before the conflagration; and though the Potala was a mile away and I was known to be in Sonam's apartments the whole time, some people wondered if my dark influence did not have something to do with the accident. Fortunately the idea did not spread, or I should probably have had a bad time of it.

Because of the fact that so little wood is used in

the construction of houses in Tibet there are comparatively few serious fires. Generally they are extinguished in the early stages either with buckets of water or else with buckets of the coarse soda which is found near many lake-beds. This seems to be the earliest known form of fire-extinguisher.

In the present instance it was only one wing of the Potala which was damaged, and the damage affected only the interior of a few rooms. These were not the apartments of the Dalai-lama but those of the special ecclesiastical school which is housed in the great palace.

It will be remembered that there are a large number of monk officials inside the secular Government of Tibet; e.g., that there is a priest governor as well as a lay governor of each province. These monk officials are not chosen, for the most part, from among the members or minor officials of the great monasteries but are priests who have reached a special preliminary training in the Tsetrung college. They enter the school as youngsters and on graduation receive some minor appointment and then work up the official ladder.

The lay officials have no such preliminary training college. They usually learn to read and write the official language by means of private tutors, often monks, and then by influence are selected as assistants in the Tsikang, finance or treasury office, where they learn to cook accounts in the time-honored way and then are appointed to real official posts.

The Chinese introduced the Tibetans to a system of gradation in official rank, giving even to Tibetan officials the equivalent of Chinese stages in officialdom. Since the forced departure of the Chinese these gradations have fallen into a good deal of confusion, but there can still be distinguished seven stages in the official ladder.

The lowest stages are the seventh and sixth ranks, held by junior officials just starting on their careers or without sufficient influence to secure promotion. The *dzongpöns* or governors of the fifty ordinary provinces are of the fifth rank. To the fourth rank belong the governors of the three special provinces, the *depöns* or generals in the army, and such special officials as the *kenchung* in Gyangtse, who has charge of negotiations with the Indian Government.

Above this there is more confusion, as the Tibetans could not aspire to the highest Chinese ranks; but in the reorganized hierarchy it may be said that those persons who have the titles of nobility known as *teiji* and *dzasa* and *ta lama* are of the third rank, the shapes or ministers as well as the *lönchen* or prime minister are of the second rank, while the Dalai-lama is himself of the first rank.

One of my most interesting visitors was the head of the Mohammedan inhabitants of Lhasa. Although Lhasa is the center of the intolerant Tibetan Buddhist monks, there are two mosques or Mohammedan places of worship in the city, though both of them are exclusively for the use of the few foreigners who are allowed to enter the city. One of them is the Chinese mosque, for a considerable number of the Chinese merchants who used to have the privilege of coming to Lhasa were followers of Islam; but since 1912 this congregation has fallen on evil days.

The other mosque used by the Mohammedan traders from far-away Kashmir and Ladak in the West is still in a flourishing condition and has, so my visitor told me, about two hundred members. These Moslems are all Indians, and though the Koran is read aloud in the original Arabic at the Friday services, this is practically unintelligible to most of the auditors, and so there follows a commentary in Urdu, the language spoken by most Indian Moslems. My visitor added sadly that many of the congregation were very slack and paid only scanty attention to the Islamic rules of diet and prescribed times of prayer, and that there was but little real learning in the Prophet's lore among his Lhasa followers.

I was much interested to learn something of the status of these Mohammedans and the other foreigners who are permitted to reside in Lhasa. Tibet has always been very erratic and inconsistent in her long-contrived policy of exclusion. In spite of her vindictive refusal to allow strangers to pollute her soil, a certain number of foreigners have always found entry. Quite naturally the Sikkimese and Bhutanese have generally been permitted to go and come at will, for these people are really Tibetans living on the south side of the Himalayas. Mongolians (i.e., the inhabitants of Mongolia) have entry also, for the religion and institutions of Mongolia are the same as those of Tibet. But in addition to these a limited number of Chinese, Nepalese, and Kashmiris escaped the ban of exclusion. Before

1912 there were a number of Chinese officials and soldiers placed in Lhasa, and also a number of Chinese merchants, though the Chinese authorities themselves, in deference to Tibetan prejudices, limited the number of Chinese who could come to Lhasa, and general immigration into Tibet was strictly prohibited. Since 1912 the Chinese officials have disappeared, and with them most of the Chinese merchants, only a tiny number of special exceptions, mostly petty traders from the south of China, being permitted to stay; and, for the Chinese in general, Tibet is now as much the Forbidden Land as it is to the European.

But there is still a considerable Nepalese community in Lhasa, and Nepal keeps a minister or consul-general there. Most of the skilled artisans, metal-workers, and craftsmen are Nepalese. They enjoy certain extraterritorial privileges, and in most cases are tried by their consul and not by the ordinary Tibetan courts.

I met only some four or five of the Nepalese while I was in Lhasa, but one of them proved very helpful to me. He was somewhat acquainted with the mysteries of photography, and while I was cooped up as a prisoner he went around the city and took several pictures for me.

The Kashmiri Mohammedans constitute the only other group of foreigners in Lhasa. What is so strange is that though these Kashmiris by long-established custom are permitted to come to the Sacred City, other Indians, whether Hindu or Mohammedan, are not. A man from Kashmir is permitted to go from Lhasa to Darjeeling and return, but he is not allowed to bring back with him a cousin who may live in Darjeeling.

Not only Indians but all other Orientals, Japanese, Siamese, Burmese, Ceylonese, etc., as well as all Europeans, are rigidly excluded.

The Kashmiris are British subjects, and my visitor, the leading man of the community, had been given the title of *khan bahadur* by the Indian Government; and as no European is permitted to reside in Lhasa, he is more or less the unofficial representative of the Indian Government there. Diplomatic negotiations, however, do not pass through his hands but are conducted either by correspondence or through meetings of the *kenchung* and the British trade-agent or the political officer of Sikkim at Gyangtse.

Another mixed nationality presented itself a few days later in the person of a fat and jovial merchant who was a Sharpa (often pronounced Sherpa). The Sharpas are persons of Tibetan blood, speaking a Tibetan dialect, who reside in Nepal, in contrast to the Nepalese proper, who are a mixed people but of predominating Indian blood and speak an Indian language. The Sharpas live quite apart from the most of the Nepalese in little isolated valleys, thickly wooded, just south of the Himalaya Mountains. Formerly they owed allegiance only to Tibet, but of recent years the Nepalese Government has insisted upon its territorial rights, and it sends an official each year to the Sharpa villages to collect taxes. Apart from this the Sharpas are left very much to themselves, and on local matters, according to my Sharpa friend, they are practically autonomous. They are divided into nine groups, each ruled over by a chief, an office which seems to be largely hereditary though not necessarily so. The people are all Lamaistic Buddhists. In recent years a reformed or yellow-hat temple has been erected, but all the others belong to the old unreformed red-hat group. As far as I could find out the Sharpa territory has never been visited by any European, but of recent years a number of Sharpas have found their way to Darjeeling, where they have been found to make very useful and reliable servants.

My Sharpa friend, who is now one of the leading merchants in Lhasa, paid me several visits, but I remember particularly well the first time he called. He had been in India and thought he was well acquainted with the tastes of sahibs, and so he brought as an introductory present (one must always take presents when one calls in Tibet) two bottles of brandy. It so happened that I was feeling particularly unwell when he came and did not feel equal to the strain of a long conversation, and so I sent in my apologies and told Satan and Lhaten to entertain him for me in the next room.

In order to help out the party I ordered the brandy which my new friend had brought to be opened and served. I had forgotten the unamiable disposition of Satan when under the influence of any drink stronger than chang, but I was soon to be reminded of it.

At first, of course, things went very well. Songs, jokes, and laughter followed in quick succession, but at the end of the first bottle Satan took exception to a witticism of the visitor, and a violent quarrel began. At first it was a question of words; then it came to blows; and here the Sharpa, though none too sober himself, proved more than a match for Satan; and so Satan seized his sword and made a savage lunge at his adversary, inflicting a nasty-looking wound, though it proved to be nothing serious. Every one now joined in the fray, trying to keep the two principals apart, but things seemed to go from bad to worse until, ill as I was, I staggered into the next room; and by slashing Satan in the face with my pony whip I brought him to his senses.

The Sharpa was a very important man in Lhasa, and if he had been killed by Satan (as we thought for a time he was) there would have been very serious consequences not only for Satan but for me. Even as it was, I was afraid our visitor would be mortally offended, and so I gave him an elaborate apology and invited him to dinner the next day. Fortunately he was a very jovial soul, and thereafter he came frequently and we became fast friends.

I was afraid to dismiss Satan for fear he might cause trouble with the hostile elements in Lhasa and incite them to a further attack against me. But I gave him a long harangue and insisted upon his finding quarters elsewhere, as I could not have Sonam's apartment upset by his drunken sprees. The Lhasa crowd had now somewhat abated, and he found no great difficulty in securing accommodation with a young and rather attractive grass-widow.

Here a romance of true Tibetan fashion developed. Satan already shared a wife in Darjeeling with another priest, but he now determined to leave the way of polyandry for that of monogamy. He wrote a letter to the

Darjeeling woman announcing that he gave up all claims on her—this was his idea of a divorce—and immediately constituted himself the spouse of the young lady in Lhasa, who in return for his affections gave him free board and lodging, though he continued to draw living allowance from me. The union was without benefit of clergy, for Satan was a priest, and in Tibet a little loose living on the part of the priests is more excusable than a legal wife. He tried to keep all knowledge of the affair away from me, but of course I heard all about it; as both parties were satisfied, I felt that it was no affair of mine. I was glad to hear, however, that the lady was said to be more than his equal for temper and vindictiveness.

There can be no doubt that the moral life of Tibet is of a low order. This has nothing to do with polyandry, for both polygyny and polyandry can be quite in keeping with a strict moral code; but in urban Tibet, particularly in Lhasa, even among the upper classes, there is a good deal of moral laxness, both among the men and women. A great many of the Lhasa women are prostitutes, and in all lay circles adultery is regarded as a minor offense. Curiously enough the real cause of this is, I think, the ideal of absolute celibacy instilled by the church. Theoretically the only true moral life is a life of absolute sexual abstinence, and if a person is unable to live up to this standard it makes little difference what he or she does. "It is as well to be hung for a sheep as for a lamb."

CHAPTER XIV

LAST DAYS IN LHASA AND THE RETURN TO INDIA

ON the evening of March 13, after the great Maitreya festival, the monks began to leave Lhasa in great numbers. The two lords of misrule handed their authority back to the ordinary civil officials. Large numbers of pilgrims returned to their native heaths, and by the next day the population of Lhasa had sunk back to its normal size. After the huge crowds to which I was accustomed, it seemed almost deserted.

With the departure of the monks, most of the danger from attack was gone, and my imprisonment was relaxed. Without waiting for formal permission to do so, I began to leave the courtyard and to wander around the city and its environs, though always, of course, in Tibetan clothes and with my face muffled up so as not to attract too much attention. Very refreshing it was to feel once more at liberty.

Several times I went around the great Outer Circle, a parallel to the Inner Circle. This Outer Circle is a pathway which encircles the whole of the city of Lhasa, as well as the college of medicine and the Potala, and is, of course, frequently circumambulated by pilgrims.

Near the eastern side of the Outer Circle are to be seen the curious huts made of horns and mud in which are housed the ruffian outcasts of the city who, in addition to begging and pilfering, play the part of scavengers and corpse-cutters. In former years they were very turbulent and caused the city authorities a great deal of trouble, but now the strong measures of Tsarong, backed by his army, have very considerably checked their power.

During my numerous excursions, nearly all the chief sights in and around Lhasa were seen and reseen. The cathedral, the four lings, Ramoche, Norbulinga (the private palace of the Dalai-lama, about a mile west of the Potala), and the home of the Lhasa oracle, a magnificent building or rather groups of buildings lying not far away from Drepung.

But quite as interesting to see and to visit were the stalls and shops constituting the Lhasa market, which lay around the Inner Circle and on the adjoining streets. The stalls were even more numerous than the shops. Most of these stalls had umbrellas or awnings over them to protect the traders and their customers from the fierce heat of the midday sun. It was interesting to see the large number of stalls kept by women, for women play a large part not only in the social but also in the economic life of the country. Some of the smaller articles sold at fixed prices, but for the more valuable articles there was always interminable bargaining and haggling before anything could be sold.

In the larger shops, many of them kept by Nepalese or Kashmiri merchants, were sold woolen and silken clothes, and a little, a very little, cotton. The wool, of course, came from Tibet, while most of the silk came from China. People never buy their clothes ready-made in Tibet but procure the material and then have their private tailors make them up. Hats of all shapes, designs, and colors there were. Apart from the officials, the Tibetans never seem to have hit upon a national head-dress. The women, of course, never wear any hats whatever, on account of the elaborate *partuk* or head-decoration which they wear; but in recent years the men have taken to wearing European felt hats, which look very much out of place with the rest of their outfits.

Other shops housed the sellers of precious stones, chiefly coral and turquoise; for the Tibetans prize these above everything else, and good specimens fetch fabulous prices.

Many of the stalls were devoted to religious emblems—prayer-wheels, bells, rosaries, little portable charm-boxes containing images, butter-lamps, and offering-bowls; other stalls sold only tea-bowls, mostly of wood, and at a few chop-sticks were procurable, for though the peasants eat with their fingers, the nobility have learned the use of chop-sticks from the Chinese; but of knives and forks I saw no evidence, though many steel daggers and short swords were in evidence.

Food-stuffs were a very important item of merchandise, and the sellers of brick-tea of various quality, but nearly all imported from China, did a roaring business.

Tibet's boycott of foreign people does not apply to

foreign goods, and a number of articles were on sale which had been brought back from Kalimpong. These included scissors, cheap looking-glasses (a great favorite with the peasant women from the country, many of whom had never gazed on their own beauty before), matches, candles, and an occasional box of highly perfumed soap.

Matches and candles have made a real conquest of Lhasa, as they are so much more convenient than their respective Tibetan prototypes, the tinder-box and butter-lamp. The presence of the soap was very surprising, considering the known filthiness of the Tibetan, but I found that very little of it is used for washing purposes. The peasants like to smear it on their bodies as an additional precaution against the cold and because of its pleasant smell. I even heard of cases where this perfumed soap was placed on family altars as a cheap and more lasting substitute for incense.

The international trade of Tibet is, of course, very small. Miscellaneous food-stuffs (chiefly tea), materials for clothing (chiefly silk and hats), and various metals and manufactures from metals, such as copper for the mint, knives, and other tools, form the principal imports.

The principal export is wool, followed at a great distance by furs and by musk—the musk-deer of Eastern Tibet are very famous; a certain amount of borax from the lake-beds also finds its way down to India, chiefly through Nepal, while a large number of mules, ponies, sheep, and goats are also sent to foreign markets.

There are three main trade routes connecting Lhasa with the outside world. One goes to Peking in China, passing through Tachienlu, though this route, formerly the one most used, is largely blocked owing to the hostilities which exist between Tibet and China. The second route goes from Lhasa through Shigatse to distant Ladak and Kashmir. At one time this was of great importance, but it is less so now on account of the great distance to be covered. The third and now the greatest trade route is that which runs from Lhasa through Gyangtse, Pari, Yatung, and the Chumbi Valley to Kalimpong. This seems to be the line along which Tibet's trade stream now flows, though I am convinced that a much more natural outlet into India would be from Kampa Dzong down the Tista Valley. This would do away with the terribly steep ascent and descent of the Jelap Pass, for along the Tista Valley route a cart- and even motor-road could easily be made.

So easy in fact is the ascent that it should prove no insuperable difficulty even to the railroad builder; and certainly, once arrived at the Tibetan plateau, the building of a railroad across the plains would be a comparatively easy matter. But it is doubtful if any such project will be carried out for many years to come. Quite apart from the continued desire of the people for rigid isolation, it is doubtful whether the present resources of Tibet would warrant the expense. Tibet can never be a great agricultural country, and though its wool and live-stock trade could be enormously increased under favorable conditions, these alone would hardly excite the interest of the railroad builder.

Finally comes the question of Tibet's mineral resources. All adequate development of these has been greatly hindered by the religious superstitions of the monks, who assert that to delve into the earth is to disturb the subterranean demons and to destroy the crops and the people. In spite of this, however, the Tibetans themselves have opened up a number of gold-mines, chiefly for placer mining, which can be operated without undue damage to the prejudice against digging. Some of these gold-mines have been operating for the last century or two, though, of course, on a small scale and with very crude and rough methods. Many of these have proved paying undertakings, but as yet no great mother-lode of gold has been discovered.

Tibet is full of iron ore, and this will probably be developed in the future. No great deposits of coal are known to exist, but many persons assert that great oil-wells lie hidden under some of its plains. This assertion is largely due to reasoning by analogy, for no borings have as yet been made.

Another great source of interest to me, in the days following my release, was to go out to the Settam plain and watch the soldiers of the new army hard at work at their training and drilling. The new army, of which mention has already been made, is entirely the result of the independence which Tibet achieved in 1912. The Dalai-lama was insistent that a strong army be organized to maintain the country's newly won independence and also to secure internal order. The Younghusband expedition had taught him the immense superiority of European tactics and equipment; consequently in the creation of the new Tibetan corps, the British army served as the model.

Theoretically every family with more than one son can be called upon to send one to serve in the army, but this system is not yet enforced, because of lack of equipment, money, and accommodation, and up to the present time the soldiers form a special professional class, increasing every year in numbers.

There are already engineering, transport, cavalry, and artillery units, though the artillery has, as yet, only some light mountain-guns. The greatest attention, however, has been paid to the infantry.

The infantry is armed with Lee-Enfield long rifles and short bayonets, and the uniform and equipment resemble those of the British—khaki cap, tunic, trousers, and puttees—with the exception that some battalions wear a sort of turban instead of the service-cap. In the winter fur caps are issued. Regimental badges are being adopted after the British style but of Tibetan design. Battalions are distinguished by numbers (Tibetan numerals) cut out of colored cloth and sewed on the sleeves just below the shoulder-straps. N. C. O.'s are distinguished by stripes on the sleeve after the British fashion. Officers wear the British-pattern tunic with collar and tie, Sam Browne belt, breeches and puttees, leggings or field boots. Rank is indicated by badges on the shoulder-straps.

Some of the battalions have bands that play, as we have seen, British tunes. The performance of at least some of these was very creditable.

The organization of the infantry battalions is that

of four double companies with sixteen platoons, and the officers and N. C. O.'s are correspondingly distributed.

Machine-gunnery is being practised, and the Lewis gun has been adopted; and this, on account of its portability, is well adapted to the country.

The Tibetan troops parade well and seem to be keen on their work, which includes everything from squad drill to manœuvers across the fields, musketry, and signaling with flags and heliograph. Altogether they provide evidence of most excellent material for the shaping of a most formidable force, which may well give a good account of itself should future necessity arise.

The weakest points in the service, as far as I could see, were the officers. They were all recruited from among the rather degenerate Lhasa nobility, few of whom seemed to possess ordinary physical courage.

Some of the guns and uniforms were imported direct from India, while others were manufactured in Lhasa in exact imitation of the European models. Those things which were imported from India were secured with the knowledge and consent of the Indian Government.

The Tibetan army has also learned much of its drill from English commissioned and Indian non-commissioned officers. None of these, of course, have been allowed to come to Lhasa. But it will be remembered that the British keep a military outpost at Gyangtse, and the Tibetan Government has arranged to station various groups of her soldiers in Gyangtse in order that they may see and copy the English tactics. Of recent years an arrangement has been reached whereby

British officers are allowed to give the Tibetan soldiers direct courses of instruction. When one group of soldiers has been fairly well trained, it is brought back to Lhasa and a fresh batch sent down to Gyangtse.

Considering the great indebtedness in which Tibet stands to the British in this respect, it is surprising that Lhasa has not become more open to the British. It will be remembered that when our first party came to Gyangtse and asked for permission to come to Lhasa, they had come as a body recognized, even though not directly supported, by the British Indian government. Their object in wanting to pay a visit to Lhasa was an entirely friendly one, and yet a decisive refusal was given them. My own subsequent secret journey through Tibet was, of course, entirely and absolutely a private venture and was undertaken without the sanction or even the knowledge of the Indian Government.

Of great interest, however, is the attitude of the British Government toward the Governments of China and Tibet. England and China are on friendly terms. China has never recognized the independence of Tibet and refuses to do so, and will, as soon as military conditions permit, once more invade the country. It is largely for this reason that Tibet is preparing her new army.

Officially England is entirely neutral on the dispute between China and Tibet. Probably it would be officially declared that England would like to see an autonomous Tibet under the technical suzerainty of China, and undoubtedly many officials in the diplomatic service of England have very pro-Chinese sympathies in the matter; but certainly the India Office, while maintaining its neutrality, manages to make it a very benevolent neutrality in favor of Tibet. The Indian Government would probably like to see Tibet an independent buffer-state, not entirely devoid of British sympathies and influence, and so while the Indian Government refuses to recognize the Dalai-lama's claim of independence from China, it has placed no difficulties in the way of allowing the Dalai-lama so to increase his power and his fighting forces that China will be unable to enforce her claim over Tibet. Certainly diplomacy is a very marvelous affair, and as the result of diplomacy we are likely to see some very interesting developments in Asia in the next few years.

Almost every day of my long stay in Lhasa brought forth some new item of interest, but I was already looking forward to the time when I could return to India on my way back to England. My leave of absence had long since expired, urgent business called me back, and my health continued to be very unsatisfactory, and so at last I asked the Kashak for permission to depart.

I am sure that most of the Tibetan officials were very glad to get rid of so troublesome a visitor; but a large number of details cropped up which prevented my leaving, and in the end I had to bring a good deal of pressure to bear before the Government would give me my official papers which would allow me to make my way back to India in safety.

But in the end not only was I given the necessary papers but I was also supplied with transport-animals to take the place of my own animals which had died and was given permits which allowed me to stay at all government rest-houses en route. Finally I was given an armed escort, probably to safeguard against further escapades, but also to see that no attack be made on me by a fanatic.

Eventually, March 24 was chosen as the day of departure, and on the morning of that day a number of my new-found friends gathered to see me off and to load me down with farewell presents. Long and elaborate farewells took up the whole morning, and it was afternoon before I could get off.

For the first few days the road coincided with that over which I had come to Lhasa, but after reaching Yase I continued along the highway to Gyangtse, reaching that city on Good Friday and leaving on Easter, April 1. Thereafter I went over the old Gyangtse-Pari route down to the Chumbi Valley, and at Yatung (reached April 7, for I was traveling double stages) I met my old friend Mr. MacDonald, the trade-agent, who was as jovial and hospitable as ever. How delightful it was to see known faces once more! I also met there two charming Englishmen, Dr. Bishop and Mr. Easton of Calcutta, who had had special permission to come as far as Yatung, and with them I traveled back to India.

A very merry party we made of it, but on April 16 we arrived in Kalimpong, and I was back in British India at last. That same day I went on to Peshok to be the guest of Major Bailey, the political officer in Sikkim. We had a number of things to talk over, as I was sorry to find that my little escapade had quite unintentionally caused the Indian Government a good deal of trouble; but, business matters having been settled, Major Bailey once more became the charming and cultured host, and amused the party that night by tales of his own most interesting adventures.

The next day, April 17, was a most memorable one, because it was then that I reached Darjeeling and rejoined my good friends, Knight, Ellam, and Fletcher.

The Tibetan adventure was at last at an end, but I had still with me vivid memories of the Sacred City, the far-off and forbidden abode of the gods, to which in the end I had penetrated in spite of every obstacle; and these memories were worth all the terrible hardships which the journey had cost.